LOST LIONS OF JUDAH

LOST LIONS OF JUDAH

JUDAH

HAILE SELASSIE'S MONGREL FOREIGN LEGION 1935–41

CHRISTOPHER OTHEN

AMBERLEY

First published 2017

Amberley Publishing
The Hill, Stroud
Gloucestershire, GL5 4EP

www.amberley-books.com

Copyright © Christopher Othen, 2017

The right of Christopher Othen to be identified
as the Author of this work has been asserted in
accordance with the Copyrights, Designs and
Patents Act 1988.

ISBN 978 1 4456 5983 1 (hardback)
ISBN 978 1 4456 5984 8 (ebook)

British Library Cataloguing in Publication Data.
A catalogue record for this book is available
from the British Library.

Typesetting and Origination by Amberley
Publishing.
Printed in the UK.

CONTENTS

PART III: Win or Fall

PART IV: Between the Firing Squad and the Throne

ACKNOWLEDGEMENTS

This book could not have been written without Nicholas Bołtuć; Agnieszka Egeman; Nigel H Jones; Oktawia Kruczek; my parents Maureen and Michael; my brother Phillip and nephew Jacob; Tron and Tristian Tyrie; and Magdalena Wywiałek. Contact me via www.brightreview.co.uk.

INTRODUCTION

Dessie, 6 December 1935

When the first bomb exploded, Vienna's finest trauma surgeon was elbow deep inside a patient's guts somewhere in northern Ethiopia. Dr Valentin Schuppler kept his scalpel steady as shock waves blew in the hospital windows. The Red Cross on the roof was being used as a target by Italian airplanes.

Dessie Hospital was an unhygienic pile of bricks in a backwater town whose best feature was its juniper trees. Any patient mobile enough had gone running for the hills when the first Fascist planes appeared. Schuppler stayed in the operating theatre and worked on a patient who was going nowhere without a mile of stitches and a dose of morphine.

The Italians had come over the frontier two months ago. Fascist dictator Benito Mussolini wanted an empire in Africa, and Ethiopia was the last free nation on the continent. His war machine targeted civilians. Adwa got hit back in October and other historic towns followed it into the dirt. Most raids were straight terror bombing but today's assault on Dessie had a specific aim: to kill Haile Selassie, the Ethiopian emperor.

Haile Selassie had set up military headquarters in the town, bringing with him thousands of barefoot troops and a non-combatant army of foreign journalists, photographers, and cine-cameramen. Italian spies knew his location within days and the generals sent in two wings of Caproni bombers.

The planes droned into view at 8 a.m. and bombs started whistling down. Ethiopian military encampments around Dessie opened up with machine guns and rifles. Haile Selassie jumped on an Oerlikon anti-aircraft gun near his tent and started shooting. Courtiers tried to keep the flies away by draping a sheet over the emperor's shoulders as he wriggled around, plugging bullets into the sky.

A bomb fell a few feet away and knocked out a gaggle of soldiers. The bank in the centre of town was hit. The royal palace was hit. Schuppler's hospital was hit. A bomb went straight through the stars and stripes painted on the roof of the nearby Seventh Day Adventist medical centre. Smoke rolled through the streets. Doctor Loeb of the Red Cross, a German veteran of the First World War, hustled newsmen over to the body of an Ethiopian woman with both legs and one breast hacked off by shrapnel.

'This is the best proof of the benefits of civilization I ever saw,' he shouted bitterly over the gunfire.

Journalists carried wounded to the hospital. The Associated Press boys turned their truck into an ambulance and gave up a trunkload of medical supplies. Schuppler calmly stitched gaping shrapnel wounds. He amputated limbs. Blood spattered into his precisely side-parted and lubricated dark hair while a bucket filled up with hands and lower legs. A twenty-four-year-old Associated Press photographer called Franz Roth put down his camera and helped with the anaesthetic. He was another Austrian, smooth around the jowls, with hair growing low enough on his forehead to give a touch of the werewolf. Schuppler wiped his rimless glasses clean with a rag and went to work on another patient.

'Dozens of helpless women and many children were wounded or killed,' wrote a reporter out on the Dessie streets. 'I heard and saw survivors weeping and beating their breasts, some with eyes torn out or their mouths mangled. Many had their legs crushed and some had deep holes in other parts of their bodies.'

The injured kept coming. Schuppler and Roth continued to operate, barking terse comments at each other in German. Both men were from Vienna; both supported Haile Selassie. And both were fanatical Nazis.

Schuppler had quit Austria in a hurry after police started sniffing round his role in the failed 1934 Nazi coup that left undersized Austrian dictator Engelbert Dollfuß bleeding to death on the chaise longue in his office. Roth was a member of Vienna's Nazi Stormtroopers, pro-Hitler Brownshirts – illegal enough to get him two months in prison.

Why were two Nazis risking their lives to save Africans from Italian Fascist bombs?

*

Ethiopia is a parched slab of land in east Africa and the mother to all humanity. The first *Homo sapiens* walked out of here 200,000 years ago. By the time scribes began to write, it was a mixing pot of Africans and Arabs who thought big and liked the idea of crowns.

The D'Met kingdom led to the Aksumite Empire, which led to the Zagwe Dynasty, which led to the Solomonic Dynasty, which led to many more. Somewhere along the line Ethiopia converted to Christianity, except for a few iconoclasts who preferred Islam. The country was an autocracy from the start. Some emperors were strongmen who kept their land unified with fists and torture; others were weak figureheads pushed around by the *rases*, aristocratic warlords with private armies.

The country looked inward, distrusted foreigners (*ferengi*), and remained embroiled in civil war. Locals even disagreed on what to call their land: for some it was Ethiopia, to others Abyssinia. Every time an emperor died, the *rases* tore each other apart trying to put their own man on the throne. Only inhospitable terrain and an unexpected ability to unite against outsiders spared Ethiopia becoming a colony during Europe's imperialist land grabs of the nineteenth century.

The Italians tried to swindle their way in by backing Emperor Menelik II against his rivals. They got Eritrea in return, then part of northern Ethiopia. Success led to overconfidence. Soon Rome was claiming treaty clauses entitled them to more land. Menelik was not fooled:

> We cannot permit our integrity as a Christian and civilised nation to be questioned, nor the right to govern our empire in absolute independence. The Emperor of Ethiopia is a descendant of a dynasty that is 3,000 years old – a dynasty that during all that time has never submitted to an outsider. Ethiopia has never been conquered and she never shall be ...

In 1896 Menelik's men hacked the Italian army to pieces at the Battle of Adwa. Ethiopia had proved its independence. Italy never forgot its 7,000 dead soldiers rotting in the sun.

Menelik was followed by his grandson Iyasu V, who was deposed in 1921 by aristocrats who hadn't forgiven him for playing gugs (a game like polo but without a ball or much respect for life) instead of mourning his grandfather. Iyasu's aunt Zewditu became empress, the first woman to rule Ethiopia since the Queen of Sheba. No one trusted a female to run things so a man called Ras Tafari Makonnen became her regent.

Zewditu died in 1930 and a lot of people in the capital, Addis Ababa, thought Ras Tafari had poisoned her. He succeeded to the throne as Emperor Haile Selassie, King of Kings, the Elect of Zion, and the Conquering Lion of the Tribe of Judah. The new emperor did his best to modernise the country, putting down roads and encouraging foreign investment. Ethiopia remained poor and backward. Few could read and write; the *rases* handed out medieval punishments to anyone who broke their laws; slavery was tolerated and sometimes encouraged.

'The Abyssinian maintains that the Bible contains no prohibition of slave-owning,' said a European observer, 'and they point out that Moses commanded the Israelites to enslave their prisoners and make them work.'

Within a few years of Haile Selassie's coronation, Italy renewed its imperial ambitions. The land of Dante and Caravaggio was now a boisterously aggressive Fascist state under Benito Mussolini. Provocations at the border led to war talk and demands for compensation. European powers tried to intervene but could not afford to alienate Mussolini, who was needed onside to counter-balance the growing threat of Nazi Germany. In October 1935 Italian Fascist legions kicked aside the half-hearted diplomacy and marched into Ethiopia. Bombs, bullets, and mustard gas started raining all over Haile Selassie's empire. The rest of the world wondered if the invasion was the opening shot for a new global conflict.

*

By the autumn of 1935 they were cheering the boys off to war down at the Buenos Aires docks. Around 200 of the Italian community's finest were on board the *Augustus*, heading back to the motherland. Mussolini had put out a call for volunteers to join the fighting. Italians abroad rushed forward, most enthusiastically in the Americas. The *Augustus* had calls to make at Rio de Janeiro and Montevideo before it crossed the Atlantic.

'Things in Africa had and continue to have a feverish interest for Italians in Brazil, rich and poor, large and small,' said Trento Tagliaferri, a leftist exile in Rio. 'Everything about troop movements, shipments, bulletins, is avidly read and discussed. There are those who speak, among our countrymen, of enlisting for Africa. There is – why not say so? – a great thirst for revenge.'

Émigrés were not the only men who wanted to fight. Thousands of mercenaries and fascists from around the world – including 536 Romanians, 300 South Africans, and five Iraqis – wrote to Rome offering their services. Mussolini's generals considered creating an Italian Foreign Legion until someone pointed out the different flavours of extremists might not play well together.

Haile Selassie's fans were just as keen to fight. Volunteers from places as distant as Britain, Finland, and Japan walked into Ethiopian consuls and tried to sign up. African-Americans held mass protest rallies. Zulu kings swore to help their black brothers. Worried western governments scrambled to stop volunteers from the colonies heading for Addis Ababa, fearing a race war that could roll back into Europe.

Imperialists weren't the only ones concerned about the international effects of the war. The peacekeepers at the League of Nations could see foreigners turning Ethiopia into an ideological swamp of opposing causes: white supremacy, fascism, pan-Africanism, communism. League diplomats urged both sides to shut the door on foreign help. Only Haile Selassie agreed. The emperor was being pragmatic. Having the League on his side was worth more than a few extra brigades. And he knew his fellow Ethiopians distrusted strangers whatever side they supported.

'You take too much notice of foreigners,' Ras Mulugeta Yeggazu, Minister of War, told him. 'This is foolish and against tradition. Rely on your own countrymen.'

Even with the ban, Ethiopia was soon up to its knees in outsiders. Hundreds of journalists turned up in Addis Ababa with typewriters and cameras and motion-picture equipment. British novelist Evelyn Waugh was in town, his cynical pen sharp as ever, while a German convert to Islam calling himself Harun al-Rashid Bey drove around with a blonde wife and a manservant named Fritz. Celebrity American reporter H. R. Knickerbocker snatched the best rooms by paying in gold. He was notorious for his expense accounts ('To entertaining generals, etc.: $10,000') but his reports were worth it.

The Red Cross arrived with ambulances and a team of doctors from around the world, including Dr Schuppler. If anyone wanted to know why the Austrian was backing a black emperor, they only had to look to Berlin. Schuppler's hero Adolf Hitler was selling guns to the Ethiopians as part of a complicated plot to get his hands on Austria; Nazi emissaries were all over Addis Ababa negotiating with the locals about some poison gas. Ethiopia thought the Third Reich was its friend.

Mixing with the medics and newsmen were foreigners who wanted to fight. Despite Haile Selassie's promises to the League of Nations, about forty managed to slip through the net and join the Ethiopian forces. The emperor could have done with experts to modernise his medieval army and give it a chance against the Italian war machine. What he got was a crazy gang of mercenaries who could barely shoot straight and skewed even further to the right than Mussolini.

Hilaire du Berrier was a sociable monarchist from Paris, whose accent gave the game away: he was born plain Harold Berrier in North Dakota, where he ran a failed flying circus and made advertising hoardings; the paint washed away in the rain. Along with drunk English sidekick Hugh de Wet (who had hated school so much he smashed his hand with a hammer to avoid an exam), Du Berrier tried to recruit a mercenary air force for Ethiopia. No one who knew the pair was surprised how that plan turned out.

Alejandro del Valle was a Cuban veteran of three unsuccessful far-right coups in South and Central America. He had escaped a Havana firing squad thanks to a talent for bribery and ended up machine-gunning Italians for an Ethiopian warlord. Del Valle lost faith in his new African friends after watching them dismember live prisoners, joint by joint.

Lieutenant-Colonel Léopold Reul ran a thief's dozen of ex-soldiers all connected with the *Légion nationale*, an unashamed fascist group from Belgium. Reul could not raise his voice thanks to a wartime wound and ran the quietest infantry-training programme in history. His fascists marched around Addis Aba in uniform and argued with other Belgians over who should do the saluting.

Not everyone on the crew was right-wing. German pilot and engineer Ludwig Weber was an enthusiast for communism. Not all were white. Hubert Fauntleroy Julian was a Trinidadian parachutist, arms dealer, and unstoppable self-publicist who called himself 'The Black Eagle'. He had been thrown out of Ethiopia back in 1930 for flying Haile Selassie's private plane – into a tree. Now he was back training local soldiers ('I'll teach those goddamn black bastards how to drill if it's the last thing I do') and hating it. The Black Eagle should have been friends with John Robinson, an African-American pilot from Chicago known as 'The Brown Condor', but the pair ended up in a knife fight.

Along for the ride were Swedish advisers who would rather have been fighting communism, French pilots who preferred race cars, a Turkish trio who spent months building defences in the southern desert that impressed no one, ultra-right Japanese secret societies backing a penniless Tokyo princess in her hunt for an Ethiopian husband, and a pair of Czechoslovak travellers in the wrong place at the wrong time.

This ragtag foreign legion tried to hold back Mussolini's war machine. It would not end well.

*

Haile Selassie moved into the former Italian consulate after the bombing of Dessie. It was the only place left in town with a decent roof and a flower garden. Survivors wandered through the town, mourning homes flattened by high explosive. The damage could have been worse: the British Military Attaché told London that 70 per cent of the bombs dropped on Dessie did not go off. Enough had exploded to kill fifty-three locals.

Journalists poked around the carnage for a positive angle. A delegation of cameramen got the emperor to pose heroically at his Oerlikon anti-aircraft gun and faked some captions claiming the pictures had been been taken during the attack. Schuppler's bravery in refusing to leave the hospital made it into the news agency reports, although his politics were ignored. Roth got a mention as anaesthetist. Airplanes versus civilians. Bombs versus flesh. White versus black. Things didn't look good for Ethiopia.

None of the newsmen had been hurt, but some of those bombs had hit close. It had all been much safer a few months previous, before the war, when the press corps spent its time lounging around Addis Ababa drinking expense accounts dry. Back then the only story worth covering was the misadventures of Hubert Julian, the would-be head of Haile Selassie's air force. Julian made for good copy, with his fights and lies and loans that never got repaid. He knew more about Ethiopia than any other foreigner. He'd been a hero here as far back as 1930. But that hadn't lasted long.

PART I

THE ALPHA
AND THE AXIS

I

THE EMPEROR'S PAL

A Trinidadian Flyer in Ethiopia, Summer–Autumn 1930

When you came up the stairs from the 135th Street Subway there was Lenox Avenue, cutting through Harlem like a main vein. At night it pulsed with jazz and bootleg hooch and laughter. During the day it was a dirty and crowded home to disreputable people, like the man in the walk-up apartment at No. 24: Hubert Fauntleroy Julian aka the Black Eagle.

On 19 April 1930 the thirty-two-year-old Trinidadian was sunk in a busted armchair, listening to an art deco radio that looked like a miniature wooden church. The news was gloomy. There was not much money around after the Wall Street Crash and even less employment. When someone knocked at the door Julian thought it might be his wife Essie, back early from her job-hunting. He opened up and found a thin, light-skinned African man with a moustache.

'I am Melaku Bayen,' the man said. 'I am studying medicine at Howard University. My cousin is Ras Tafari, soon to be crowned emperor of Ethiopia.'

News of Julian's exploits had reached far-away Addis Ababa. The Black Eagle was too arrogant to be surprised. He had never doubted things would come right.

Julian came from a well-off family of plantation managers, who had inadvertently diverted him from the family business when they attended a 1913 air show in Port of Spain. Flying that day, American pilot Frank Boland banked through the sky, performed a loop the loop and crunched his biplane into the ground nose-first. Locals pulled his body from the wreckage. Death did not bother Julian. He knew within moments of seeing Boland take off that he wanted to be a pilot.

As an adult, Julian was tall, good-looking and athletic. And he knew it. Family money gave him a private education in Europe and a plummy posh accent, which he followed up with a stay in Canada perfecting his French. One chilly afternoon he persuaded fighter ace Billy Bishop – seventy-two kills and a Victoria Cross – to give him a flying lesson. By 1919 Julian was among the first black pilots in the world.

He crossed into America in the back seat of a McFarland touring car, driven by a white chauffeur ('I wish we'd get more niggers like you over here,' said an impressed border guard) and set up home in New York. Julian soon made a name for himself with a series of parachute jumps over Harlem, playing the saxophone as he came down. The *New York Telegram* dubbed him 'the Black Eagle' after he crashed through the window of the 123rd Street police station and got arrested. Julian liked the nickname and ignored the sarcasm.

As the 1920s rolled on, the Black Eagle got serious. He joined Marcus Garvey's United Negro Improvement Association (UNIA). To publicise its pan-African/Brotherhood of Black Men ideas, Julian offered to fly to Liberia in a sea plane and collected money from supporters to fund the trip. The money piled up but Julian kept delaying the flight.

'Julian and Garvey were both frauds, robbing the gullible for their own aggrandizement,' said George Schuyler, an always acerbic African-American journalist.

Only the threat of arrest for mail fraud eventually forced Julian into a disorganised attempt from the Harlem River that saw him dumped him into Flushing Bay five minutes after take-off. He was a better parachutist than pilot. UNIA dropped him and Julian's career zipped through one scheme after another as he barnstormed for money, ran bootleg liquor and drugs for New York gangster Owney Madden, and tried and failed to start his own Black-American association.

By 1930 he was a married and penniless former celebrity, still buoyantly confident his talent would be recognised. Then Melaku Bayen knocked on the door. The Ethiopian wanted a black parachutist to perform at Ras Tafari's coronation later that year for $1,000 a month plus expenses. Julian accepted.

*

Addis Ababa was a great town if you liked camels. From his room at the Hotel de France, Julian could see endless caravans of the sour-faced, one-humped beasts bringing in spice and hashish from the provinces. The town had a core of single-storey brick builds with rusty roofs, home to Europeans, and an aureole of pointy mud and wattle houses for the locals. Camel caravans covered both districts in dust.

Julian ogled the brown-skinned local girls, supple and dark-eyed in their white robes. Then he thought about Essie and felt guilty and slid his eyes over to the priests riding mules through town. Servants trotted barefoot alongside them, holding sun umbrellas over holy heads. The priests' jeweled skullcaps glittered in the hard sunlight. Julian's eyes slid back to the local girls. His marriage was not in good shape.

Crockery had got smashed back in Lenox Avenue when Essie found out her man was heading to Ethiopia. She thought Africa was uncivilised and dangerous, and there were jobs in Harlem. Julian tried to explain that a Trinidadian flyer at the Ethiopian coronation would unite black people across the world. Essie looked for another plate to throw. Julian kissed her goodbye and strode out the door.

He and Bayen enjoyed first-class staterooms on the German SS *Europa* on a six-week journey via Marseille along the Suez Canal, through the Red Sea and down the Straits of Bab-el-Mandeb.

At Djibouti, the harbour town of French Somaliland, the pair boarded the *Chemin de fer franco-éthiopien* (Franco-Ethiopian Railway) and set off for Addis Ababa. They arrived the evening of 25 May. Julian unpacked his extensive wardrobe in the closest thing the Hotel de France had to a suite.

Five days later the Royal Chamberlain, wearing a blue cape, was giving Julian a quick lesson in etiquette outside the throne room in Ras Tafari's palace. Barefoot guards stood around, carrying swords and pretending not to eavesdrop. Bow three times to Ras Tafari. Be formal and humble. Julian promised to try.

Then the huge carved doors to the throne room swung open. At the far end sat a small, light-skinned man with a beard and a dignified glow. His throne was made of red velvet and gold. Ras Tafari's feet almost touched the oriental carpet.

The emperor-to-be spoke French and English better than Julian, but tradition dictated an interpreter had to be present. The go-between whispered back and forth as the trio talked stunt flying, military applications of air power, and the future of aviation. Julian glossed over his failed attempt to fly to Africa for the UNIA.

After the polite chat, Ras Tafari got to the point: he wanted to show the world Ethiopia was a modern power. His cousin Melaku Bayen thought that an air display at the coronation would be a good start. Could Julian provide a parachuting audition in four days? Julian gave his broadest smile. Of course he could.

The Royal Ethiopian Air Force was run by a squat, blond Frenchman with the kind of head that could have been chiselled by a sculptor who liked cubes and wasn't keen on expressionism. Today Captain André Maillet looked especially unhappy. A tall, black figure in jodhpurs and brown suede jacket was striding towards him across the air field, swinging a leather pilot helmet by the straps.

Maillet only had three airplanes: a Junkers, a Potez 25, and a shiny white Gypsy Moth, the last a present from the Selfridge's mail order team as thanks for all the business Ras Tafari was putting their way. Something about Julian's jaunty appearance that afternoon made the Frenchman worry for his planes.

The decision to get Ethiopia airborne had been made the previous year when Ras Tafari sent his diplomats on a hunt for an experienced foreigner who could build air power from nothing. They found Maillet in Paris, a thirty-four-year-old war hero looking for a new challenge. The former baker had served three years in the artillery before getting airborne in May 1917 with the *Service Aéronautique*. A German biplane knocked him out of the sky a year later but failed to kill his love of flying. After demobilisation Maillet trained Japanese pilots and set up an airline in Indochina. He spent his spare moments risking his life as a race car driver. Maillet's friends thought he was addicted to speed; his wife thought he had a death wish. Addis Ababa signed him to a three-year contract.

Ras Tafari bought a Junkers from Germany and the Potez from France – both countries keen to make friends with the last independent nation in Africa. On Sunday 18 August 1929 the planes arrived in Djibouti. The gaunt German aristocrats with the Junkers were presented with a wad of French customs forms thick enough to choke a camel. Maillet and the Potez 25 were waved through.

Ethiopia's first airplane landed on an improvised strip near Addis Ababa, guided in by a policeman waving a flag. A happy crowd surged forward and was nearly chopped to pieces by the propeller. Ras Tafari, binoculars around his neck, gave Maillet a glass of champagne while the staff of the French consulate stood nearby and looked pleased. The Junkers arrived three weeks later.

The Germans soon got squeezed out and the Ethiopian air force became a French concern. Maillet was a straight mercenary but his second-in-command, the tall and toothbrush-moustached Lieutenant Pierre Corriger, was a pilot seconded from the *Aéronautique Militaire* in a friendly gesture by Paris. The pair built up a staff of pilots from back home and a more cosmopolitan ground staff that included a Romanian and an Armenian. Geston Vedel, a smug-faced flyer from Carmaux with slicked-back hair, got to work training a handful of Ethiopian pilots. No one seemed happy to see Julian at the air show. He put it down to fear of losing their jobs to a black man.

'Those French pilots are not gentlemen,' he said.

That was Julian's story. The French claimed things only went wrong when Julian stroked the flank of the Gypsy Moth and announced the emperor might be more impressed if he flew today, not just parachuted. A brief interrogation by Maillet established Julian had only a few hours in the air and no licence. The Frenchman refused to let him take the controls. Instead, Julian and the Armenian mechanic Jacob Sarafian would strap on parachutes and jump at the same time from different planes.

It was Ethiopia's first parachute jump and 5,000 locals had turned up. Ras Tafari arrived in a red Rolls-Royce. Servants guided him to an outdoor throne on a piece of carpet, shielded from the sun by an open tent. An ocean of faces around him tilted towards the sky.

Julian's white silk chute opened and dragged him up as it plumped with air, then floated him down; he landed within fifty feet of Ras Tafari's throne, hitting the ground in a cloud of dust. The crowd went merrily crazy, cheering and stomping feet. Sarafian landed further away and missed all the attention.

Ras Tafari gave Julian a cup of tea, the Order of Menelik medal, and Ethiopian citizenship. Vedel, roping down the Junkers in a pasture, gave him the Gallic death stare. Only Maillet had warmed up and the pair posed for a photograph, arms around each other. The Black Eagle towered over the Frenchman.

Julian accompanied Ras Tafari back to Addis Ababa in the Rolls-Royce. He watched peasants pressing their faces into the dirt as the emperor-to-be passed.

*

Champagne, claret, *poulet chasseur*, fresh-caught fish on silver platters. The Trinidadian pilot was now a court favourite. He learnt the tune, but not the words, of the national anthem '*Ityoppya Hoy Dess Yibelish*' (Ethiopia Be Happy).

'Brother, once I got there it was just willpower and personality – that's the Alpha and the axis,' said Julian.

His new uniform arrived at the Hotel de France: white jodhpurs, blue tunic, pith helmet with the royal crest and spurred black leather boots. Julian got changed and moved into a villa with an aide-de-camp and servants. The high life had finally arrived. He peacocked around town. The impressed local ladies did not need to know about a wife in New York called Essie.

Royal courtiers noticed with interest that Julian had a weakness for gossip and settling scores. The Black Eagle was already blaming Maillet's refusal to let him fly on white power sabotage. Julian's grousing was weaponised by a backstabbing clique of the court that disliked the Frenchman, and fired off. It led to needling questions, rows over delays to the coronation air show, and loud arguments conducted in French, with things said that could not be taken back.

Maillet's contract was terminated and he left the country at the end of August 1930; he would die four years later in an air crash at Orly. Pierre Corriger took over as head of the air force. He could barely keep the contempt off his face any time Julian's name was mentioned.

The Trinidadian missed the drama of Maillet's departure. By that time he was on his way back to America on a special mission for Ras Tafari. He cheerfully shared his thoughts about Ethiopia with any journalist he met on the way.

'The emperor-elect is a fine man with a beard,' said Julian, 'who looks a little something like I do.'

Ras Tafari looked nothing like Julian. The Black Eagle also claimed to be Ethiopian Minister of the Air, Ras Tafari's private pilot and a colonel with responsibilities in the upper ranks of the armed forces – all of which would have surprised the crowd back in Addis Ababa, who knew him as a novelty parachutist with a strictly honorary title. Friends rationalised the lies as cover for Julian's real task: recruiting black American professionals to modernise Ethiopia. Around 100 African-Americans already lived in the country ('troublesome and often impecunious American negroes,' said the US consul) but most scratched a living as farmers. Haile Selassie wanted engineers, chemists, pilots, machinists.

That seed fell on stony ground. Washington refused to help and African-Americans weren't keen either, remembering Julian's hustling days in New York. Harlem newspapers wondered how much money the Black Eagle planned to take them for this time. No one signed up. Even UNIA members – whose anthem was 'Ethiopia, Thou Land of Our Fathers' – failed to see the benefit in swapping the comforts of racist America for a country still seemingly in a medieval stage of development.

Julian's luck stayed bad on the homefront, too. His wife Essie had thrown herself into his arms when he reappeared at 24 Lenox Avenue, but she refused to visit Africa.

'No great man is honoured by his own people,' said the Black Eagle sadly, before he sailed for Addis Ababa on the SS *Europa* at the end of August. He spent the trip monopolising the ping-pong table.

Back in the land of dust and sun, Julian reported his lack of success to Ras Tafari. The emperor-to-be sympathised but seemed more interested in discussing the Ethiopian air cadets trained by Gaston Vedel for the coronation show. He had ordered a full dress rehearsal for 31 October. Julian promised to give the pilots a pep talk.

The airfield was crackling with excitement that Friday when Misha Babichev, a Russian-Ethiopian, and Asfaw Ali buckled on flying helmets and climbed into their planes. Ras Tafari leapt off his throne in excitement as Ethiopia's first pilots wobbled into the air: progress, modernity. He immediately gave Vedel a medal.

The pilots were touching down again after some gentle stunts when someone noticed the white Gypsy Moth missing from its usual space on the airstrip. Julian was driving it out of the hangar and down the runway.

'I wanted to give the emperor a thrill. After all, even an emperor deserves a thrill now and then.'

After a few dramatic banks in the air, Julian gunned the Gypsy Moth towards the ground. He could see people waving and jumping up and down. He decided they must be enjoying his display. Then the controls froze. The emperor-to-be's present from Selfridges flew into a eucalyptus tree, the wings bent back, and the engine made a crunching noise and died. In the silence, members of the royal entourage fetched ladders and pulled Julian from the wreckage.

Ras Tafari spent the rest of the day debating whether to jail the Black Eagle or to deport him. His advisers pointed out the cost of feeding prisoners. Julian was expelled back to America.

'They have more planes to destroy than Ethiopia,' said Ras Tafari.

Corriger and Vedel waved sarcastic goodbyes at Addis Ababa train station. A month later, Julian was sailing up New York's Hudson River aboard the Îsle de France in a freezing December fog. Journalists buzzed around him like flies.

'I can state categorically the emperor and I were the best of pals when I left,' Julian said. 'The emperor loved me like a son – if only the foreigners had left me alone.'

Two nights later Julian was guest of honour at the Benefit Promenade and Grand Carnival of all Nations, sponsored by the Brotherhood of Sleeping Car Porters. He looked good in white tie. His speech pushed self-improvement: anyone could rise from the streets of New York to best friends with an emperor-to-be if they took his advice. But he had harsh words about Ethiopia.

'I will never return to that country,' he said, his rich voice rolling around the crowd, 'even if they offered me the crownship. Harlem is my home. It was good enough for me when I was an unknown and it is good enough for me now.'

Julian missed the coronation: a bearded Coptic patriarch intoning in Ge'ez, a language only dusted off for coronations; a chariot once owned by Kaiser Wilhelm II pulled by eight white horses; the British government presenting a pair of jeweled sceptres almost correctly inscribed in Amharic. It was, said the newspapers, a spectacular sight. But not for the British novelist Evelyn Waugh. He attended the coronation for a lark. What he saw up close in November 1930 made him support Fascist Italy five years later.

2

NO DARKER THAN A SPANIARD

The Coronation of Haile Selassie, 3 November 1930

The road to Ethiopia started in the old library at Pakenham Hall, a turreted Gothic mansion buried deep in Ireland's County Westmeath. Frank Pakenham's guests liked to spend their afternoons wrapped up in conversation and laughter while the walls of leather-bound books creaked around them like an old sailing ship.

Pakenham was a wealthy young man who had invited a gang of upper-crust friends to liven up the boring August of 1930 with a house party. Poet John Betjeman was clowning around singing Victorian hymns; a camp young man from the Foreign Office complained about an upcoming post in Cairo; the daughter of a Harley Street eye surgeon was quietly in love with the host; and Evelyn Waugh drank too much and brooded about his approaching conversion to Catholicism.

Waugh was twenty-seven years old, short, delicate faced, bad tempered, angry-eyed. He looked like a faun who had skipped out of woodland and started a new career as a boxing promoter. That summer he was the best-known young novelist in Britain, famous for comic bestsellers like *Vile Bodies* and a bitter divorce in which his wife left him for a man who worked at the BBC.

'I did not know it was possible to be so miserable and live,' he told friends.

The failed marriage haunted him. Waugh tried to block out the chaos screaming round his ears with gin and casual sex and travel. But the only thing that seemed to lower the volume was long conversations with a Catholic priest in Mayfair. The public saw a successful satirical novelist; the priest saw a man in need of a spiritual safe harbour. Waugh's conversion was scheduled for September.

Religion was in the air that afternoon at Pakenham Hall. The man from the Foreign Office told everyone about an awkward lunch he'd had with two Ethiopian princes who wore capes and bowler hats and didn't speak a word of English. The only thing he learned, through a lot of miming and pointing, was that the Ethiopian Coptic church had canonised Pontius Pilate.

Waugh refused to believe any Christian church could consider Pilate a saint. Pakenham's guests raided the library shelves for information to settle the argument and found only equally bizarre stories: the legitimate heir to the throne was imprisoned in gold chains; slavery was legal; polygamy widespread; locals ate with their hands and wiped food grease into their hair. A recent newspaper turned up the fact that Ras Tafari Makonnen was being crowned emperor in November.

It passed the afternoon. The party moved on to dinner followed by the gossip and parlour games that fueled the get-togethers of rich folk. Waugh kept thinking about Ethiopia. His celebrity had trapped him in a world of socialites, bottle parties, and black-tie dinners. It was getting stale. Half the people he met reminded him of his ex-wife. The next day he asked his agent to find a newspaper willing to sponsor a trip to the coronation. By the time Waugh got back to London, *The Times* had agreed to pay for his ticket.

On 29 September Waugh was received into the Catholic Church by Father Martin D'Arcy at the Church of the Immaculate Conception in Mayfair. Two weeks later he was on his way to Djibouti, heading for the coronation of Emperor Haile Selassie I.

*

The Ethiopian Empire had its roots in the squabbling lands of Abyssinia, four mountain kingdoms with little in common except Coptic Christianity and an enthusiasm for fighting each other. In the middle of the nineteenth century an alcoholic emperor called Kassa, son of a tapeworm remedy seller, forcibly united them. He hit the bottle full time as reward. The next emperor, Yohannes, left the heavy lifting to his lieutenant Menelik, who expanded Abyssinian territory by invading tribal lands to the south. The newly conquered populations, often Muslim, were not happy to find themselves taking orders from Christian overlords.

Yohannes got himself shot fighting some Sudanese jihadists and Menelik replaced him as emperor after defeating other contenders in a vicious civil war. His victory was helped along by Italian support and a batch of rifles brought in by crop-haired French gun-runner (and one-time poet) Arthur Rimbaud. The Italians got Eritrea for their efforts; Rimbaud was still trying to get paid when bone cancer put him in a French provincial cemetery.

Menelik wasn't long on the throne when Italy started hustling for a larger chunk of Abyssinia. The new emperor turned them down. Rows and threats led to an armed confrontation at Adwa on 1 March 1896. By the end of the day 7,000 Italian corpses were bloating in the sun, including many who had made the mistake of surrendering only to be castrated and left to haemorrhage. In the aftermath the Abyssinians grabbed more territory from tribes in the north who had backed the wrong side. Menelik became master of a patchwork realm of different cultures, religions, and languages that he named Ethiopia; he united the new country with ruthless tax collection and the Lion of Judah flag. His less enthusiastic subjects called it the Abyssinian Empire.

'The Abyssinians had nothing to give their subject peoples,' said Evelyn Waugh after scanning a few books on the subject, 'nothing to teach them. They brought no crafts or knowledge, no new system of agriculture, drainage or roadmaking, no medicine or hygiene, no higher political organisation, no superiority except in their magazine rifles.'

Menelik's successor, Lij Iyasu, was arrogant and disrespectful and believed by some of the intensely Christian royal court to be Muslim. The *rases* kicked him out and crowned Menelik's daughter instead. One of the men involved in the conspiracy to remove Iyasu was a short and quiet type called Ras Tafari Makonnen. Within ten years he would manoeuvre himself onto the imperial throne.

*

Ras Tafari was born in 1892 at a village near the walled city of Harar, a place known for its fresh greenery, pink flamingoes, and coffee plantations terraced up the hillsides. His father was a war hero who had helped crush the Italians at Adwa; his mother was daughter to a ruler of a northern province. Both were dead by the time Tafari was fourteen years old.

He was a slim and serious child who grew up to be a slim and serious man, smart enough to see Ethiopia needed two things: centralised control over the powerful but worryingly independent *rases*, and enough modernisation to discourage the circling European wolves looking for a new colony. The young nobleman kept his views to himself through a series of minor provincial posts until he joined the 1916 coup against Lij Iyasu. Ras Tafari's modesty and apparent lack of ambition made him the plotters' choice for regent when Empress Zewditu took the throne.

The little man had to prove himself almost immediately, when Lij Iyasu escaped the conspirators and declared war on the new state. It ended badly for the former emperor. Iyasu managed three-and-a-half years of guerrilla warfare before capture and imprisonment in a remote corner of the country; Tafari confined him in gold chains as a concession to status. Iyasu would escape in 1932, only to be recaptured and die back in chains a few weeks after the Italian invasion. Not everyone thought the timing a coincidence.

Ras Tafari had shown the strength of the new dynasty. It gave him the confidence to start concentrating power in his hands, using a combination of a silver tongue and quiet intimidation. He had support from a few progressives, but Ethiopia's reactionaries didn't trust him. They sneered that his famous dignity and wisdom were little more than strategic silence and a solemn face.

'Half man, half snake,' said Dejazmach Balcha Safo, the ruler of a southern province paranoid enough about gossip to cut out the tongues of his household servants. When Balcha openly challenged the regent's authority, Tafari showered him with tributes at a feast and bribed Balcha's men to desert the same night. The *dejazmach* found his camp empty and government soldiers waiting with rifles. He served two years behind bars and never spoke against Ras Tafari again.

A more serious revolt occurred in the late 1920s when Empress Zewditu's former husband made a play for the throne. Ras Gugsa Wule raised an army in Wollo province and headed for the capital, claiming foreign plotters controlled Ras Tafari like a puppet. Traditionalist-minded warlords and friends of Dejazmach Balcha joined the rebellion. Everyone else waited to see who came out on top. Neither side could muster much manpower, although Maillet and Corriger took to the air and dropped leaflets excommunicating anyone who challenged the throne, followed by hand grenades.

After a bitter struggle Ras Tafari's men surrounded Ras Gugsa Wule and his bodyguard. The rebel leader refused to surrender and was hacked to death on the last day of March 1930. Two days later, Zewditu died. The official cause of death was stated as shock from the daily ice bath of Holy Water the empress thought was curing her diabetes, but the timing was so ripe that many suspected Ras Tafari of murder. The regent declared himself next in line for the throne. No one argued.

*

The coronation began early on 3 November and was still going at lunchtime. Waugh found himself sitting next to Professor Thomas Whittemore, a hollow-cheeked American enthusiast for the Coptic language taking a holiday from some fresco work in Istanbul. The fifty-nine-year-old Whittemore was a gentle and well-connected man, better at fundraising than translating Amharic. He kept a running commentary through the ceremony.

'They are beginning the Mass now ... that was the offertory ... no, I was wrong; it was the consecration ... no, I was wrong; I think it is the secret Gospel ... No, I think it must be the Epistle ... how very curious; I don't believe it was a Mass at all.'

Waugh had arrived in Djibouti ten days earlier aboard the *Azy-le-Rideau*. The journey had been dull; a fancy dress party on the last night had not cheered him up. As he disembarked, two exhausted couples were still dancing to a wind-up gramophone while a Chinese steward mopped around them.

A train crowded with international diplomats took him to Addis Ababa. The city smelt of rancid butter and red peppers and burning cow dung. The Ethiopian aristocracy paraded around in elaborate capes, waving swords and animal-skin shields. Their barefoot serfs carried gifts, and local bands competed with British Royal Marine musicians from the HMS *Effingham* to make the loudest racket. The diplomats headed out to their legation compounds on the outskirts of the capital. Waugh got a room at the Hôtel de France and worked up some local colour pieces for *The Times*.

He had expected barbarous splendour but got shabby processions and flea bites. Waugh filed unimpressed stories about Ras Tafari ordering screens for the capital to hide the poorest parts of town; policemen chasing lepers and mutilated beggars off the streets; prostitutes being thrown out of their open-door cabins; and attempts to bury some of the hyena corpses that piled up on the side roads.

The stories were mean-spirited, but no one had ever accused the *Vile Bodies* author of being charitable. Waugh quickly decided the Coptic Church was ridiculous, as were the dancing priests, the stuffy diplomats, the barefoot Ethiopian soldiers, the cab drivers who overcharged, and the xenophobic courts that found against foreigners without bothering to check for evidence. The bar that sold homemade spirits in bottles hand-labelled 'Very Olde Scotts Whiskey' and 'Koniak' was ridiculous and overpriced.

European powers took the country more seriously: Ethiopia was the last independent nation on the sub-continent and a growing market. The coronation was a chance to push open the door. Guests came from Belgium, France, Holland, Poland, Sweden, Turkey, and Italy. Germany presented 800 bottles of Hock and a signed photograph of President Paul von Hindenburg. The Greeks gave statues. Egypt sent some bedroom furniture.

Problems of race and colonialism were defused by the Ethiopians' refusal to see themselves as black, claiming instead to be swarthy Caucasians. Diplomatic outsiders were happy to follow their lead, especially when describing Ras Tafari.

'Like many of the members of ancient Abyssinian families,' said the Reverend Ashley Brown, Chaplain of Aden, 'he is no darker than many a Spaniard, with clean-cut features. Indeed in his person he preserves the tradition of the personal beauty in the House of David. He has great charm, great dignity and superb self-control.'

More complicated aspects of the Ethiopian racial worldview were ignored. When an American journalist told locals about a lynching back in America, a lighter-skinned Ethiopian courtier quietly advised him not to repeat the story.

'If you were ever to tell the Abyssinians what you have been telling us about how they treat the colored people,' said the courtier, 'they would rise and kill all the white people here. And since we are light-coloured they would treat us in the same way since they don't know the difference.'

The coronation itself was lower-key than journalists would have liked. Many slipped away to the nearest bar and made up extravagant details about marble halls, ancient traditions, swordsmen, and glittering gold. The actual droning Ge'ez ceremony took place in a cathedral full of dusty frescoes, and overran by an hour. No one told Corriger. His carefully rehearsed display of Ethiopian air power began on time. Two biplanes thundered low over the Church of the Trinity and blotted out the priests' intonations. None of the diplomats saw the parachuting display. By the time Emperor Haile Selassie emerged into the dry heat, Corriger's pilots had finished the show and gone back to base.

There then followed a week of official functions: processions, legation dinners, race-meeting, military parades, church services. Waugh was bored. A trip to Debre Libanos to visit a famous Coptic monastery didn't help. The ancient holy relics he had been promised turned out to be illustrations clipped from a nineteenth-century German newspaper. The monastery was surrounded by thieving baboons and diseased young men. As a newly minted Catholic, Waugh could feel only contempt for the Ethiopian branch of Christianity. On the trip back to Addis Ababa his car ran out of petrol and Waugh freewheeled down a hill into town as the night came in, hyenas yapping at his tyres.

The diplomats drained out of the city the following week. Waugh took a long journey back to Djibouti via Harar and managed to fall out with the daughter of the British Envoy Extraordinary ('the ugly Miss Barton') and her fiancé on the way. It had been a boring and dispiriting trip to an odd backwater of the world. He hadn't even been able to discover if the Coptic Church canonised Pontius Pilate. Waugh told friends in London that Haile Selassie's country needed a European power to come along and civilise it.

But he had enough material for a new novel with a snappy title. *Black Mischief* came out in October 1932. It sold well and offended everyone from the League of Nations to more sensitive members of the Catholic Church.

Waugh had no intention of ever returning to Ethiopia – but he would be back within five years. It all began when a gnawed bone got thrown at someone's head in a remote oasis and the bullets started flying.

3

HOT MACARONI

The Belgian and Swedish Military Missions
Teach Modern Warfare, 1931–34

The League of Nations had fifty-eight member states, aspirations to end all war, and a white stone headquarters in Geneva with peacocks roaming the grounds. The League liked to talk big about power-broking but spent its days issuing reports that no one read on slavery, child labour, working conditions, border changes, refugees, and international cooperation in archaeological research.

Nothing proved the peacekeepers' lack of muscle more than Manchuria. In 1932 the Japanese invaded northern China and established a puppet state under Henry Pu Yi, an emaciated descendant of the Qing dynasty in thick-rimmed glasses. The men in Geneva ordered the intruders to withdraw and seemed genuinely surprised when the Japanese quit the League instead. No one wanted war and the few countries who supported sanctions couldn't afford to lose trade with Japan. The League settled for issuing another unread report, and Hirohito's army stayed in Manchuria. Japanese nationalist ideologues like Kita Ikki boasted that they had proved international peacekeeping a sham.

The League was a toothless tiger, but Ethiopia had failed to get the message. In December 1934 Haile Selassie made the mistake of asking Geneva for help.

Walwal was a little piece of nothing in the middle of nowhere, home to a cluster of water wells and not much else. Ethiopia claimed the town sat inside its southern frontier but Italian maps figured it somewhere in the north of their Somaliland colony. Walwal was too insignificant for anyone to care much. Ethiopian tribes and Somali soldiers squatted in the same oases and drank side by side.

In late 1934 a British border commission team arrived in Walwal to sort out the competing claims. It should have been a quiet few weeks, penciling frontiers on maps and debating the difference between nautical and statute miles.

Things got violent when a Somali soldier deserted to the commission's Ethiopian escorts. His commanding officer wanted him back but Haile Selassie's men sneaked their new friend away and tried to look innocent. The resulting shouting match escalated into cocked rifles and a fiery political exchange between Addis Ababa and Rome. Then Italian tanks rolled up. On 5 December, nerves stretched tight, an Ethiopian sitting at a campfire threw a bone at a passing Somali and the shooting started. By the end of the day 107 Ethiopians were dead and forty wounded. The British commissioners barely got out alive. Haile Selassie appealed to Geneva for intervention.

Some observers thought the emperor was making a mistake in approaching any kind of international body, even one as ineffectual as the League of Nations. The Italians might have been persuaded to walk away from Walwal when it was just a minor border clash, but they had too much pride to quit once the world started paying attention. Others thought Mussolini didn't much care who Haile Selassie approached: the confrontation at Walwal had been intended from the start as an excuse to squeeze territory out of the Ethiopians.

The emperor's peacemaking was unpopular with both sides. Fascist Blackshirts marched in Rome demanding war. Amharic graffiti appeared on walls in Addis Ababa: 'When you want to eat macaroni, don't delay; chew it while it's still hot.'

After another fracas at the end of the month, the two dictatorships pulled their troops apart but continued lobbing threats at each other. Haile Selassie seemed confident the League of Nations would resolve the situation. He had faith in foreigners: he had been using them to modernise Ethiopia for the last four years.

*

Major Auguste Léopold Dothée was a round little Belgian with teeth like smashed pottery. He had soft hands and a double chin, and had been awarded the Croix de Guerre for killing Germans in the war. In 1934 he was a thirty-something professional soldier teaching at L'École de Guerre when the army asked him to lead a military mission to Ethiopia.

Catholic, conservative Belgium had got rich from imperialism. Settlers in the Congo dug up the jungle and discovered diamonds and enough copper to corner the global market. Most of the money went back home but enough stayed to fund the *Force Publique*, an army of African soldiers with white officers. The *Force Publique*'s performance against the Germans during the war impressed many Ethiopians. Haile Selassie hoped his new friends from Brussels would sprinkle some of their military magic over his own troops.

By the autumn, Dothée was running a training school at the walled city of Harar. The major and his fellow Belgians stood around wearing pith helmets and shouting orders while squadrons of Ethiopian soldiers rode past on camels. The advisers made such an impression that twenty years later white visitors to Harar would be greeted by locals saying, 'Beldjik! Beldjik! Doté! Doté!'

The Harar training school wasn't the first Belgian mission in Ethiopia. Haile Selassie had originally got in touch with Brussels at the time of his coronation, painfully aware the official Ethiopian army (known as the Mehal Safari) was outmanned and outgunned by the *rases*' private militias. He wanted to redress the balance.

The emperor already had foreign experts updating Ethiopia's infrastructure: an Englishman advised on the abolition of slavery, the Swiss constitutional lawyer Auberson helped with legal issues,

Swiss soldiers had created the Addis Ababa police force, a young American from Harvard called John Spencer acted as the emperor's personal legal adviser, Everett Colson of the US State Department did the finances, and Greek Dr Adrien Zervos was the emperor's private physician.

The modernisation of the Ethiopian military required caution and a low price tag. Too fast a programme and the more independent *rases* would fight back; too expensive and the royal treasury would bleed out funding it. Haile Selassie started small by asking Brussels to create an elite Imperial Guard. The Belgian government smelled opportunity.

'The sending of a military mission must be considered a great start for encouraging Belgian expansion in Abyssinia,' wrote Belgium's Minister of Defence to King Léopold III, 'and likely to lead the Abyssinian Government to request other technical missions.'

Brussels sent a five-man group of advisers under Major Ernest Polet, a beak-nosed and slope-shouldered old soldier who had seen plenty of action; the language barrier was a problem until the Belgians hired a local Armenian émigré who had done time in the French army. By 5 July 1930 Polet's men had trained a 600-strong infantry battalion and a cavalry squadron of 125 riders.

Other Belgian soldiers arrived to flesh out the instruction programme, including a team of policemen under Captain Leclaire, which tried and failed to improve the Addis Ababa police force. Polet blamed the workload: Leclaire had to equip and teach illiterate policemen, draft traffic regulations, and create a secret police unit. The less diplomatic Leclaire blamed the Ethiopians: the police chief refused to work with foreigners and the locals were lazy. Haile Selassie noted politely that the night shift had actually got worse under the Belgians.

In 1934 soldiers of the Imperial Guard's first battalion stood to attention to receive a richly embroidered Lion of Judah banner. They looked impressive from the ankles up in their European uniforms, but Haile Selassie had insisted they remain barefoot to preserve their fighting spirit. After the ceremony, the Guard marched off to secure the national armoury at nearby Koremash village, a set of stone storehouses packed with lion skin wardrooms and rifles already antique when Menelik acquired them from Rimbaud.

Polet returned to Europe with his team later that year. He recommended Dothée as his replacement, and the major arrived with eight men in September. Like his predecessor, Dothée worked slow and steady. Haile Selassie seemed pleased. The chubby Belgian couldn't understand it when a rival group of Swedish soldiers arrived early the next year.

*

The man behind the military competition was Major General Eric Virgin, a twinkly-eyed fifty-eight-year-old Swede who had been Haile Selassie's chief adviser for a year. Virgin was an aristocratic career soldier who'd seen some action in the trenches with the Germans during the last war and had gone on to become head of the Swedish air force. He ditched his planes when Stockholm suggested a trip to Ethiopia.

Haile Selassie had been inviting Swedish missionaries and teachers to work in his schools since the coronation. The more patriotic among them got annoyed by the Belgian military missions swaggering around and wrote home to see if one of their own could be sent over to restore national prestige. Expatriate hopes weren't high. Sweden was a chilly and conventional social democracy where everyone went to church, everyone approved the new welfare state, and everyone agreed not to talk about the ongoing programme to sterilise the disabled. The nation wore its neutrality like a medal and the government avoided any overseas entanglements.

But after some discussion among its upper echelons, Stockholm decided there was no harm in sending one man to a remote corner of Africa. Virgin arrived in the punishing heat of Ethiopia and immediately had a mild heart attack. He shrugged it off quicker than the doctors thought smart and went to work advising Haile Selassie. Despite his health problems, Virgin was clever and charming. Soon the Swede had so much influence other foreigners were calling him the 'white emperor'.

Virgin saw a gap in the market for a new officer corps. Most local military commanders were old, reactionary, and hostile to modern ideas. Virgin put together a plan to bring over a group of experienced Swedish soldiers to pass on their cutting-edge tactical knowledge to a fresh generation of leaders. Haile Selassie was enthusiastic, although his courtiers made it clear they preferred Belgian war veterans to peaceful Swedes. Virgin soothed their egos by making French the language of instruction.

In early 1935 five Swedish officers arrived in Addis Ababa, each employed on three-year contracts. Their leader was thirty-nine-year-old Captain Viking Tamm, a tall and sour-faced career soldier in the Svea Livgarde (Swedish Royal Life Guards), who strongly believed communism was the real enemy and expected Soviet tanks to roll into Stockholm any day soon. He had been keeping an eye on the Finnish border when a newspaper advert asked for soldiers to join an overseas mission. Tamm applied and was accepted. His bosses told him to put the red-baiting on hold and head for Ethiopia.

Tamm and his men set up the Ecole de Guerre Haile Selassie 1er (Haile Selassie I School of War) cadet school near the emperor's summer residence in Oletta, west of Addis Ababa. They selected their students from two schools popular with sons of the aristocracy. Forty-five students began infantry training, with another fifty split between cavalry and artillery courses. Tamm's men found the boys smart, overconfident, and not keen on exercise.

The training programme ran so smoothly that Tamm had time for a little light backstabbing. He had no respect for Virgin's legendary charm or his press briefings, now given from bed after another heart attack. The major general was all over the papers, calling the Italians lousy soldiers who lost wars and Haile Selassie a great leader who welcomed an invasion as a chance to defeat Mussolini. Tamm thought it all reflected badly on his country's reputation for cold, competent technocrats.

The Svea Livgarde captain told Stockholm all about Virgin's health problems, which had somehow been kept quiet until now. By the spring of 1935 Virgin was under pressure to go home. He took the hint and packed his bags, but at the last moment miraculously recovered and decided to stay. Tamm returned to the backstabbing and watched his superior's health perk up every time he was ordered home; Virgin wasn't going anywhere. Tamm couldn't decide if he was watching a masterclass in gameplaying or the vacillations of a sick and indecisive man.

A bigger problem intervened. Italy had been making enquiries about Tamm's plans in case of war. The Swedish government made reassuring noises about the military mission mirroring Dothée's Belgians and returning home. Tamm did not agree.

'You may not stay in Ethiopia in the event of war,' wrote the Foreign Ministry.

'Can you please send us gas masks?' Tamm wrote back.

The government saw its precious neutrality getting shot full of holes and tried to change Tamm's mind with urgent telegrams. He ignored them. The politicians didn't know that Colonel Af Klercker at Swedish Army Command had privately authorised the mission to resign from the army in the event of war, serve with the Ethiopians, and then resume their positions afterwards. Tamm and his men intended to stay and fight.

*

By February 1935 Italian divisions had begun lining up on the Somali and Eritrean borders. Fascist agents spread bribes around the *rases* in the north, sending a lot of Maria Theresa silver thalers to Dejazmach Haile Selassie Gugsa, a drunk in Tigre province with a Greek mistress. All Ethiopian aristocrats took money if it was offered. They had huge retinues to support ('A man to put the master's hat on,' wrote *Times* journalist George Steer, 'a man to support him into the saddle, a third to hold the left side of the mule's rump in the street'). The emperor did not seem to care.

'Most of my chiefs take money from the Italians,' said Haile Selassie. 'It is bribery without corruption.'

He trusted the League of Nations to step in and defuse the situation. To encourage the peacekeepers, the emperor refused to respond to Italian provocations. Minister of War Ras Mulugeta made sure everyone saw his disgust when Haile Selassie pretended not to hear the violent rhetoric being spewed out in Rome.

'It is better to live one day as a lion,' barked Mussolini from his balcony, 'than 100 years as a sheep.'

Haile Selassie saw the advantages in acting like a sheep. He told his foreign advisers to keep a low profile and closed the door to any more, except for a few specialists from neutral countries who could be slipped across the border without anyone noticing. The emperor didn't want conspicuous outsiders hanging around his capital.

That summer Haile Selassie was being driven to church when he did a double take from the back of his Rolls-Royce. Among the supplicants lining the road with outstretched hands and grievances was a tall Trinidadian, towering over them like a glossy black lighthouse in a sepia sea.

Hubert Julian was back in town.

4

RETURN OF THE BLACK EAGLE

Hubert Fauntleroy Julian Prepares for War, Spring–Summer 1935

Joe Liebling of the *New York World-Telegram* had interviewed palm readers, horse clockers, baseball pitchers, drug pushers, wrestlers' agents, boxing promoters, gut-shot gangsters, the misanthropic French novelist Louis-Ferdinand Céline, and a dapper colonel who claimed his cannon could control the weather.

'I can write better than anybody who can write faster,' said Liebling, 'and I can write faster than anybody who can write better.'

The New York fur trade had given Liebling's Jewish immigrant parents a ladder from poverty to middle-class respectability. Their twenty-nine-year-old son preferred the seedy side of life, cheerfully trawling the city's dive bars and fleapit hotels for larger-than-life New Yorkers. On 18 February 1935 he was up in Harlem with one of the very largest: Hubert Fauntleroy Julian.

The Black Eagle had spent the last four years bouncing around America and Europe. After a spot of whisky-smuggling over the Canadian border, he joined an all-black flying circus called 'The Blackbirds'. They put on a good show with parachuting and wing-walking, and dodged racism in the South by pretending to be aristocrats from the colonies.

'Hey, these ain't no field niggers,' said an impressed gas station attendant when they rolled up one evening. 'They're African princes.'

Julian screwed a monocle into his eye and gave the man a tip. The good times didn't last. Rural American soon got bored of African princes hanging by their toes from airplanes. Julian returned to New York and got serious about politics again, reconnecting with a faction of the UNIA still loyal to ex-leader Marcus Garvey. That went well until he ditched a UNIA delegation during a trip to London and ran off after a black chorus girl famous for her high-kicks.

The girl eventually high-kicked off with someone else, and Julian switched his attention to the MacRobertson Trophy Air Race, a London to Melbourne effort sponsored by the inventor of the Freddo Frog chocolate bar. He sent a telegram to Addis Ababa for permission to name his aeroplane 'Haile Selassie I'.

'Do as you like,' said the Ministry of Foreign Affairs.

Julian interpreted that to mean they still liked him, but he never got around to entering the race. By 1934 he was in Chicago, haggling over a transatlantic flight with African-Americans John Robinson and Charles Coffey, owners of the Challengers Aero Club; the duo were tough businessmen and they knew enough about Julian not to offer a discount. The Black Eagle threw them out of his hotel room and moved back to New York.

A few months later Joe Liebling was schlepping his way up the stairs to Julian's Harlem apartment. The climb was a challenge to a man who liked his food but the *World-Telegram* wanted the facts on a juicy story. Sources in the African-American community claimed Julian was heading back to Ethiopia to fight Mussolini.

Liebling had been warned that Julian would keep quiet about his plans but the newsman had a trick to squeeze out the facts. Silence. He would do a Trappist monk impression until the Black Eagle cracked, blabbing every secret just to hear a human voice. It was a good technique but not required against Julian, who started talking the moment Liebling entered the apartment and didn't stop until they parted company on the street a while later.

'Italy, of course, is making a terrible mistake,' Julian said. 'The only disparity between the combatants is in the air. Once that's remedied, Ethiopia should have nothing to fear.'

Julian had the remedy. He was planning to buy American aeroplanes for Haile Selassie ('at cost, of course') using money siphoned out of advance funds handed over by a British lady who thought Julian was flying her to India any day now.

'After all, India is always there,' he said. 'It can wait until I get back from the war.'

The Black Eagle was also spearheading a boycott against New York's Italian icemen, fruit vendors, and spaghetti house owners. Julian thought that Haile Selassie would appreciate the economic guerrilla warfare. He had visions of first-class tickets to Addis Ababa and a job running the air force.

Not many journalists would have taken Julian's plans seriously, but Liebling appreciated egotism with a dash of style (he got his own *World-Telegram* job by paying an unemployed Norwegian sailor to parade around with a 'Hire Joe Liebling!' sandwich board) and promised a sympathetic write-up. He was warned to make sure the Black Eagle's name was spelled correctly.

Julian put on a white silk muffler and a furry black overcoat that made him look like a suave teddy bear. He had a boycott meeting to address. The two men headed down to the street.

'Remember,' said Julian, 'no monkey business with this story. It is very serious and dignified.'

He strode off into the February cold to organise some Black Power. Marcus Garvey would be proud.

*

Over in Jamaica among the palm trees and Union Jacks, Julian's political hero was getting increasingly sick of his wife. Marcus Garvey had married Amy thirteen years before, and it was starting to feel like an unfairly long sentence for a crime he hadn't been keen on committing in the first place. Garvey had recently bought a boat ticket to London, where he intended to start a new political life. Amy and the kids would stay behind.

It wasn't a nice move but whatever geniality the tubby forty-seven-year-old possessed had been squeezed out of him over the last decade. In 1925 the UNIA head found himself in an Atlanta prison doing four years for mail fraud; he blamed it all on white oppression and discovered some racial prejudice of his own in the aftermath.

'I would have been freed,' he said, 'but two Jews on the jury held out against me ten hours and succeeded in convicting me, whereupon the Jewish judge gave me the maximum penalty.'

He was deported to Jamaica on release. His old colleagues would have preferred him to fade into Caribbean obscurity while fresh faces took over in Harlem. Garvey had too much of an ego for that. After some angry letters he started his own UNIA branch in Kingston. A row over ownership of the organisation's assets led to court cases and seizures. Sloppy bookkeeping and a grandstanding speech about corrupt judges put Garvey in prison again. He got out bitter and determined to continue his political crusade overseas.

The UNIA was never big in Jamaica. The island had too much sunshine and sentimental affection for George V to allow racial tensions to get close to American levels. Whatever dissatisfaction the locals felt for white rule got displaced into a love of pan-Africanism that saw brotherhood in every black face around the world. In 1930 Jamaicans celebrated when Haile Selassie became emperor. The UNIA held a few joyous marches, and dreadlocked dope-smokers calling themselves 'Rastafarians' adopted Ethiopia's new leader as a living god.

Five years later Garvey was getting ready to pack his bags for London when news came in about the confrontation at Walwal. The UNIA leader took time out to lead thousands of protesters around Kingston, holding up life-size photographs of the Ethiopian emperor and family. Soon the whole island was protesting against the Italians.

'A very considerable degree of interest,' wrote the Colonial Secretary, describing events to the mother country, 'amounting at times to undesirable excitement.'

The British began to suspect that Bolshevism and race war lay behind the protests. Local authorities shut down a Biblically worded petition from 1,400 Jamaicans who wanted to fight for Ethiopia. The same thing happened on the neighbouring Caribbean island of St Lucia.

Over on Hubert Julian's homeland of Trinidad, black longshoremen refused to unload Italian ships. Occult-minded types in a village near Port of Spain sacrificed turtles and goats to gain supernatural support for Ethiopia. A mob in the Trinidadian capital that didn't know its flags attacked a Portuguese family's house, thinking them Italian. The action surprised Lisbon, where the right-wing military dictatorship supported Haile Selassie and locals tied Ethiopian flags to their cars. Portugal owned a spread of African colonies and didn't appreciate Rome muscling in.

Anti-Italian protests spread around the Caribbean. Riots on the island of St Vincent targeted whites and left many injured. More peaceful campaigners raised $5,000 for the Ethiopian cause. Barbados held mass prayer meetings and collected for the Red Cross. The local *Barbados Advocate* ran Ethiopian news on the front page and cash-grabs from local businessmen in the classifieds.

'The Ethiopians' lack of modern war equipment has been a handicap to them,' ran one ad. 'Why be handicapped by old-fashioned cooking appliances? See the modern gas appliances at the gas showrooms.'

The former French colony of Haiti was in favour of sanctions against Italy, telling the League of Nations: 'The period of colonial wars is now closed.' The island's anti-imperialism had been excited by the recent ejection of US occupation forces, who had been around for nineteen years. Down in Guyana, a British colony on the northern edge of South America, 500 black veterans of the First World War petitioned King George V to allow them to fight in Ethiopia.

'Twenty years ago Negroes fought to save white civilisation. Surely, they cannot now be refused permission to fight for what they regard as a symbol of their own civilisation?'

The king ignored them. Georgetown authorities banned Paul Robeson's racially explosive film *The Emperor Jones* but failed to stop rumours that Italian spies had slipped poison into the local sweet factory, leading to school closures, weeping mothers, and a white education inspector beaten half to death in a riot.

The occasional spot of cynicism crept in. A letter to Jamaica's *Daily Gleaner* suggested sending all pro-Ethiopian locals to live in Addis Ababa, where slavery and bandits would soon change their minds. A few fellow cynics chuckled but nothing stopped the protest rallies. Some activists seemed to be looking forward to war. Amy Garvey told a UNIA meeting that an Italian invasion would be a blessing from God, uniting black people across the world. Her husband rolled his eyes and counted the days until London.

While Marcus Garvey waited for his ship, news came in that Hubert Julian was in *The New York World-Telegram* threatening to join Haile Selassie's air force. Garvey liked Julian well enough but had seen too many of his plans fall apart to take him seriously. He couldn't see the Black Eagle making it back to Ethiopia.

*

Addis Ababa had changed. From his room at the Imperial Hotel, Julian could see cars rolling down paved roads in the centre of town. Traffic police in blue uniforms and pith helmets stood at intersections shepherding locals onto freshly built pavements.

'In the name of the emperor! Walk on the right!'

The roads soon branched off into camel tracks that bounced cars around like a ship in a storm. But it was progress. Everything in the Ethiopian capital was busier and more modern. Cinemas and clubs had opened. Locals embraced capitalism by selling off possessions in the city's markets, getting good money for beds still warm from the relatives who died in them that morning. Some of the police even spoke French. Warriors from distant provinces wandered around barefoot with their spears and antique rifles, gawping at the twentieth century.

Julian's arrival, on 12 April 1935, surprised everyone in New York who had dismissed the *World-Telegram* piece as another publicity stunt. Opinion was split over whether Julian was finally showing some altruistic heroism in the name of Black Africa or just wanted a taste of the $1,000 a month he'd earned for the coronation. Some Harlemites wondered if he had left town in a hurry after being pressed to return the money for that India flight. The newspapers leant towards sarcasm just to be sure.

'IL DUCE NOTE', ran a *Chicago Times* headline, 'BLACK EAGLE SAILS FOR ABYSSINIA'.

Not even Julian knew if Haile Selassie would allow him back in the country. To lower the odds of being turned back at the border, the Black Eagle talked up his heroism to anyone he met en route. At a suite in the Stafford Hotel, near Buckingham Palace, he told reporters he was willing to die for his adopted country.

'I would like to go down in flames over Ethiopia,' he said, 'taking a few of the others with me.'

Addis Ababa remained silent so Julian travelled on to Paris, where the Ethiopian embassy refused to give him travel documents, then Marseille before embarking on a freighter to Djibouti in French Somaliland. He bribed a visa out of someone and took a hotel room in the Ethiopian capital. Local boys struggled up the stairs behind him, carrying suitcases stuffed with enough clothes for two wardrobe changes a day.

The Imperial Hotel was more basic than it sounded: a two-storey building with a billiard table and one bathroom. It had started to fill up with journalists who smelled war coming and wanted a head start. Its Greek owner Bollolakos quickly got bored of British journalists giggling at his name and retaliated by stuffing guests four to a room until the hotel bulged at the corners. New arrivals complained that rooms on the ground floor had obviously been used to pen livestock in the recent past. It didn't help that every reporter turned up with trunkloads of equipment: rifles, telescopes, ant-proof cases, medicine chests, gas-masks, pack saddles, sometimes a motorcycle and usually a canoe.

Julian used some of the India money to bribe Bollolakos into a single room and set off to catch Haile's Selassie's attention. Every day the emperor's red Rolls-Royce drove out to St George's Cathedral, an octagonal building that stood opposite a huge tree creaking with the bodies of hanged criminals. Suppliants, beggars, and bystanders lined the route, many in rags. Julian joined them in a sharp blue suit, a bowler hat, and a monocle. His chin was cocked at a 45-degree angle to the world.

The emperor saw him one morning and recoiled in his seat. He turned his head to look out of the other window. The Rolls-Royce nudged its way through the crowds and on to the church.

'The Ethiopians frown on ballyhoo,' said Baltimore's *Afro-American*.

*

Julian tried the silent but dignified route for a few more months then bribed his way into an audience with the Royal Chamberlain. He talked big about buying American aircraft and using his flying experience for Ethiopia. The Chamberlain offered Julian a training post in the army for $100 a month, and confided he was only up for the job because Selassie's young daughter, Princess Tsahi, had a crush. Otherwise the Black Eagle would be on his way home. Julian took the post.

By June 1935 he was striding around Addis Ababa in a uniform of his own design (part-Canadian, part-British) and claiming to be a colonel again. His job was to turn 1,000 Ministry of Public Works officials into a fighting force. Julian got them crawling under barbed wire, doing jumping jacks, and practising hand-to-hand combat. Every morning he led his men around Addis Ababa on a white horse, diverting regularly past the palace to lead them in chants of '*Ebalgume!*' (Kill the enemy!)

In the evenings Julian slumped into a chair in the Imperial Hotel and chatted to passing journalists. Newsmen liked him: colourful personalities gave them something to write about in the absence of an actual war. Soon the *New York Times* was telling its readers that Julian would make a fine leader of the Ethiopian air force. Julian liked the idea. Machine-gunning Italians from the air would be more fun than huddling in a trench.

Ethiopia was all over the *New York Times* that summer. The war drums could be heard everywhere, from front-page headlines all the way through to the sports pages, where an Italian and an African-American were doing their best to beat the hell out of each other in a boxing ring at New York's Yankee Stadium. Primo Carnera versus Joe Louis: six rounds and a $130,000 purse.

It was a big fight. Everyone expected New York to be at war by the time it was over.

5

THE GREAT WHITE HOPELESS

Primo Carnera vs Joe Louis in New York, 25 June 1935

It was a beautiful right cross, straight to the jaw. The big Italian folded up in the middle of the ring. He got up and fell to his knees; he got up again but he was swaying.

Yankee Stadium was full with 64,000 people tonight. A scrum of men in suits and ties and hats, plus a few women who didn't mind getting blood on their mink wraps, all roaring down from the stands at a boxing ring the size of a postage stamp. The Italian-Americans were telling Primo Carnera to stay on his feet and keep his guard up, their black hair glossy in the lights; African-Americans shouted at Joe Louis to finish him! Joe, finish him! and shadow-boxed with whatever fist wasn't holding a cigarette. Commentators ringside talked fast into their microphones for the folks at home. Photographers popped off another bulb in cameras big as a box of groceries. Louis stalked a glassy Carnera around the ring.

Boxing men had their money on the Brown Bomber. Carnera was a bum. A shambling mountain of a man from an Italian village no one could find on the map, Carnera, known as 'the Ambling Alp', had been mobbed up since his first fight in America. Everyone knew Jack Sharkey took a dive two years ago. Only the gangsters who managed the Italian Giant knew how many of this former circus strongman's other opponents got paid to hit the canvas.

The kind of men who preferred to hang around bars instead of going home to the wife had been arguing for weeks over whether this fight was rigged. The conclusion was always the same: no chance, pal. No one alive had enough money to persuade an Italian or African-American to take a dive in the summer of 1935. Not with Ethiopia all over the front pages and war marching closer every day. Not with New York's Italians and African-Americans at each other's throats.

Ethiopia meant something special to Black Americans. No one had wanted to go live there when Hubert Julian came recruiting five years ago, but they loved the country as a showcase for black pride. Everyone knew that Italy had attempted an invasion a few decades back and got beaten to a paste by the Ethiopians at a place called Adwa – just like Joe smearing Carnera all over the canvas tonight. Haile Selassie's turf was a symbol of black defiance: the last unconquered nation in Africa.

That's why there were 1,500 policemen outside the stadium, the largest riot squad New York had ever seen, with truncheons and guns and tear gas, waiting for the trouble to start. They could hear the crowd inside roaring as the big Italian tried to shake some sense into his skull.

Carnera had guts. It was round six and he was still upright. But all 6'5" of him was hurting. Joe Louis, fresh as rain, ducked inside the giant's clumsy hooks and chased him to the ropes. The African-Americans in the stadium cheered every time Louis landed a punch.

*

'Why don't you fight lynchings, peonage, bastardy, discrimination and segregation?' said the front page of the *Chicago Defender*, one of the biggest black newspapers in America. 'Why don't you fight for jobs to which you are entitled? Why don't you fight for your own independence? What advantage is there in your rescuing Ethiopia from the Italians and losing your own country to tyranny and prejudice?'

The *Defender* liked Ethiopia as well as anyone, but there were limits. African-Americans were not long out of slavery. Down south, Jim Crow laws gave them separate water fountains and seats at the back of the bus. Up north, property prices and low wages corralled them into ghettoes. The Ku Klux Klan lynched them, the police force beat them, and justice was for white people.

The past few decades had been all about pushing back. Marcus Garvey's UNIA and the National Association for the Advancement of Colored People (NAACP) fought the battle for civil rights an inch at a time. W. E. B. Du Bois and other intellectual types up on Sugar Hill were in the front row of a black cultural renaissance. And even the snobbiest music critic had to acknowledge that jazz was a real art form.

Then Mussolini moved his soldiers to Ethiopia's borders and Black America forgot about its own problems. Everyone wanted to talk Haile Selassie. The boys in the *Defender* newsroom put up with as much as they could take then let loose on the front page. They had strong words for the community: drop this crazy talk about fighting in Ethiopia and concentrate on homegrown problems.

No one listened. That summer Chicago was full of rallies and leaflets as Black America projected its fantasies about living free and proud onto a baked slice of inhospitable bushland. Up in New York you couldn't walk between 125th and 145th Streets in Harlem without tripping over someone with a megaphone and a collecting bucket and an Ethiopian flag.

African-Americans followed Hubert Julian's example and boycotted Italian shops, ice cream parlours, and icemen. Letters to newspapers poured in from correspondents calling themselves 'Count Him In' (Brooklyn), 'Would Die for Abyssinia' (Lancaster, PA), 'How Ethiopia Must Win' (Philadelphia), 'Six War Vets Ready' (Hampton, VA), and 'Wants to Help Ethiopia' (Cleveland). Black students in New York organised an Africa vs. the Imperialist Powers mock trial. Black churches held prayer meetings and reminded everyone that Haile's Selassie's empire was mentioned in the Bible (Psalms 68:31 – 'Princes shall come out of Egypt; Ethiopia shall soon stretch forth her hands unto God').

The UNIA got in on the action. Back in the glory days of the 1920s Marcus Garvey's men had marched through Harlem in uniform, a biplane flown by Julian swooping overhead. Garvey's deportation to Jamaica put the UNIA into a long-term hiatus but it was reactivated when his successor in New York, Captain Alfred L. King, started protesting Haile Selassie being pushed around by Italy.

Captain King had plenty of competition. The Pan-African Reconstruction Association (PARA) talked about sending volunteers to fight, the African Patriotic League made a lot of noise, and the Provisional Committee for the Defense of Ethiopia (PCDE) got the biggest numbers by bringing together Elks lodges and other national organisations.

Haile Selassie's supporters had enthusiasm but not much practical knowledge about Ethiopia. The country was a big, blank, symbolic spot on the map. In the 1920s the Tutt Brothers, toast of black vaudeville, ran a show that claimed jazz came from Ethiopia. No one argued the point. Hubert Julian knew the country first-hand, but he was out in Addis Ababa mixed up in all kinds of intrigue. In his absence the UNIA found itself suggesting everyone read articles from the pulp rag *Adventure* and follow them up with L. M. Nesbitt's *Hell Hole of Creation*, a book not much subtler than its title.

This lack of information meant Ethiopia's friends welcomed any well-informed white folks who wanted to help out. No one cared if the new arrivals were red as Moscow. Groups like the PCDE were happy to work with the Communist Party and pretended not to notice when the comrades mixed Marxist thought with their support for a black emperor; a united front seemed more important than red-baiting and white-hating.

Only journalist George Schuyler, a socialist apostate and eventual hero to the small contingent of African-Americans who leaned so far right they were practically horizontal, took a contrarian view and told the world what he thought of the community's new white friends.

'Professional Negrophile busybodies and self-appointed shepherds of the Negro races,' he said, 'who believe nothing can be done by or for Negroes unless a white man is directing it.'

Most of the action, left-wing or not, took place up north. Down south things were quieter because no one wanted the Klan turning up at midnight. But all parts of the country were listening to the radio when Joe Louis went up against Primo Carnera at Yankee Stadium.

*

Carnera went down again with another right cross to the jaw. He was on one knee in the ring and the referee was pushing Louis back. Then the Italian giant was upright with the dull panic of a man taking a beating he can't stop.

Anyone would panic with the Brown Bomber coming at them. Joe Louis was a young heavyweight with a sulky look on his face and a talent for killer knockouts. The son of dirt-poor Alabama sharecroppers with a dash of Cherokee on his mother's side, Louis took up boxing to stay out of trouble when the family moved to Detroit. Yankee Stadium was another stop on the road to the heavyweight championship. Carnera was just another obstacle.

The referee checked the Italian's eyes and got out of the way. Louis went in swinging. Howls of support from the Brown Bomber's fans rolled around the Stadium. This was the kind of direct action on fascism they could get behind.

Thousands of black men had already signed up to fight for Ethiopia, drawn by idealism, racial solidarity, and the promise of a steady job. Samuel Daniels of New York's PARA and Harold H. Williams of the Ethiopian League of America travelled cross-country signing up volunteers. By the time Louis stepped into the ring they had 1,000 in New York, 1,500 in Philadelphia, 8,000 in Chicago, 5,000 in Detroit and 2,000 in Kansas City. Daniels had no problems getting rich off a good cause: he charged 25 cents per enlistment, with higher rates for officers.

A group calling itself the Black Legion under Sufi Abdul Hamid, aka Eugene Brown (a Muslim convert known as the 'Black Hitler' for his anti-Semitic speeches), claimed to have 3,000 volunteers at a training camp in upstate New York. Another group talked about chartering a freighter to take 2,000 volunteers to Africa. Journalists and police were never allowed to get close enough to see if anyone was telling the truth.

Ethiopia wasn't much interested in foreign volunteers, but a courtier's diplomatic reply when black newspaper *The Pittsburgh Courier* sent Haile Selassie a telegram on the subject was misinterpreted as something more positive. The resulting story inspired thousands to contact Melaku Emmanuel Bayen, Ethiopian doctor and the man behind the pan-Africanist *Voice of Ethiopia* newspaper. They figured he had some pull as Haile Selassie's cousin. They'd even forgiven him for recruiting Hubert Julian back in 1930.

Bayen knew his relative well enough to turn down volunteers. He advised everyone to follow his example and work peaceably with a white-run group like the Ethiopia Research Council. Privately, Bayen disagreed with cousin Selassie's stand on foreigners and had already sent a black pilot called John Robinson down the pipeline to Addis Ababa.

The dogs of war did not give up easily. Would-be mercenaries contacted the Ethiopian consul in New York, a sad-faced and big-nosed businessman called John H. Shaw. It was another dead end. Addis Ababa had already instructed the white forty-eight-year-old to turn away anyone who wanted a visa. Shaw did as he was told and got thanked by having to pay the rent on his own consulate when the Ethiopians forgot about him.

Washington put the final shovel of soil on the coffin by announcing new penalties for anyone enlisting in a foreign army against a nation not at war with America. The mix of African-American uproar and leftist agitation triggered the politicians into handing down three-year sentences in prison and $2,000 fines. Haile Selassie's most fanatical defenders claimed they would still find a way. The government told the FBI to keep an eye on them and refused to issue passports to anyone heading for East Africa.

Only white Americans (then about 88 per cent of the population) could support Haile Selassie without the government getting too concerned. Most thought Italy should stay out of Ethiopia – a surprise to opinion pollsters who knew how popular Mussolini had been until recently. A lot of folks saw Italian Fascism as a supercharged patriotic capitalism, bombastic but unthreatening. They covered their ears when Il Duce's speeches threatened to burst the bubble of peace.

'War is to man as maternity is to women,' said Mussolini. 'I do not believe in perpetual peace; not only do I not believe in it but I find it depressing and a negation of all the fundamental virtues of man.'

White America finally realised the man in Rome was serious when Blackshirt soldiers began sailing for Africa. By the summer of 1935 enthusiasm for Mussolini had dropped away. Soon only Italian-Americans were left to cheer on Il Duce and his dreams of a reborn Roman Empire.

*

Out in the lonely centre of Yankee Stadium, Primo Carnera was a shambling mess. The Italian's hands were drooping and Louis was taking him apart. Carnera's face took a hard right cross that sprayed sweat over the ringside seats. The Italian went down for the third time. The referee pushed Louis back. Carnera made it to his feet, but the big guy was wobbling all over the ring with no more fight left in him. The referee waved his arms and ended the punishment. Technical Knockout. It was Louis' twentieth win out of twenty matches, and his seventeenth knockout. The ring filled with the fighters' people; the crowd's shouts rolled across the stadium like a thunderstorm.

Police checked their riot gear and got ready to crack some skulls as Yankee Stadium drained into the streets. But to everyone's surprise there was no trouble that night: African-Americans were too happy and Italians too depressed to throw punches. The lights went out in the spaghetti district while Black Harlem erupted with waves of cheering, with men climbing lamp posts to pose for the cameras.

'Everything is hotsy-totsy and the goose is hanging high,' said a correspondent for the *Pittsburgh Courier*.

Things weren't so hotsy-totsy over in Addis Ababa. The Italians were on the border, and Haile Selassie had begun to realise the League of Nations wasn't going to intervene. The only foreigners around were newsmen hunting down stories and adventurers looking for action. One of them, a mercenary pilot called Hugh de Wet, was heading in right now from Djibouti, a coastal town nobody loved. And he needed a drink.

6

MURDERING OUR OWN MOTHER

Hugo de Wet Volunteers His Services,
Summer–Autumn 1935

Djibouti was a French hellhole on the Gulf of Aden. The sun-scorched port stank of fish, and locals kept their women hidden indoors. Sailors got so girl-hungry they danced cheek to cheek with each other while the bar gramophone scratched up a 78.

Hugh William Arthur Oloff de Wet wasn't that desperate for female company. But after a week in the capital of French Somaliland he was getting close. De Wet liked puppy-eyed French girls, dark-haired Irish gypsies, and art-smart bohemian upper-class types. All the French port had to offer was a pair of exhausted French whores working themselves to death in a brothel on the outskirts: fifteen minutes for thirty francs. The girls did not get a lot of rest. The black shadows around their eyes made them look like pandas.

De Wet was waiting for the *Chemin de fer franco-éthiopien*. He had a second-class ticket for Addis Ababa. By late summer the CFE had transported over a hundred journalists, diplomats, photographers, cine-cameramen, and arms dealers into Ethiopia. The Italians were gathering on the frontiers and everyone believed it was only a matter of time before the shooting began.

The railroad did not keep much of a timetable. Barefoot black porters in faded blue uniforms shrugged when asked what time the train departed. 'Perhaps tomorrow, maybe the day after tomorrow ...'

De Wet was stuck in town. He watched French civil servants going slowly mad in the heat. They spent their days in white-hot offices and their nights cruising the town in car convoys, trying to catch a breeze. Then they queued for the brothel.

Nothing grew in Djibouti except rocks and sand. Trees died within days of being planted. A story did the rounds that the French governor had offered a cash prize to anyone who could make something grow. A Greek settler unveiled a garden of juicy leafed palm trees. The governor had the money in his hand when he looked closer. The trees were made of painted metal, scalding in the sun.

De Wet needed a drink.

*

The would-be mercenary picked up his taste for alcohol back at Sandhurst, Britain's premier military school, all white neoclassical buildings, rolling lawns, young men in uniform marching up and down. De Wet hated it.

The school had been his father's idea. De Wet senior was a naval man, descended from a famous Boer general but happy to serve Britain everywhere from Middle East diplomatic missions to the evacuation of Constantinople. His son learnt Arabic in Egypt, attended school in Brussels, and entered Bath's upper-crust Monkton College at twelve.

De Wet was soft-spoken and well-mannered but had a streak of anarchy in his soul. His father sensed it and enrolled him in Sandhurst at eighteen, hoping military discipline would send back a conventional son of empire. Instead, De Wet discovered alcohol. He quit classes for the nearest pub, skipped essays for hidden bottles of whisky, and gave up his military career for the warm alcoholic glow of drifting nowhere with no ambition.

'I learnt to abhor discipline,' he said. 'They solemnly warned me that to command men one must learn to obey. But I – I have never had the slightest desire to command anyone.'

He began to dodge any work heading his way. When a tough exam came along, De Wet bashed his hand with a hammer to avoid it. In 1932 he dropped out entirely.

He respected his father enough to give conventional life another try and joined the Royal Air Force. De Wet got a neat blue uniform and a pilot's licence. Things seemed to be going well until a car crash put him on the sick list. A medical commission asked stupid questions and the devil on his shoulder made De Wet give stupid answers in his polite, educated voice. The RAF kicked him out.

De Wet senior handed over a wad of money and told his son to go make something of himself. A few months later Hugh was back, the stitches falling out of his suit and wallet empty. He had a story about travelling around Ireland with a gypsy family. No one believed him until he was spotted talking Romany with some gold-toothed men at a local horse show.

By now it was the summer of 1935. Newspapers talked about the coming war in Ethiopia and Haile Selassie's shortage of specialists, particularly pilots. De Wet was twenty-three years old, tall and skinny with dark hair sealed in brilliantine. He wore a moustache and a permanently distrustful expression. His father handed over a final wad of cash and bought him a ticket to Addis Ababa. Make something of yourself, Hugh. Or else.

*

Someone in Paris had thought it would be a good idea to name the engines of the *Chemin de fer franco-éthiopien* after animals: Rhino, Turtle, Camel, Elephant. Ornamental Abyssinian hieroglyphics carried the names on one side of the boiler and neat French letters on the other: *Rhino, Tortue, Chameau, Éléphant.*

Every train heading for Addis Ababa was a rank sweatbox. The third-class carriages were full of Somalis squatting on the floor with their spears stacked on the luggage rack. Second-class was Europeans on a budget. The rich travelled first-class in carriages identical to second-class but with ticket prices that kept out the riff-raff.

De Wet forced his way through the hundreds of locals crowding Djibouti station, a flat white building behind a picket fence, and climbed aboard a second-class compartment. He had a cluster of suitcases and two books to read on the long journey: the RAF manual and a large-print volume of *Carmen*.

The engine steamed and the train rolled out. Just over the Ethiopian border was Dewele station, a tin shack in the middle of nowhere, where police climbed aboard and checked passports. A discreet bribe could get a visa, as Hubert Julian had discovered. Lozenge-faced Hungarian journalist Ladislas Faragó of Associated Press found the same thing when the guards pretended to be unable to understand the visa already stamped in his passport. The newsman had seen too much of the world to get upset.

'These station police are a ragged lot dressed in miserable uniforms,' he said. 'On their shoulders they carry rifles of the pre-flood period which Menelik got in return for the railway concession. However, they keep wonderful order on the platform.'

Cash changed hands. The new visa was a flamboyantly beautiful design of Amharic lettering surrounded by lions, crowns and angels. The train moved on. From the carriage window De Wet watched barefoot Ethiopian infantry marching across dust and crumbling volcanic lava against a background of a few unimpressive mountains on the horizon. Everywhere was sand and desert, a few stone huts, and some bare-breasted Ethiopian girls nursing babies as the train passed. Eastern Ethiopia looked as dry and fissured as a cracked heel.

Nervous travellers warned everyone in second-class about bandit raids. In January 1931 thirty-one people, including a French government official, had died in an attack near Djibouti. More experienced types knew the real risk was the train rolling off the track where locals had ripped up the rails to make spears.

It took three days to reach Addis Ababa. Rainy season clouds hung low over the city. The tiered roofs of the capital's station shone white in the weak sunshine and raindrops spattered a golden statue of an Abyssinian lion holding the flag just outside the entrance. Taxi drivers mobbed the new arrivals. One ripped

De Wet's luggage out of his hands and threw it into his car. The Englishman shrugged and got in.

De Wet asked for the Hotel d'Europe and got a tour of Addis Ababa on the way: bleating mules and stinking camels; armed soldiers on horseback galloping past; street corner orators; low buildings and muddy wide roads. De Wet was more interested in the distinguished-looking men who perched in tin booths near the markets. The taxi driver tried to explain in broken French. The men are a judge to make the law. *Comprenez-vous?* If a man who sell cloth and a man who buy his cloth argue over how much material is sold, they go to the judge. We use a measure of fingertips to elbow. The man who buy have longer arms than the man who sell. The judge tell them to use the distance halfway between their two arms and give him the leftover cloth. Everybody happy.

The Hotel d'Europe was run by a German and infested with bed bugs and mosquitoes.

'If I had a penny for every flea,' muttered a Czech guest as he tried to sleep, 'I could buy out Rockefeller.'

The next morning De Wet went to see Thadessa Mechecha, Ethiopian Minister of the Air. It was time to become a mercenary.

*

The Ethiopian war machine was slowly waking up. Ras Mulugeta continued to argue for full mobilisation, aggressively pushing back against Haile Selassie's efforts to paint Ethiopia as a nation of peace-lovers. The emperor compromised by starting a training programme for civilians in the cities and allowing the *rases* to shuffle their private armies closer to the frontiers.

The Ethiopians were sure any invasion would come from Italian Somaliland in the south. The xenophobic but energetic Afework Woldesemait dug in at a stone fort on the yellow Gorahai plain with 600 men and two machine guns. Nagradas Basha had 500 men at Tafere Ketema. Balambaras Tafare had 300 at Gerlogubi. Ras Nasibu Zeamanuel, an intellectual in jodhpurs soon to be promoted commander-in-chief of the southern front, was setting up defensive positions near Harar. More soldiers trudged in every day.

Watching them from across the border was Rodolfo Graziani, Somaliland's thick-haired and toweringly tall Fascist governor. His two divisions and jumble of assorted units had dreams of military glory (one Blackshirt gang had the motto 'The life of a hero begins after he dies') but Graziani knew something they did not. The south was a backwater in the Italian plan. The main strike would come through the mountains in the north, the soft spot in the Ethiopian skull.

Up there all the country had to offer was Ras Seyoum Mengesha marshalling his men in the foothills and Dejazmach Haile Selassie Gugsa doing the same in Tigre, an independent-minded province that preferred its own language to Amharic. Neither man realised the Italians were building roads and buying mules and employing locals on the other side of the mountains.

Mussolini had prepared a huge strikeforce on the northern border. Divisions were assembling with army veterans, volunteers, Fascist students, veterans of nineteenth-century colonial wars, and survivors from Gabriele D'Annunzio's 1919 adventure in Fiume. Tank crews baked in the sun while their bottles of Chianti evaporated. The Duke of Pistoia commanded the 23 March Blackshirt division. The Duke of Bergamo was second-in-command to the Gran Sasso army division. Shaven-headed Futurist artist Filippo Tommaso Marinetti joined the air force. A journalist asked him what would happen if Rome lost again.

'That was another Italy,' said Marinetti. 'Now we are going to win.'

The Italians had plenty of newsmen to record their efforts: 200 Fascist reporters, joined by forty right-leaning foreigners like Nazi Germany's Captain von Strunk (*Völkischer Beobachter*), Britain's Major-General J. F. C. Fuller (*The Morning Post*), and Frenchmen Henri de Montfried (*Le Petit Soir*) and Raoul Salan (*Le Temps*, and also spying for the French government).

Reporters who preferred to get their news from the Ethiopian side headed for Addis Ababa. Among the British contingent was Evelyn Waugh, who had arrived on 21 August 1935 to report for *The Daily Mail*. Waugh disliked Ethiopia even more intensely than his last visit and couldn't hide his enthusiasm for an Italian victory. The other newsmen muttered snide remarks and steered clear of him. The author of *Black Mischief* was too tough-skinned to care. He dismissed his fellow newshounds in a terse letter home: 'The journalists are lousy competitive hysterical lying.'

Waugh's brand of pro-Italian feeling was equally unpopular at home. The telephone jangled all day in the Ethiopian embassy near Hyde Park with offers from Britons to fight for Haile Selassie. Letters arrived by the sackload. Expatriates from Turkey and Czechoslovakia and Hungary also volunteered, along with White Russian exiles. The British government reminded the Ethiopian ambassador that it was against the law to accept volunteers. Addis Ababa didn't need the hint; it was already committed to appearing defenceless for the League of Nations and turned away at least 3,000 men who applied. Many of those lining up to fight were white but the flame burned just as bright among black British subjects.

'Letters simply poured into our office from blacks on three continents asking where could they register,' said Ras Makonnen (aka George Nathaniel Griffith) of British Guiana, recently deported from Denmark for left-wing activities. 'I've got money. I can pay my fare across to Ethiopia and I'll buy my own rifle even.'

Makonnen's office was the 'The International African Friends of Abyssinia', a pro-Selassie outfit in London run by a gang of pan-Africanists. Jomo Kenyatta was a member, as were Trotskyite cricket writer Cyril James and George Padmore, a black leftist recently kicked out of Nazi Germany. Padmore wrote about Ethiopia for American readers, placing articles in NAACP magazine *The Crisis*.

'It is the duty of every black man and woman to render the maximum moral and material support to the Ethiopian people in their single-handed struggle against Italian Fascism and a not too friendly world.'

Britain's few pro-Italian voices came from right-wing Catholics like Waugh and G. K. Chesterton, who supported Mussolini partly out of religious feeling; backbench Tory iconoclasts led by Winston Churchill; and far-right types like American expatriate poet Ezra Pound. Both Chesterton and Pound wrote articles for *The British-Italian Bulletin*, a newsletter for Italian Fascists abroad. Alongside comments on Italy's need to expand its limited territory, Pound praised Rome as the birthplace of European civilisation. It had to be supported against Africa. Anything else would be 'murdering our own mother'.

Hugh de Wet didn't mind such matricide. But he found Ethiopia more reluctant to accept mercenaries than his father had predicted. De Wet explained his RAF credentials to Thadessa Mechecha and volunteered for the air force. The minister waffled politely then told him to come back the next day.

'Tomorrow?' asked De Wet.

'*Ishy naga.*' Yes, tomorrow.

De Wet returned the next day.

'*Ishy naga,*' said the minister.

It was the same reply every day. The minister never revealed that Haile Selassie didn't want foreigners around and, even if he did, Corriger had more pilots than planes. The air force was not hiring.

Addis Ababa was a bad place to kill time. It was 40 degrees centigrade at midday. De Wet went to the hotel bar and stared down the barrel of a whisky and soda. He was laying down the foundation for a good all-day drink when a whip-thin man in a pith helmet and pencil moustache slipped onto the stool next to him.

The man introduced himself. He was a French aristocrat with an American accent, fresh from Paris. He had a plan to make a lot of money with a mercenary flying legion and needed a partner. He bought De Wet another drink.

7

THE BARGAIN BASEMENT ARISTOCRAT

Hilaire du Berrier in Montparnasse, Autumn 1935

La Closerie des Lilas was a stylish café in the heart of Paris where Pernod cost three francs a glass and flower girls went table to table selling violets by the bunch. A statue of Marshal Ney stood across the road behind an iron railing, faded to a pale aquamarine by sun and rain and birds. When the drunks on La Closerie's terrace were feeling patriotic they slipped the flower girls a few coins to lay a bouquet at Ney's feet.

Hilaire du Berrier sometimes took a terrace table and imagined the marshal leading his troops across a smoke-shrouded battlefield. The French hussar had been one of Napoleon's best. After Waterloo the new government had executed him for his loyalty. It was a lesson in never being too devoted to any cause.

'Make your friends on one side of the river, Hal, make them good and strong,' warned Vincent Minor Schmidt, a dark jowly pilot and drinking partner who believed in integrity.

Du Berrier would nod at Schmidt's advice but never took it seriously. Ney only got a statue after he was long dead. The last orders he ever gave were instructing his own firing squad to shoot straight for the heart. So much for loyalty.

When the terrace scene got old du Berrier would head up the rue Notre Dame des Champs. A Russian art lover ran a restaurant called Dominique's, where borscht was two francs fifty and painters ate for free. The staff was a gang of exiles from the old country too busy arguing politics to get the orders right.

'There was a sporting element to dining there,' said Du Berrier, who liked a bit of a gamble, 'which made it doubly attractive.'

Then back to the cramped apartment where du Berrier lived rent-free with a seventy-year-old prince called Charles and the old man's twenty-three-year-old mistress. In exchange for this perch near the Hôtel Lutetia, du Berrier had to pose as the girl's fiancé whenever the prince's divorce lawyers came sniffing around. It was a good deal. In long, lazy days at the Jockey Club and the Club des Cent, Charles showed him how a French aristocrat behaved: elegant manners, fencing lessons, the right places to be seen.

'In brief,' said du Berrier, 'Charles taught me how a gentleman should live. Whether or not either of us would ever be able to afford it was another matter.'

Some days du Berrier hung out with a tougher crowd. Americans like Schmidt and Charles Sweeney and Granville Alexander Pollock were mercenary pilots, drinking Paris dry while they waited for the next war. They were a charismatic bunch: Ernest Hemingway had been an admirer. They told stories about skirmishing in the Mexican Revolution, shooting down German biplanes over the Somme, flying rich men on African safaris, barnstorming in the USA, helping Poland stop Bolshevism at the gates of Warsaw, and fighting for Sultan Yusef ben Hassan of Morocco against Rif rebels.

Du Berrier had done his own share of flying, sometimes over Chicago hanging from a rope ladder, but nobody had been shooting at him. He bought drinks for his flyer friends and soaked up their adventures. Being a soldier of fortune sounded an interesting life. He just needed a war.

*

By the autumn of 1935 Addis Ababa was packed out with local warlords, parading troops, prostitutes and pimps, merchants raising their prices, foreign journalists – including a skinny Latvian ex-circus ringmaster with a monocle, and shaven-headed Harun al-Rashid Bey, a forty-nine-year-old German Muslim convert whose parents knew him as Wilhelm Hintersatz – cine-cameramen, diplomats, arms dealers, two mysterious Japanese men in horn-rimmed glasses who spent their time playing table tennis, a Greek claimant to the Bourbon throne, an aging British foxhunter who thought he could teach Haile Selassie lessons learned in the trenches of France, a pair of Czechoslovak explorers who seemed unaware of the Italian threat, and a black South African representing, according to Evelyn Waugh, 'another world league for the abolition of, I think, the white races'.

Grey rain clouds hung over the town. Periodic downpours rang the corrugated iron roofs like a bell. The authorities refused to let anyone leave Addis Ababa for the front lines, and journalists hung around the railway station looking for a scoop. All they got was crowds of refugees leaving for Djibouti, Indian soldiers arriving to protect the British consulate, and the occasional arrest of a currency smuggler.

Everyone went crazy waiting for the inevitable Italian invasion, coming slow as a glacier. In early September a bar fight left one man dead and ten in the hospital. The Ethiopians made some arrests and shook their heads.

Evelyn Waugh tried to amuse himself by buying a pet baboon but had to sell on his new friend when it began masturbating in public. One night he had a scuffling fight about English literature with H. R. (Hubert Renfro) Knickerbocker, the aforementioned half-blind celebrity American journalist who paid sources in gold and submitted outrageous expenses. Knickerbocker liked the work of Aldous Huxley; Waugh hated him. The pair rolled around in the mud for five minutes while the rest of the press corps looked on.

On 9 September Haile Selassie sent a message to Rome via the peacekeepers at the League of Nations. He offered major concessions and a border change. Mussolini turned him down; war crept a little closer.

Journalists got desperate for stories. Americans telegraphed home lifestyle pieces about the challenges of living in Africa. Europeans paid off spies for scraps of information ('It is stated in some quarters ...') that always turned out to be untrue. There was no army of Yemeni Arabs ready to help Ethiopia, no Egyptian division sailing to the rescue, no troops sent by Haile Selassie's friends in Imperial Japan. A Spanish newsman who couldn't afford the telegraph posted huge wedges of typescript back to Madrid every few days.

Some of the colourful foreigners infesting Addis Ababa were good for a paragraph. Hugh de Wet got some ink for his new living arrangements: a palatial house in the centre of town. The Greek owner had been kicked out of the country for reasons no one seemed willing to talk about and his house was a cheap rent. It had a stable full of horses. An aggressive black Staffordshire terrier barked at any journalist who got too close.

De Wet's housemate was worth a few sentences. He was a recently arrived French count out of Paris with a gas mask concession and plans for an air squadron flown by mercenary pilots. Some of the reporters suspected he might really be American.

*

If Walt Disney had anthropomorphised a polecat and slapped on a pencil moustache, the result would have looked a lot like Hilaire Du Berrier. He was slight and skinny with slicked-back hair and a winning smile that never lasted more than a few seconds. And he wasn't French.

He was born Harold Berrier in the small town of Flasher, North Dakota, in November 1906. His father was an all-American success story who had started a fur business in a remote piece of nowhere and built the town around it. He worked himself into an early grave when Harold was nine years old.

The family moved to Humbolt, where Berrier's mother founded the town's first newspaper. Her son had a talent for art but ran wild as a teenager and got packed off to Pillsbury Military Academy. Berrier, now calling himself Hal, endured the discipline for a few terms then ran away. He ended up at his friend Joseph Chamberlain's house where he borrowed fifty cents from Chamberlain's father and used his artistic skills to make some cash.

'He bought water paints,' said Chamberlain, 'and made signs for windows, etc., for lawyers and such. Collected. The first rain all signs were gone and so was Hal.'

Berrier returned to Pillsbury but was expelled a few months before graduation. He headed off to Chicago for art school and a job in department store advertising. But Berrier's dream was to fly. The thrill of watching a biplane juddering through the sky at an airshow when he was six had never left him. He signed up part-time with the Heath School of Aviation. By now he was calling himself Hal du Berrier, having decided his family had roots in the French aristocracy. Five minutes of research would have shown the Berriers came from Poland. But du Berrier preferred romance to reality. At twenty he earned a pilot's licence, quit his job, and joined a flying circus as a stuntman. His mother cried. Joseph Chamberlain, his friend from Flasher, saw him perform.

'He came to Iowa from Chicago; he was a stunt performer on flying airplanes. Parachute jumps, standing on wings, hanging on a rope ladder. He put on a show at Fort Dodge Iowa and took me with him. It was a day to remember.'

Du Berrier loved the danger and told stories about how a rival tried to kill him by painting acid on the rungs of his ladder before takeoff. That didn't stop him putting together his own flying circus, but the pilot entrepreneur went into business at the wrong time. In 1927 Washington passed tough safety and maintenance regulations that forced many barnstormers into early retirement. Du Berrier exchanged one precarious living for another and became a journalist, studying at college before hitting the Chicago newsbeat.

In 1931 a Berrier uncle was appointed US representative to a commission in Paris. Du Berrier guilt-tripped a monthly allowance out of his mother and went with him. The legendary lost generation of expat writers had packed its bags when the economy had collapsed a few years earlier but there were enough Americans still around to make du Berrier welcome. His mother's allowance transformed him into a debonair man-about-town and he started turning up at cafés with cane and spats and monocle. In breaks from coffee and cigars he wrote poetry and dabbled in journalism for the capital's English-language newspapers.

Du Berrier had a gift for languages and picked up French. He became Hilaire du Berrier and began spending more time with the natives. Politics took a bite out of his life. He joined *Action française*, a reactionary monarchist group with a literary edge. Du Berrier had, as always, a romantic-sounding explanation:

> When I was nine years old I was given a book on Napoleon's cavalry, and my mind was made up. One of the first things I did when I came to Paris was to join the French monarchist party. I think that one of the most sublime speeches a head of state ever made was the reply that King Alphonso XIII gave to the men from Madrid who came to ask him to abdicate.
>
> His Majesty was in the Maurice Hotel in Paris, heard them through and when they were finished he stood up, addressed them and said: 'You have asked me to abdicate. But abdicate I cannot. For I am not only the King of Spain, but I am the King of all the Spaniards. And I not only have my own reign, but those of my family who have gone before me, for which I must someday give a rigorous accounting.'

That played well in letters back home to Humbolt. Du Berrier didn't mention that *Action française* was an extreme-right movement that hated Jews, liberals, and democracy. Its youth section, *Les Camelots du Roi*, brawled on the street with leftists and policemen and anyone else who got in the way. More mature members discussed anti-Semitic conspiracy theories and how to turn the clock back to the *ancien régime*.

Du Berrier was about as far right as you could get without jack boots. But he had charm. Not many right-wingers could have talked Louise Bryant into bed. She was the widow of John Reed, American author of *Ten Days That Shook the World*, a book about the 1917 Bolshevik Revolution no reviewer would ever call unbiased. When du Berrier met Bryant she was in her late forties and drinking herself to death. Du Berrier rarely drank to excess but was happy to feed Bryant double gins on the terrace of Le Select as he pumped her for Bolshevism's dirty secrets.

'He combined the promiscuous sociability of a billy-goat,' said someone who knew his lifestyle and didn't much care for it, 'with the predatory viciousness of a rattlesnake.'

His *Action française* contacts got him an introduction to that French aristocrat who had a spare room in Montparnasse and needed an alibi for his young mistress. Du Berrier soon found he couldn't live an aristocratic lifestyle on a North Dakota allowance. He left Paris for Monte Carlo to manage a nightclub run by a White Russian exile. When the club went under, he joined a perfume business.

It made money but du Berrier was bored. All those *Action française* meetings had convinced him he was a man of action. He just needed the right setting.

*

Du Berrier's mother died in the summer of 1935 and left him a lump sum. With a full bank account and no maternal overwatch, he quit the perfume racket and looked for adventure. Ethiopia was all over the newspapers. His *Action française* friends supported the Italians; du Berrier wasn't much fond of anyone non-white himself, but consistency was never his strong point. Haile Selassie was a monarch in an exotically remote nation. Du Berrier chose Ethiopia.

He reached out to his pilot buddies in Paris. Du Berrier had always admired the Lafayette Escadrille, a squadron of Americans who flew for France in the First World War with a pair of lion cub mascots named Whiskey and Soda. He suggested building a new squadron to fight for Ethiopia. Vincent Schmidt and Granville Pollock liked the idea and roped in ten other pilots. They were smart enough to stay in Paris until du Berrier produced a signed contract from the Ethiopians.

First there was a duel to fight. Du Berrier had got into a row with an off-duty Italian infantry officer in a Monte Carlo café. Slaps were exchanged; seconds made arrangements.

'The Riviera was agog at the chance of witnessing its first duel in years,' said the *Pittsburgh Post-Gazette*. 'Du Berrier was given an odds-on chance to come out victorious because he was a prize pupil of M. Mondoloni, famous Paris fencing master.'

The Monaco police intervened and du Berrier got sent back to Paris before any blood was spilled. The Ethiopian consul there had encouraging words about the air squadron, but insisted the matter had to be discussed in person at the Air Ministry in Addis Ababa. A French munitions company bought the ticket in exchange for du Berrier pushing their gas masks to the Ethiopians. In September he was on his way to Djibouti.

He wrote to his sister Helen, a regular confidante, about the boat trip. Crates marked 'condensed milk' contained guns and ammunition, and most passengers were soldiers for the French garrison in Somaliland: 'Dirt ... three sheep ... four cats ... 20 priests ... a number of journalists ... 200 soldiers and 40 officers and the rest ... the merriest band of fighting, drinking, swearing soldiers it has ever been my pleasure to meet ... all bound for hell and Ethiopia.'

It was raining in Addis Ababa. He got a room at the Hotel d'Europe, now calling himself Comte Hilaire du Berrier, and headed off to talk airplanes and gas masks with Haile Selassie. He got as far as the palace door. The courtiers were polite, diplomatic, and refused to help. *Ishy naga*. Every day, *ishy naga*. Du Berrier settled down in the hotel to see if things would change when Italy invaded.

In a bar he met Hugh de Wet and signed up the Englishman for his theoretical squadron. De Wet got evicted from the Hotel d'Europe shortly after when his allowance failed to turn up. The pair relocated to an empty house in the centre of town and du Berrier put down a deposit. American journalist Benny Arnold joined them and the trio lived in style with servants and horses. The pilots spent the last days of September trying to get an audience at the palace. *Ishy naga.*

On 3 October 1935 a drum began to beat slow and solemn in centre of Addis Ababa. Crowds gathered at the palace to hear the Royal Chamberlain read a proclamation.

It was war.

PART II

LIONS AT WAR

8

TWO BOHEMIAN
ADVENTURERS

Adolf Parlesák and Vilém Breyer in
Debre Tabor, 3 October 1935

Adolf Parlesák sat in a room at the Swedish Seventh Day Adventist missionary station in Debre Tabor, spinning the dials on a battered radio transmitter. It had arrived an hour earlier.

'Ras Kassa sends you a talking box,' said the messenger.

Parlesák put on the headphones and dialled through the static, wondering what Kassa expected him to do with this antique bit of kit. The twenty-seven-year-old Czechoslovak had been in Ethiopia since the summer; every day saw him sinking deeper into the quicksand of Haile Selassie's confrontation with Italy.

It was a long way from his home town of Brno, a sprawl of café squares and coffee-coloured apartment blocks that got its yearly adrenaline jolt hosting the Czechoslovak Grand Prix. Parlesák grew up there in a family rich enough to put him through engineering college and fund a stay at a Prague business school. He got good grades but preferred travel to studying. As a teenager he cycled through Austria, Hungary, Romania, and Poland, picking up new languages on the way. After studies he joined the Lloyd Triestino maritime shipping company, sailing around the Middle East and roasting himself dinners of grasshoppers over an open fire on the banks of the Nile.

In 1928 Parlesák got back on his bicycle to explore the Balkans, the Near East, and parts of Africa. He got as far as Ethiopia where Ras Tafari, preparing for the coronation, was impressed by the solemn charm of the fox-faced Czech whose dark hair jumped up like bristles on a brush.

Back home in Brno, Parlesák had to choose between an engineering career and rolling the dice on something riskier. He took the gamble. By the early 1930s Parlesák was a full-time explorer, who supported himself selling travel articles to the Czechoslovak press. Readers liked his colourful descriptions of eating shark fin in China and grappling with poisonous sea snakes in the Pacific Islands. In the summer of 1935 Parlesák took another trip to Ethiopia, hoping to explore the north of the country. He didn't pay much attention to the Italian threat.

In the baked port of Djibouti he met fellow Czechoslovak Vilém Breyer waiting for the *Chemin de fer franco-éthiopien*. A mystery man with a dry sense of humour, Breyer had recently been kicked out of Nazi Germany for reasons he didn't like to talk about. He was heading to Ethiopia for adventure.

They shared a train carriage into Addis Ababa with a Greek merchant who spent the journey moaning about the many problems in his life: how the railway company controlled all trade to Ethiopia, pushing prices high and profits low; how it was impossible to keep trade secrets when the Addis Ababa post office handed telegrams not in Amharic to any passing white man. It was a hell of a country and he didn't know why he was going back. Parlesák and Breyer ditched him in the crowds at Addis Ababa station and rented themselves a four-room apartment on the city's main road.

Accommodation was basic. Breyer haggled a table, kerosene lamp, and two folding camp beds from a man in the market. The pair hung their clothes on nails hammered into the wall. Parlesák made friends with an Ethiopian teacher, who took him to visit a school for the children of freed slaves out in the suburbs.

'About 200 pupils of all shades of skin colour and all ages from five to fourteen years, lined up at the orders of headmaster in the spacious courtyard to sing the Abyssinian national anthem. Then they demonstrated athletics and floor exercises, a sort of pocket editon black *Sokol* [Slavic youth movement] rally.'

Evenings were spent drifting through the city, keeping company with journalists and adventurers. A cinema in the main square showed old movies from America. The Greek owner of a nearby bar cranked up the gramophone and raised his prices as customers got drunker.

Some of Haile Selassie's courtiers remembered Parlesák from his earlier trip and invited him to a party honouring the emperor's birthday. Rows of cages lined the palace driveway, and Haile Selassie's pet lions roared and snarled and stank behind the bars. In the banquet hall, a band played the latest international hits to a horde of foreign dignitaries; good food on silver plates, alcohol flowing like a river. Two Belgian military advisers taught local ladies the tango.

Haile Selassie claimed to remember Parlesák. After some social chat, the emperor promised to think about granting permission to explore the north. The Ethiopian leader's polite smile, normally oblique as the Rosetta Stone, looked strained.

The next day Belgian advisers could be seen shaking off their hangovers marching groups of soldiers through the streets. On the other side of town Hubert Julian taught civil servants how to shoot. Addis Ababa was slowly mobilising. Parlesák and Breyer hung around the cafés and listened to foreigners and locals talking over the future.

'The Italians cannot win the war …'

'In a week they will be in Addis Ababa …'

'The war will last a hundred years!'

'Ethiopians are invincible in their own country …'

'How will they defend themselves against tanks? The Italian Air Force will destroy Addis Ababa on the first day …'

Everyone had an opinion, including Parlesák's own corner of Middle Europe.

*

'I feel sorry for the Abyssinians, because they have only knives and spears, while the Italians have tanks and aircraft,' said a Czechoslovak schoolboy to a reporter from *Mladý Svět* (Young Word). 'If I were rich, I would buy the Abyssinians planes so they could defend themselves.'

He deserved top marks for spotting the importance of air power in modern warfare. But no one was buying planes in Czechoslovakia. The government, determined to stay clear of any coming conflict, had suspended all weapon sales to Ethiopia. That didn't stop liberal newspapers carrying editorials condemning Italian empire building; communists talking about fascism, imperialism, and race; or churchgoers pushing Ethiopia as a Christian nation under attack, whose unfortunate habit of slavery should be ignored. A missionary from Parlesák's home town of Brno wrote the pamphlet *Habeš a její osud* (Abyssinia and its Fate), which claimed slaves had a sad life but not much worse than the average European worker.

The Czechoslovak right remained unimpressed. They preferred to debate civilisation versus barbarism and the stupidity of anyone who opposed white imperialism. Many rightists saw racial extinction on the horizon. Newspaper *Národní Politiky* (National Policies):

Our young intellectuals, who might know a few representatives of the coloured intelligentsia, either through accidental meetings, or from somewhere in their college books and more or less exotic novels, favour further freedom and equality for people of colour, and fail to think of the white race's future, which is thus digging itself a grave.

Fellow Slavic nation Poland, freshly independent after two centuries of partition, liked Ethiopia enough to have sent its *chargé d'affaires* from Cairo to attend Haile Selassie's coronation. The emperor's envoy in Paris returned the favour by visiting Warsaw. The diplomacy led to a 1934 treaty (which included 'unshakable peace and eternal friendship') and a plan to settle Polish peasants in Ethiopia. The peasant idea collapsed before it could start, and Poland did its best to stay neutral when Mussolini cast his shadow over Africa.

Romania announced it would support any action dreamt up by the League of Nations but continued to sell oil to Italy. Its neighbour Hungary, a far-right dictatorship under Admiral Miklós Horthy, made no secret of its admiration for Fascism. Mussolini had plenty of friends in Budapest: he was a strong supporter of Hungary's efforts to reclaim land stripped away in the aftermath of the First World War.

'As soon as the Italian troops cross the Ethiopian border,' Prime Minister Gyula Gömbös told his military attaché in Rome, 'go see the Duce and assure him of our solidarity and comradely cooperation.'

Around twenty Hungarians lived in Ethiopia, most educated men and women with backgrounds in engineering, medicine, or teaching. A taxidermist and hunter called Gajdács Mátyás was the richest of them, but the most successful may have been Dr Kerestély Irma, who taught French to the Imperial family and wrote the first Amharic–Hungarian dictionary.

Another doctor, the forty-five-year-old Sáska László, got himself some publicity by claiming to have spotted a previously unknown animal in Lake Abaya three times bigger than a hippopotamus. If it ever existed, no one saw it again. More practical work was done by Dr Ferenc Pádár, who lived in Harar and specialised in tropical diseases. A Swedish mission paid him to treat the locals. The money wasn't good enough to keep Pádár's equipment up to date and half the test tubes in his lab had been replaced by beer bottles. He spent most days administering syphilis tests.

The émigrés were careful not to take sides on any coming conflict but their countrymen back home cared less about neutrality. Before the invasion a Budapest veterans' group recruited 3,600 men to fight on the Italian side. Rome wasn't interested in the project.

Only a few Hungarians supported Ethiopia, people like writer and politician Imre Csécsy, who made his feelings known in the magazine *Századunk* (Century): 'I am a moral being who can never be in solidarity against the aggressor, even if it's only black people being attacked,' said Csécsy. 'I don't see how these feudal black slave-owners could be any more savage or stupid than we are.'

*

A wooden castle dominated the northern town of Debre Tabor. Ras Kassa Haile Darge had ordered it built to a traditional design and added a few modern tweaks, like glass-paned windows that allowed the Ethiopian sun to stream in and fade everything it touched. Outside, the locals lived in a permanent twilight in their windowless huts.

On 26 September 1935 Parlesák and Breyer had received permission from Haile Selassie to visit the town if they took along a letter for Kassa, the emperor's cousin and an important warlord in the area. They agreed.

The emperor shook their hands. His face was lined by lack of sleep. A courtier drove them to the airstrip in the early hours of the morning, car headlights illuminating the glowing green eyes of hyenas alongside the road. Mechanics prepped the airplane as the sun came up. The Ethiopian pilot told them not to worry about parachutes, then strapped on his own and checked it carefully.

The pair found Ras Kassa sitting on a frayed Persian carpet in a first-floor room of his castle. The *ras* was a stocky and bearded fifty-something with sparse grey hair clipped close to the skull. He wore a black cloak fastened with gold lion-head clasps, and a pair of folding half-lens spectacles with gold frames that he liked to show off when reading. Parlesák handed over Haile Selassie's letter. Kassa scanned it through and looked depressed.

'Will the Italians use gas in the war?' he asked.

'Absolutely,' said Parlesák. 'Mussolini is capable of anything ...'

The *ras* showed them gas masks his son had made by sewing circular glass eyepieces into a canvas hood. Parlesák did his best to look impressed. The masks had no air filter and were useless. No one knew that Hilaire du Berrier and his gas mask concession were being politely knocked back by Haile Selassie's courtiers down in Addis Ababa.

The two Czechs were given a room at a local Swedish Seventh Day Adventist missionary station. They shared it with a man called Jacob, an Ethiopian of Egyptian descent who handled Ras Kassa's finances and proudly wore a European suit, more patches than original fabric. The next day they were guests at Meskel, a festival that officially marked Saint Helena's discovery of the True Cross in the fourth century but was mostly celebrated as the end of the rainy season.

Ras Kassa sat under a silk umbrella flanked by anti-aircraft guns while warriors rode horses around him, shaking their swords and spears and shouting about the Italians they had killed and would kill.

'I have with this spear pierced fifteen lions and can kill a hundred times as many Italians!'

'I was with the famous Menelik at Adwa! I cut with this sabre ten Italians!'

Then more feasts in huge tents. Ras Kassa was the only chief not eating with his hands. Dignitaries wiped food grease into their hair and beards (as Waugh had found out at Pakenham Hall) – an economical bit of grooming in a country where rancid butter served as brilliantine for men and perfume for women. Kassa made sure Parlesák and Breyer had filled up on the local mead before asking if they would put their exploring on hold to train his soldiers. Breyer the adventurer was keen. Parlesák agreed to stay with him.

The training was supposed to begin at seven in the morning at a meadow outside of the town. The soldiers straggled in at nine. A handful of NCOs who had been instructed by the Belgians acted as translators. It took the Czechs two days to teach the Ethiopians how to line up in formation and march in the same direction.

The troops paraded for Ras Kassa and Debre Tabor locals. Trumpets, lines of barefoot men, officers on horseback; stop, march, present arms, bare feet clicking heels together. *Gra-Ken-Gra-Ken-Gra-Ken* (left-right-left-right-left-right). The discipline impressed onlookers, but no one could understand how marching in lines would help beat the Italians. Ras Kassa came to the same conclusion. The next day Parlesák was presented with a battered metal box covered in wires and dials. He and Breyer were now radio operators.

On 3 October he was in the missionary station listening to a speech breaking through the white noise. The broadcast was Italian.

'Abyssinia! ... We waited for forty years! ... Now, enough!'

It was Mussolini. The Italians had invaded Ethiopia that morning. Parlesák ditched the headphones and went to find his boss.

Ras Kassa and his son had already heard the news. The emperor had sent orders to gather together troops and confront the Italians in the far north. Kassa's warlord façade crumbled. He went into his room and cried for a while, then spent the rest of the day praying in a Coptic church. It was said he had once wanted to be a priest. The next day he gave Parlesák and Breyer the choice of staying to help or going home. They stayed.

The town was an ant hill of activity. New rifles handed out; horses saddled; mules loaded; young warriors happy and laughing; wiser chiefs silent and sad. In the afternoon a plane droned over the town and bumped down into a soggy meadow. Misha Babichev had brought orders and equipment from Haile Selassie.

'When are you coming back?' asked Parlesák. 'I have some letters to send to Europe.'

Babichev shook his head. The Italians already controlled the skies.

'It would be suicide.'

He told them Mussolini's air force had bombed Adwa in the far north, avenging Italy's nineteenth-century defeat by Menelik.

A few days later, an African-American pilot nicknamed the Brown Condor would turn up in Addis Ababa with a dramatic story about Adwa involving dogfights and destroyed hospitals and dead nurses. The newsmen ate it up. Only Evelyn Waugh thought he might be lying. Waugh was right.

9

THE MAN FROM CHICAGO

An African-American Pilot in the News,
6 October 1935

The Ethiopian army was no place for snappy dressers. Warriors headed for the front wrapped in metres of white cloth, unwashed since the last time they fell in a river; the *rases* preferred shabby black cloaks and lion skin hopping with fleas. Only pilots had a sense of style. Misha Babichev raced a sports car through Addis Ababa with a silk scarf fluttering around his neck, while fellow flyers opted for jodhpurs, leather jackets, and sweaters with Lion of Judah designs. The best dressed among them was an African-American a long way from home, doing his best to look sharp in the middle of a war.

It was the Saturday after Italy crossed the border. John Robinson was getting measured for a new uniform in one of the capital's tailoring shops. The thirty-two-year-old had a neat moustache, hair straightened with the hot comb, and a slight smile permanently on his lips. The tailor got busy with tape and chalk while Robinson talked over his head to a British journalist, who wanted an eyewitness account of Adwa's fall to the invaders.

It was a good story, told in a calm southern voice: bombs falling, the hospital exploding, the corpse of a dismembered Swedish nurse in the flaming ruins, Robinson's plane tussling with two Fascist fighters high over the town, then the shot-up crate limping all the way back to Addis Ababa.

'Mr Waugh,' he said, 'do you realise I might have been killed myself?'

Waugh nodded but Robinson could smell his scepticism. He'd smelled it all his life. Things could be tough for an ambitious African-American and Robinson had wasted a lot of years getting white people to take him seriously.

He grew up in Mississippi in an era when hooded vigilantes hanged black men from trees at midnight. Then it was the casual racism of co-workers at a Detroit cab company and the sneers of white teachers at a Chicago flying school who wouldn't give lessons to African-Americans. Robinson fought them all. Today he was chief instructor of the Royal Ethiopian Air Force and the man America's black newspapers called the Brown Condor.

The tailor finished his measurements and hustled around the shop looking for pins. Robinson retold his story and piled on more detail to convince Waugh.

He had flown up to Adwa on Wednesday with dispatches for Ras Seyoum. He stayed overnight. Next morning he was sitting in the hospital with a Swedish nurse, drinking cocoa when the Italian planes attacked. The nurse was good-looking and 5'5" tall, blonde. The hospital was clearly marked with a red cross and Adwa inhabited only by women and children. Robinson ran for his Potez 25 biplane when the bombs started falling. It was impossible to take off. He returned to the town and found the hospital in ruins and the nurse dead. He flew back to Addis Ababa, dog-fighting Italian planes on the way, and told the emperor about the bombing. The emperor was distraught.

And that, Mr Waugh, is what really happened.

Robinson gave his most sincere look across the tailor shop and hoped the Ethiopian government appreciated the performance. It was mostly lies.

*

Haile Selassie had been expecting an attack from the south. All he got was Graziani's men scampering around some border posts as decoy for the Fascist war machine invading through the other end of the country. In the early morning of 3 October 1935 three columns of Italian cavalry, lorries, and mules crossed the northern frontier from Eritrea.

'We have been patient for forty years,' said Mussolini. 'Now we too want our place in the sun.'

Ras Seyoum's men folded under aerial bombing and fled for the Tembien mountains; many had never seen an airplane before. The other defender of the north, Dejazmach Haile Selassie Gugsa, had been taking bribes for months. He defected to the Italians and surrendered his capital, Makale. Unhappy locals burned down the *dejazmach*'s palace before Blackshirt troops arrived. Any remaining resistance was beaten down by aerial bombing. Adwa, Enticco, and Adigrat fell in days.

Rome ruled the air. Haile Selassie's air force had eleven planes, none armed and not all flyable, manned by a team of Ethiopian pilots padded out with foreigners like the German Ludwig Weber. The fliers stayed safely behind the lines: the Italians would have gunned them down at will anywhere near the front. Only the Brown Condor, caught in Adwa the day before the invasion, saw some action. But one of Pierre Corriger's new hires got a closer look at the action when he found himself in Adwa the day before the invasion.

As a child of seven, John Charles Robinson watched from the Mississippi Sound beach when pilot John Moisant skimmed a pontoon biplane along the water and set it down in one piece. Robinson spent the rest of his childhood flying kites in Gulfport and dreaming of airplanes. He wanted to be a pilot when he grew up.

'Nine-tenths confidence plus one-tenth common-sense equals successful aviator,' Moisant told the world shortly before falling out of a plane and breaking his neck.

Robinson had a hard work ethic. As a schoolboy he shined shoes, delivered groceries, and drove a truck. He kept a bad temper locked away behind the feet-shuffling, eye-rolling minstrel show that America expected from her young black men. Nothing good came from getting angry with white folks in Mississippi. An aptitude for mechanics got him a place studying Automotive Mechanical Science at Alabama's Tuskegee Institute, a private college and the only place around where African-Americans could get an education past their teens.

Four years later Robinson was a mechanic for the Yellow Cab Company in Detroit, working with white co-workers full of casual racism. He cooled off by hanging around a local airfield and earned his first passenger flight as reward for repairing a pilot's stuttering biplane engine. It reawakened Robinson's dream of flying. By the end of the 1920s he had moved to Chicago and a room in the YMCA while he badgered the admissions desk at the Curtiss-Wright School of Aviation. They turned him down: white students only.

The best Curtiss-Wright could offer was a janitor job. Robinson took it and sat in on lectures, fishing old textbooks from the trash bins out back when everyone else had gone home. He met Cornelius Coffey, another black mechanic and would-be pilot at the YMCA. Together they built a kit plane around a motorcycle engine and showed it off to a lecturer at Curtiss-Wright. A few weeks later they were the first African-American students in the school's history. Robinson claimed his plane-building skills had impressed the school into lifting its colour bar. Curtiss-Wright staff remembered Robinson's temper breaking out of its cage when he threatened them with legal action.

Robinson and Coffey did well enough at their studies that Curtiss-Wright offered the chance to teach an evening class if they could come up with some African-American students. *The Chicago Defender* publicised the scheme; thirty-five people turned up for the first night. The class evolved into the Brown Eagle Aero Club, flying a handful of airplanes out of a homemade airstrip carved into a cornfield.

The Brown Eagles put on shows for paying audiences as the Challenger Air Pilots Association. It made money but Robinson and Coffey had to dip into the profits to bail out anyone who accidentally landed in a white district. Chicago did not like airborne African-Americans.

*

By the spring of 1935 Robinson was married, running a garage, and spending his evenings talking Ethiopia with the rest of the Eagles. The gang was keen to help Haile Selassie. Claude Barnett, director of the Associated Negro Press, put them in touch with Malaku Bayen. The emperor's cousin knew how his homeland felt about foreigners but thought it might accept one pilot smuggled into the country. Robinson volunteered.

Addis Ababa made things difficult, demanding references and certificates, but Bayen pulled some strings in the royal court. On 2 May 1935 Robinson left his wife in charge of the garage and departed for Ethiopia, posing as an African tailor returning home after twenty years in America.

He reached Addis Ababa in early June and took a room at the Hotel de France. The American had dreams of swooping in and showing the natives how flying was done back in the technologically advanced USA. His enthusiasm deflated at the airfield when Corriger explained that though Robinson's 600 flying hours was impressive, he had Ethiopian pilots with more air time and several of them had done military aviation training in France. Haile Selassie had only taken on the African-American as a favour to cousin Bayen.

Corriger sugared the bad news with some good. Gaston Vedel had left for France two years previous after barely surviving a poisoning attempt in a Harar restaurant owned by a Muslim partisan of Lij Yassou. The training programme had been on hold since. Corriger offered to resurrect it for Robinson. The American signed a one-year contract to instruct new pilots.

In the middle of July, Johnson was officially introduced to Haile Selassie. He was tongue-tied in the presence of the emperor.

'He asked me if I liked the work I had been assigned to and I told him any work I did to help Ethiopia was to my liking. He asked that I say something else, but I had nothing else to say and went out.'

When he wasn't stumbling over his words in front of the emperor, Robinson cut a slick figure in a brown leather jacket with an Ethiopian lion cloth badge stitched to the left breast. He sent lying letters back home to the Eagles, claiming to be head of the Ethiopian air force and signing himself Colonel Robinson, an honorary title locals gave to any foreigner who served with them. But he was competent at his job and knew white people well enough to act humble with the foreign journalists gathering in Addis Ababa.

'He is a quiet, capable man,' said Wynant Hubbard, Harvard man and big game hunter, 'modest to a degree and reluctant to talk about himself.'

It was going well, until Robinson ran into Hubert Julian at the Hotel de France on 8 August. The Brown Condor versus the Black Eagle: a one-round bout with a bad result for everyone.

*

Back in the early twentieth century Haitian journalist Bénito Sylvain arrived in Ethiopia with a plan to end white imperialism. Sylvain had a waxed moustache, wealthy parents, and the early stages of a mad stare. He was well known in Paris for using the pages of *La Fraternité* newspaper to push pan-Africanism, and had been making regular trips to Addis Ababa since Menelik's victory at Adwa. The journalist wanted to enlist the emperor in his campaign to free the black world from its colonial chains.

In 1904 Sylvain got his chance to explain his plans to the royal court. Menelik listened politely as the Haitian talked imperialism and a new dawn for the black race.

'I applaud your theory and I wish you the greatest possible success,' said Menelik. 'But, you know, I am not a Negro at all. I am a Caucasian.'

That way of thinking had never gone away among Ethiopians. Locals were always asking John Robinson how it was possible for a black man to be an American citizen, a country they associated with technology and modernity and white skin. The pilot was patronised by courtiers, looked down on by soldiers, and continually reminded of his race. He got used to gritting his teeth.

'I can readily see for an American Negro to succeed here,' said Robinson, 'he must possess the following qualifications – First, A strong Stomach – A Silent tongue – A king Heart – An Iron hand – The Patience of Job, and above all things, know his line of work.'

In August, Robinson faced another challenge in the form of Hubert Julian. The Black Eagle had always depended more on publicity than ability and had spent the previous weeks giving press briefings to Anglophone journalists, changing outfits twice a day, and trying to strong-arm the American consulate into sending a telegram protesting Washington's lack of support for Haile Selassie. Julian believed that enough newspaper headlines would convince the Ethiopians to let him back into the air force.

Then John Robinson got the job. Calling himself the Brown Condor, a nickname clearly influenced by the Black Eagle, was just dripping lemon juice into the cut. The feud ramped up when Robinson discovered Julian was the man who had thrown him and Coffey out of a Chicago hotel room. Journalists made things worse by running stories about two black foreigners competing to run the Royal Ethiopian Air Force. Exasperated palace officials made it clear Pierre Corriger remained in charge: 'Ethiopian aviation is headed by competent foreign experts.'

Julian and Robinson met face-to-face for the first time in the hotel lobby. Guests stopped to watch as an argument turned into a fight. When it was over, each man had a different story. Julian claimed Robinson pulled a knife and slashed his arm; the Black Eagle knocked him out with a chair. Robinson told journalists his rival had been sitting in the lobby when he came down the stairs; Julian had marched over and slapped him across the face before staff pulled them apart.

Courtiers grounded Robinson and stripped Julian of his command. A week later both were quietly reinstated. Robinson went back to instructing new pilots but Julian got posted to Ambo, a calm spa town three days from the capital, with orders to turn 3,000 locals into soldiers. The day of Julian's departure, journalists were sitting on wooden benches outside Addis Ababa's tin-roofed press building and exchanging gossip when he rode up on horseback.

'It is a prodigious lie that the emperor told me he hasn't enough planes for me to crash,' Julian shouted at them. 'I am favoured by His Majesty, respected by high officials, and loved by the people. Also, this magnificent assignment is a promotion by the emperor for making soldiers in Ethiopia.'

The journalists watched as he rode off, tailed by a convoy of new recruits and assistants lugging suitcases.

Robinson got the better deal. He moved into a house with six servants and made a daily commute out to the airfield for training sessions. The flying instructor enjoyed his new life. He liked the weather, the spicy stew made by his cook, the white boot lifted off his neck. In return, the royal court expected him to lie to the press after he got caught in Adwa when the Italians invaded; the press would believe a foreigner. Another outsider, a Russian called Feodor Konovalov, had been in the town at the same time but he was still up on the northern front, and no one was sure if he was as willing to lie as Robinson.

The Brown Condor's real experience had been dangerous enough. As the bombs fell, Robinson raced for his plane, camouflaged at a makeshift landing strip a few kilometres outside the city. He doubled back to shelter when takeoff proved impossible. By 4 October the skies were clear and the Brown Condor flew to Addis Ababa. He just missed Italian soldiers dragging a monument to their dead of 1896 into the centre of Adwa. They had brought it with them all the way from Europe.

The Ethiopians knew that dead white foreigners would stir up the press and asked Robinson to claim a Swedish nurse had been killed. It was a stretch. Adwa didn't have a hospital. The Brown Condor did his best, adding in a lie about fighting off Italian fighter planes on his way home in an unarmed plane, and committed to the story in letters home: 'I dident [sic] mind being attacked, but I wish my airplane had been of a later type, I think I would have given them a wondreful [sic] lesson.'

Journalists ran the stories but got suspicious when they could find no trace of the missing Swede. The *Daily Mail* badgered Evelyn Waugh for facts on the 'upblown nurse'. He tracked Johnson down to his tailor in Addis Ababa and pumped him for information. Robinson stuck to the story, but Waugh left unconvinced. A bit of detective work revealed the truth.

'Nurse unupblown,' Waugh telegrammed London.

Robinson was all over the papers as a liar. He was happy to get out of town on 22 October and fly Haile Selassie up north to Dessie, where the emperor was moving his court closer to the action. The Brown Condor was still doing better than Julian, exiled to the middle of nowhere. De Wet and du Berrier couldn't even get an interview at the palace.

But there was one group of foreigners the Ethiopians welcomed with open arms: Belgian fascists.

HAILE SELASSIE'S FASCIST FRIENDS

Léopold Reul's Unofficial Belgian Mission in Ethiopia, October–November 1935

The *Légion nationale* did most of its marching in Liège, the heart of Belgium's coal-mining country. The fascist group had started as a gang of war veterans who liked to get together, drink beer, and complain about the government. Then frog-faced lawyer Paul Hoornaert joined. The former trench fighter juiced up the movement with uniforms and a political ideology that split the difference between *Action française* and Mussolini. Soon the *Légion* was marching through the streets with blue shirts and tricolour flags, beating drums and giving fascist salutes.

By 1935 the movement was 5,000-strong, loving the homeland and despising democracy. Hoornaert was modest enough to accept he wouldn't make much of a dictator. He preferred direct rule by Léopold III. Hoornaert's followers dreamt of forming a royal bodyguard for a new absolutist monarchy but spent most of their time fighting in the Liège streets with anyone who got in the way.

Unlike many of its fascist rivals, the *Légion* believed in national unity. Belgium was two nations lashed together by Catholicism and bureaucracy. Poor, rural Flanders farmed the north and wealthy, French-speaking Wallonia industrialised the south. By the time Mussolini invaded Ethiopia, fascist groups like *Vlaams*

Nationaal Verbond and loudmouth Léon Degrelle and his Rexists were agitating for separation. Hoornaert kept waving the tricolour and talking about togetherness.

Some days it seemed that supporting Mussolini's claims in Africa was the only thing the *Légion nationale* had in common with fellow fascists. Hoornaert applauded the invasion and harangued his government about pulling Major Dothée's military mission out of Ethiopia. The *Légion* leader was pushing at an open door. His government was equally eager to disengage from the Ethiopian swamp.

In June 1935 Brussels banned weapons sales to both Ethiopia and Italy, annoying Haile Selassie and making arms dealers' wallets bleed. In the previous two years Ethiopia had bought 16,000 rifles and 595 machine guns from Belgian companies. Brussels allowed Dothée to stay in Harar, training the last of the Imperial Guard as the clock ran out on peace, but ordered him home the day Italy came over the border. The pudgy Belgian hung around Addis Ababa waiting for his men to join him. He heard worrying reports that Lieutenant Roger Cambier was seriously ill, with Ras Desta's army in the south.

The news of Dothée's withdrawal should have brought an extra snap to Hoornaert's goose-step as he marched the *Légion* through Liège in October. But he had something new to worry about. The Ethiopians had outmanoeuvred Brussels by recruiting a private military mission of Belgian mercenaries, led by fifty-three-year-old, monocled Lieutenant-Colonel Léopold Reul.

Hoornaert knew something that made the situation sourer: Reul and his ten mercenaries were all full-blooded fascists. Until recently, most of them had been marching in the ranks of the *Légion nationale*.

*

'Europeans in general,' said Léopold Reul, 'are apt to think about the military situation in Ethiopia in terms of Europe when, in fact, it is completely different.'

Outside his office window Addis Ababa was getting ready for war. Soldiers drilled in the streets. Locals dug trenches in their gardens. Journalists slept with gas masks clutched across their chests. The suave and arrogant Count Luigi Vinci-Gigliucci was under house arrest at the Italian embassy for refusing to leave the country until he knew his consulate staff was safe. He spent his time playing cards and chatting with Evelyn Waugh. The Englishman had been the only person to attend his press conferences before the invasion.

Haile Selassie was preparing to leave for Dessie in the north. Courtiers packed trunks, rolled carpets and polished crowns. Newsmen queued at the tin shack press bureau to get travel permits stamped by the secret police. Locals craned their necks, each day expecting a fleet of Italian airplanes to turn the sky black with bombs.

All the activity reminded Léopold Reul of the First World War. The dust blowing round Addis Ababa, drying everyone's throats now the rainy season had ended, summoned up sharp memories of the day he got shot. Reul had been somewhere near Antwerp in the first August of the First World War. The Belgian army was in retreat from the Germans, and Reul was a professional soldier trying to keep his men together in the chaos of screaming artillery, wounded horses, and falling men. A bullet hit him in the side of the face and bounced around his palate and exited through the other cheek. Léopold Reul went down into the dust.

It left him with a throat that tasted like a house fire. He could not speak for a year. The wound was the start of a long political journey that led to Addis Ababa and a whispered interview in late October with French reporter Jean d'Esme, a thirty-something French journalist for the conservative *L'Écho de Paris* with a face like a granite slab and a sideline in colonial adventure novels.

Reul blamed the League of Nations for the fighting, telling D'Esme the Italians had spent nine months building up forces before the invasion while the Ethiopians did nothing except wait for the League's help. When the Italians came over the border, Geneva got busy writing reports and voting on sanctions but it was clear the peacekeepers would not get directly involved. Reul was too much a military man not to wish Haile Selassie had been more active ('not even skeleton units of trained men, so necessary when you are getting together an army') but claimed that a force was being assembled on feudal lines and would soon be at the front. No one could expect a medieval army to mobilise as fast as a modern European one. D'Esme nodded in agreement and scribbled in his notebook. The Frenchman knew all about war: he had earned the Croix de Guerre fighting in the trenches. That shared experience was the only reason Reul had given this rare interview. As the sound of marching barefoot soldiers drifted in from outside, Reul turned as optimistic as he ever was. Perhaps negotiations would end the war. No serious fighting had taken place yet: 'On the Italian side there is stagnation, a stalemate. With the Ethiopians this is a training period. But if there is to be a war it will begin shortly.'

*

As Reul gave his interview, other foreigners were leaving Ethiopia. On 9 October Hubert Julian had ridden in to Addis Ababa on an exhausted horse.

'It was the emperor's wishes,' he told newsmen and tethered his sweaty horse to a eucalyptus tree. 'I will start immediately for Adwa to help capture the city. I know how to fight the Italians. I knocked a lot of them out in Harlem – with my fists!'

He claimed to have been attacked by a pack of hyenas on his way there and offered his revolver so journalists could sniff the barrel. The next morning he got a post as aide-de-camp to Ras Mulugeta, Minister of War. As the army prepared to move north, Julian's private thoughts became less enthusiastic.

'To fight on the front is no more than an empty gesture that might cost my life,' he said. 'Everyone agrees that, with the lack of ammo and weapons, and the disorganisation in the capital, there is no hope of stopping the well armed and highly trained

Italian army. I think, too, of the old proverb: "He that fights and runs away ...'"

Others felt the same way. Swedish Major General Eric Virgin had already left, claiming the heart attacks were coming at faster intervals. Journalists suspected his rival Captain Tamm had applied political pressure in the right places. Haile Selassie asked Sweden for a replacement but got only excuses.

Tamm and his officers decided to stay on, disbanding the cadet programme and fast-tracking their students into officers for a new brigade. The Swedes' families sent telegrams begging them to reconsider, and Stockholm applied more subtle persuasion with talk about honour and duty. Tamm ignored them all and asked army friends back home to come join him. The Ministry of Foreign Affairs intervened with threats to cashier anyone who volunteered. No one answered Tamm's letters. One of his own men had already broken under the official pressure and left; another would leave in the near future.

In early November soldiers dragged Hubert Julian out of his tent near the emperor's palace and marched him inside to see the Royal Chamberlain. He was accused of plotting to assassinate Haile Selassie, not repaying loans, and cashing two paychecks. Julian collapsed when he heard the news and had to be carried out.

The murder plot turned out to be malicious gossip from Italian newspaper *La Tribuna* and the charges were dropped. Enough evidence existed on the embezzlement angle for the Royal Chamberlain to investigate deeper. Julian felt the noose tightening around his neck and quit Ethiopia. On 15 November he took a final drive around Addis Ababa. His chauffeur ran someone over and locals threw stones at the car. The next day Julian caught a train to the coast. Pierre Corriger was glad to see him go.

'This character from an operetta,' said the Frenchman, 'is said to be a colonel but is nothing more than an adventurer.'

If Julian had been drawing a double salary he had little to show for it. The Black Eagle's bankroll was so thin he had to lie his way on board a liner to Marseille and dodge the bill when they docked.

In town, a pair of photographers tried to shove their way into his hotel bathroom for a picture.

'That could never happen in Ethiopia,' said Julian, throwing a sponge at them. 'In the first place there are no bath tubs.'

He eventually reached London and shared his opinions about Haile Selassie with journalists.

'I'm sorry for the guy,' the Black Eagle told the *Daily Express*. 'I could have won the war for him.'

Not many people believed him. If any foreigner was going to win the war for Ethiopia, it would be a patriotic military man like Lieutenant-Colonel Léopold Reul.

*

'Believe me, it moves one to tears to see a people rising up in response to a sublime emotion, the love of country, the defence of native soil,' Reul told d'Esme. 'Almost without arms they are bearing their breasts to the most formidable modern weapons of warfare.'

Warfare was something Reul knew all about. After taking that bullet to the throat, he had transferred to the Belgian Congo and led the locals to victory against the Germans in East Africa. His voice remained a whisper.

Reul had sixteen medals jangling on his chest when he sailed back home in 1919 to teach strategy at military school. On the way he married the daughter of a German aristocrat. He had medals, intelligence, bravery, and a forgiving attitude towards the enemy. Reul should have been set for a glittering career in the post-war Belgian army, but his health remained poor and the voice never recovered. In May 1923 he retired. Some colleagues were happy to see him go, suspicious of his involvement with the *Comité de Politique Nationale* (National Policy Committee) of Pierre Nothomb, a reactionary troublemaker with a profile like an eagle.

'A democratic regime must necessarily ruin our civilisation,' Nothomb had said.

Within a few months of retirement Reul was supporting a coup by Ruhr separatists in the city of Aachen. The territory had been taken from Germany after the war and the *Comité* hoped to cause enough chaos for Belgium to grab a slice. After firefights and a few deaths French troops crushed the coup. The *Comité* fell apart in the aftermath but Reul stayed loyal to its ideology and became general manager of Nothomb's newspaper, *L'Action Nationale*, an outfit heavily influenced by the monarchists at *Action française*.

The war veteran felt betrayed when Nothomb, sick of being called '*Napoleon de la Marmaille*' (Napoleon of the delinquents) by the press, joined mainstream conservative politics. Reul refused to compromise. He joined the *Légion nationale*, a fascist group with paramilitary leanings that liked Mussolini but had never forgiven Germany for the war.

In the summer of 1935 Reul was dabbling in real estate and marching in Liège when the Ethiopian ambassador to France knocked on his door. Perhaps the *Légion nationale* didn't seem fascist to the Ethiopians: it had king-worship and flag-waving and dodged the customary anti-Semitism by accepting Jewish members if they were 'worthy Belgians'. Perhaps Tekle Awariathe just hadn't bothered to background-check the military veteran.

The ambassador signed Reul to a two-year contract and asked him to recruit ten more men. Reul got to work. His fellow mercenaries came from similar military and political backgrounds: war buddies, members of veteran associations, far-right political activists from the *Légion*. All were retired soldiers or in the reserves. Friends were surprised to see them packing their bags to help an African emperor.

For some it was the logical extension of their old *Action française* ideology: Haile Selassie was a dictatorial monarch freed from the burdens of democracy. *Action* leader Charles Maurras would have approved if he hadn't just joined half the members of the Académie Française in signing the pro-invasion *Manifesto of French Intellectuals for the Defense of the West*. Other mercenaries had the more practical aim of growing Belgian influence in East Africa.

Or it might have been the money. Reul got 30,000 Belgian francs a month – six times the pay of a Belgian general. Edmond Debois, Reul's right-hand man and a decorated wartime captain-turned-industrialist, earned 25,000 francs. Even low rankers like lieutenants Gustave Witmeur and Joseph van Fleteren got 10,000 a month. Tekle Awariathe waited until the ink had dried on their contracts before discussing the issue with the Belgian government. He knew Brussels might object to the recruitment of soldiers who took orders direct from Addis Ababa.

'Will the Belgian government authorise army veterans to enlist in a private capacity as military instructors?' he asked in July 1935, signing off with a smooth lie. 'This engagement will naturally end in case of war.'

Brussels reacted badly. Opposing Italy on the battlefield, even indirectly, could cause serious diplomatic problems; it didn't help that the king's sister Marie José of Belgium was married to the Italian Crown Prince. The government tried to shut down the mercenary operation with lawyer-speak about military regulations. Reul and his men got around it by stripping the insignia off their uniforms. Haile Selassie's relations with the Belgian government became strained.

'Emperor very unhappy over difficulties created by the Groupe Reul,' reported Belgium's man in Addis Ababa. 'It is no secret that Belgian industry will no longer get any orders for material or weapons.'

*

Reul's mercenaries arrived at Addis Ababa railway station on 15 September 1935. Some of Dothée's men were there to meet them. Lieutenant-Colonel Reul expected to be saluted. The official mission regarded him as a renegade who had disobeyed Brussels. They refused to acknowledge his rank. The Belgians shouted at each other as the engine steamed and passengers disembarked and rain drummed on the roof. Reul's voice could barely be heard.

'Such behaviour has never been seen before in the annals of military comradeship,' he whispered.

The eleven mercenaries marched off to their new billet in the empress' bathhouse. They had a lot of work to do: expand Imperial Guard training, set up a General Staff, establish censorship for the central news agency, and reorganise the Addis Ababa police force. Soon the team was scattered around Ethiopia. Reul and his upper-crust lieutenant, Adelin de Fraipont, whose ancestors included the rector of Liège, waited in the capital for the emperor to leave for Dessie.

D'Esme thought Reul looked strained. Team members were already reporting back with stories of unfriendly *rases* and disinterested recruits. Xenophobic members of the royal court spread rumours Reul was an Italian spy. Behind the monocle and thin smile, the mercenary leader's throat wound throbbed. A doctor had recommended another operation. The Belgian deflected D'Esme's questions about problems and talked about the apparent failure of the Italian army in the south.

'It encountered two extremely serious adversaries,' said Reul, 'the desert and lack of water.'

As he walked D'Esme to the door, the mask of confidence dropped. Reul put his hand on the Frenchman's arm. He begged him not to criticise Ethiopia.

'Before such a situation one should walk on tiptoes, softly, as one does in a house where someone lies dead.'

A few days later Haile Selassie asked Pierre Corriger to fly him up to Dessie. The Frenchman reluctantly declined: Paris had ordered him home. John Robinson took the controls instead. Reul, de Fraipont, and over 100 journalists joined them in the north. Spies told Italy about the emperor's movements within days.

On 5 December 1935 a wing of Italian bombers took off from Eritrea and flew south. Their mission was to kill Haile Selassie.

II

DOCTORS AND PROSTITUTES

The Ethiopian Red Cross under Attack in
Dessie, 6 December 1935

They shot Europe's smallest dictator as he walked out of a corner office. Sour-faced putschist Otto Planetta fired his pistol twice and hit the 4' 11" Austrian leader in the throat and armpit. Engelbert Dollfuß would spend the last hours of his life bleeding to death on a chaise longue.

Austrians used to joke that any full-figure portrait of Dollfuß on a postage stamp would be life size. The dictator had a schoolboy face to match his height but he was a war hero who grew up illegitimate on a farm and fought his way to the top of Austria's political pile. His *Christlichsoziale Partei* (Christian Social Party) had clung to power since the end of the First World War. By the early 1930s pressure from Nazis to the right and socialists to the left convinced Dollfuß to abolish parliamentary democracy and rule as dictator of the *Vaterländische Front* (Fatherland Front). He saw it as the only way to keep Austria independent; but the stress of being führer gnawed at his nerves.

'He eats too little and smokes too much,' said his wife.

The Front was Catholic and corporatist. Benito Mussolini approved and cheered on Dollfuß when he smashed the Socialists in vicious streetfighting. Homegrown Nazis proved tougher. They campaigned for Anschluß, the union of Austria with Adolf Hitler's Germany. Dollfuß preferred to stay captain of his own ship and

in June 1933 banned the Austrian Nazi party. Thousands fled
to Germany or went underground. Bombs started exploding on
Viennese streets.

On 25 July 1934 a gang of Austrian Nazis stormed the Vienna
Chancellery. The ceremonial guards on duty didn't even have
ammunition for their rifles. Planetta led a team in search of the
Austrian dictator, planning to take him hostage until he signed
over power to a more pliable politician guaranteed to rubber-
stamp the Anschluß. When the gang ran into Dollfuß as he
tried to escape the building Planetta could only think about his
Nazi comrades doing time in prison. He pulled the trigger. The
putschists dragged Dollfuß into his office and let him bleed out as
they argued among themselves.

The Chancellery attack was part of a wider coup that involved
the seizure of radio stations, telephone exchanges, and military
bases around the country. Austrian Nazi exiles did their part by
attacking a border customs post. Hitler believed his homeland
would welcome annexation by Germany but instead found Austrian
soldiers and far-right Heimwehr paramilitaries fighting back.

Italy sent troops to the Austrian border and threatened war if the
Third Reich made a move. The two dictatorships were branches of
the same fascist tree but any admiration Hitler felt for Mussolini
was unrequited. Diplomatic relations had worsened after a recent
visit when the führer lectured his hosts on the African blood
running through the veins of all Mediterranean peoples. No one in
Rome trusted the Germans.

'In my opinion, sacrificing Austria would be a colossal mistake,'
wrote Fulvio Suvich, Mussolini's Undersecretary for Foreign
Affairs. 'It is a mistake to think that Germany, getting to Brenner
and to Tarvisio, would stop there ... Germany will make every
effort to span the 100 kilometres to the Adriatic!'

With Italians tanks at the border and Dollfuß dead, Hitler
backed off and denied any involvement in the putsch. Heimwehr
men crushed the Austrian Nazis and their supporters. Arrests,
trials, jail, exile. They hanged Planetta in a prison yard. Kurt

Schuschnigg became the new *Vaterländische Front* leader. Black mourning flags hung in the capital but few believed Austria could hold off the Nazis much longer.

'You don't see anyone shedding tears over Dollfuß, do you?' said a German sleeping car porter to an American journalist as their train rolled through Austria. 'What a mad thing for him to have attempted to keep two nations apart which were culturally and linguistically so closely allied! Imagine the American president trying to keep the United States and Canada apart.'

Some Austrian Nazis involved in the putsch escaped the round-up. Dr Valentin Schuppler was one of them. He went back to his day job as a top trauma surgeon in Vienna's biggest hospital. It took the Heimwehr a year to get on his trail. Schuppler needed to escape somewhere far away where a Nazi doctor could treat patients and punish Italy for blocking the Anschluß. He headed for Haile Selassie's Ethiopia.

*

The road to Dessie was a rutted track known as the Imperial Highway that ran north-east from the capital through sugar plantations and forests alive with birds and monkeys. Travellers spent their days in bone-shaking lorries and nights round a fire hugging cups of bitter coffee. At the road's end was a city of dust and marketplaces.

Haile Selassie set up base in Dessie centre. The tubular skeleton of an Oerlikon anti-aircraft gun sat outside his tent. Journalists camped out in the nearby grounds of the Seventh Day Adventist mission and medical centre. The sound of their tapping typewriters drifted around the city.

'Nature has made Dessie the prettiest and most picturesque town of Abyssinia,' wrote French journalist Henri de Vilmorin.

Evelyn Waugh thought the Frenchman was blind. The British writer hated the town enough to spend most of his time hiking in the surrounding hills. He chatted to local Muslims and found their support for Haile Selassie distinctly ambivalent, very different to the stories in the press about the emperor's loyal subjects coming together to defend the nation. Waugh sent his take on the fragmented empire off to *The Daily Mail* and got telegrams back demanding more. The war was all over the front pages back home. Many Britons worried the fighting could escalate and turn global.

'What next? Is it war? Where will it lead? Will England be drawn in?' asked the crowds milling through Downing Street after news of the invasion broke. Waugh did his best but there was little else to write about in the backwater town. He turned out smartly written but trivial pieces about Dessie and walked them down to the airfield, a grassy stretch of land grazed by cows that had to be herded off every time a plane appeared. Journalist copy was flown out of town by British air taxi outfits like Brian Allen Aviation Ltd and Birkett Air Service. By early December Waugh was bored enough to think about going home. A telegram from *The Daily Mail* made the decision for him.

'Have much appreciated your work,' it said.

He had been sacked. Waugh hitched a ride back to Addis Ababa with a cheerful German adventurer who drove for an outfit called the Ethiopian Red Cross. On the way out of town the German pointed at a local leader's home converted into a hospital. A Red Cross flag hung from the roof next to a light machine gun. As they drove back to the capital Waugh's new friend casually shot at farmers with his rifle. He claimed to have fought for Paraguay in the Chaco War.

The German was one of the many adventurers who had turned up in Addis Ababa looking for action. Locals didn't trust them and neither did the few foreigners who had found a place in the Ethiopian ranks.

'Adventurers of obscure origins and even darker morals,' said the Cuban mercenary Alejandro del Valle, killing time in Addis Ababa before joining Ras Mulugeta's army. 'Smugglers, swindlers or, at best, men whose incomes were a mystery to us.'

De Wet and Du Berrier were still hanging round the bars and getting knocked back by palace officials. They had been joined by Du Berrier's Paris friend Vincent Minor Schmidt, a former soldier who had taught himself to fly on days off from serving with the army of occupation in Germany, then gone on to fight in the Mexican revolution, pilot rich men on African hunting safaris, and barnstorm in the USA. He had come to Ethiopia to check on the progress of Du Berrier's mercenary air squadron. Du Berrier told him the plan was in bad shape and bought a round of drinks.

The trio sometimes hit the bars with a former bodyguard for Al Capone, a huge beer-gutted man called Waldrow who claimed to be English but had a vocabulary sprinkled with everything from Portuguese to Tagalog. Waldrow claimed to have worked as a booze smuggler out of Canada during prohibition, a gold prospector in Australia, an elephant hunter in the Belgian Congo, a pirate in Madagascar, and an arms dealer in China. His main line of work seemed to be selling French pornographic postcards.

Elsewhere in town was an English retired master of foxhounds called Major Gerald Achilles Burgoyne, a sixty-two-year-old war veteran with a large moustache, monocle, and the belief that shellshock was just malingering. He imagined himself advising the emperor how to win the war. So did Arnold Wienholt, an Australian senator, war hero, and big game hunter in his late fifties. Irishmen Captain Marius Brophil and Lieutenant Hickey just wanted some adventure. Both had fought in the First World War. Brophil served with the British army in India as a doctor; Hickey was a hard-drinking publican who had done seventeen years in the Royal Army Medical Corps.

The Ethiopians thought all foreigners were spies. The secret police followed them around Addis Ababa and steamed open their letters. Waldrow and the more suspicious types got deported when the Italian invasion began. Du Berrier, De Wet, and Schmidt clung on, hoping their luck would change. The other outsiders were offered the chance to join the newly formed Ethiopian Red Cross.

They would join a ragged gang of doctors, local orderlies, and the Austrian Nazi Schuppler.

*

'Die Behandlungsarten des Schlüsselbeinbruches'. *Archiv für orthopädische und Unfall-Chirurgie, mit besonderer Berücksichtigung der Frakturenlehre und der orthopädisch-chirurgischen Technik.* December 1934.

Valentin Schuppler published his article about the treatment of broken legs five months after taking part in the Nazi failed putsch. He was a quiet, competent, self-contained trauma surgeon who trained under the best at Vienna's top hospitals. He had slick dark hair parted on the left and round rimless glasses. Schuppler was also a dedicated National Socialist who wanted union with Germany enough to overthrow his own government.

He avoided the police round up after Dollfuß's death and went back to setting the bones of accident victims. Life seemed to be getting back to normal, with publications and citations in medical journals, when he abruptly left Vienna on 18 September 1935 with some medical equipment and a ticket for Addis Ababa. The doctor did not confide in anyone but colleagues assumed the Austrian police had started asking awkward questions.

After working in Addis Ababa's hospitals for a few weeks Schuppler joined the Ethiopian Red Cross, a ragged outfit originally set up by a gang of European women living in the capital who wanted modern medical care for their adopted country. Haile Selassie already had the Ethiopian Army Medical Service, a dozen Greek doctors hired by his physician Dr Vargos, but their exclusive interest was treating soldiers far behind the front lines. The Red Cross would help civilians as well. The emperor gave his approval but objected to women being involved in medicine. He handed the project to Dr Thomas Lambie, fifty-year-old Pittsburg-born field director of the Sudan Interior Mission (SIM), a Protestant missionary organisation.

Missionary outposts often handed out basic medical care along with Bibles. Lambie persuaded the SIM and its competitors to spare five ambulances and some personnel, including Canadian Dr Ralph Hooper who hated alcohol so much he would leave the table if a bottle of wine appeared. The heavy-drinking Evelyn Waugh found him hilarious.

Most of the Red Cross' doctors had been living in Ethiopia before the invasion. Schuppler found himself working with German-Jewish war veteran Dr Loeb, Dr Stanisław Belau from Warsaw, Dr Achmet of the Indian Medical Service who wouldn't stop talking about a plan to reconcile Islam and Christianity, a Greek called Dassios, and the bitter Jewish-Hungarian Mészáros Kálmán with his violin and complaints that the gonorrheal native orderlies were 'more dangerous than the enemy's aeroplanes'. One of the few outside medical professionals was the Irishman Brophil, who signed on as doctor. His friend Hickey and adventurers like Burgoyne and others became drivers or transport supervisors wearing khaki shirts with tabs in Ethiopia's red, yellow, and green.

The Ethiopian Red Cross was a ramshackle organisation, short on medicine, drugs, and clear-sighted management. The experts in Switzerland's International Red Cross thought they could do a better job. Small ambulance units were already on their way from Britain (a twenty-strong team), Sweden (thirteen), the Netherlands (nine), Norway (five), Finland (five), and Egypt (eleven members in a Red Crescent unit organised by the 'Committee for the Defence of Ethiopia').

Geneva did its best to co-ordinate them but spent more time arguing flags with Addis Ababa. The red cross was the local symbol for a brothel and flew over prostitutes' cabins in the capital. When the Swiss suggested the Ethiopians change the symbol, royal courtiers politely suggested the Red Cross change theirs instead. Doctors and prostitutes continued to use the same flag.

By late November, Schuppler was superintendent of a Dessie house bribed off a local leader and turned into a makeshift hospital. He spent his downtime chatting with Franz Roth, an AP staff photographer from Vienna who had done prison time after the coup for belonging to an illegal Nazi Sturmabteilung in the Austrian capital. Roth's father was a doctor. The pair talked politics and medicine. They were not the only Austrian Nazis in Ethiopia: Captain Rudolf Brunner had arrived in Addis Ababa on 5 November with some machine-guns. Brunner had been a policeman in Vienna's Alsergrund district but got four months in prison for his involvement in the coup. Exiled to Berlin when he got out, Haile Selassie hired him as part of a secret arms deal arranged with between Nazi Germany, Addis Ababa, and a businessman born in Jaffa.

Brunner dodged the journalists when he arrived and was reported to be somewhere on the southern front training locals to use his guns. The Italian press preferred to claim he was head of the Ethiopian secret police.

*

War came to Dessie the morning of 5 December. Ten Caproni bombers in two V-shaped formations appeared overhead and the bombs started falling. Locals ran for the hills.

Soldiers fired into the sky. Haile Selassie jumped on his Oerlikon anti-aircraft gun. Patients in the Red Cross hospital and Adventist medical centre were carried outside on stretchers and laid in the dust. Both buildings, marked with the Red Cross, were hit. James Rohrbaugh, United Press correspondent, saw a bomb smash directly through the Stars and Stripes painted on the medical centre's tin roof.

The Associated Press truck served as an ambulance, shuttling 100 casualties to the hospital. Schuppler stayed at his hospital post to operate on the wounded and Roth quit his camera to anaesthetise the patients. Together they cut out shrapnel and amputated limbs. Outside, Adventist Dr Ragnar Stadin, a Los Angeles resident originally from Sweden, and his nurse wife ('amiable' according to De Vilmorin, who had an eye for the ladies even in a bombing raid) ran around town treating the wounded in the streets.

'A bomb fell within fifteen feet of the Emperor,' said the *Pittsburgh Press* man, 'and wounded several soldiers who were only six feet away from where "The King of Kings" was crouching on the ground, firing an anti-aircraft gun.'

The Fascist planes eventually droned away into the distance. The smoke cleared and the only sound was screams and buildings slowly avalanching into rubble. Fifty-three people had died with at least 200 injured.

'The war correspondents' camp presented a tragic sight tonight,' wrote an AP reporter. 'By the light of the full moon, the silhouettes of the wounded and dying could be seen strewn over the camp.'

Among the wounded was Belgian mercenary De Fraipont, badly hurt in the arm. He got a medal from Haile Selassie. His commander had missed the attack. Reul got into a confrontation with Ethiopian soldiers before the raid for being foreign and white and too close to Haile Selassie. The Imperial Guard had to intervene. A demoralised Reul returned to the capital.

The rest of the Belgian mercenaries were equally dispirited. Debois and Witmeur were down south being ignored by Ras Nasibu Zeamanuel, who preferred to take advice from a trio of Ottoman Empire veterans led by General Mehmet Vehip Pasha. Lieutenant Armand Frère was on his way to Sidamo province and an advisory post with Ras Desta, the nervy son-in-law of Haile Selassie. The rest were wasting their talents censoring the press in Addis Ababa or organising bored policemen far from the front line. Enthusiasm ebbed away, salaries failed to turn up, the locals turned increasingly hostile. Reul began to wonder if coming to Ethiopia and betraying his fascist ideals had been a mistake.

Dothée's official mission were on their way home via Djibouti, one man short; Lieutenant Cambier was dead. The official verdict was pleurisy or polio. Not everyone agreed. When Frère arrived in Irga-Alem as replacement he found Cambier's living quarters covered with vomit and diarrhoea and locals claiming Ras Desta had poisoned him at a farewell meal. Desta hated outsiders.

'The less foreigners visit Ethiopia, the better,' he said.

He grudgingly accepted Frère as adviser. The Belgian kept quiet about his suspicions, watched what he ate, and looked for opportunities to get back to Addis Ababa.

Other foreigners were more enthusiastic about the Ethiopian cause. Viking Tamm's Swedes were training officer cadets near Addis Ababa; De Wet, Du Berrier, and Schmidt were hustling for pilot jobs in the capital; Vehip Pasha's men were building tank traps in the south; Parlesák and Breyer were operating radios with Ras Kassa's army on the northern front; Robinson, a few Frenchmen, and the German pilot Ludwig Weber were in the air force; a Russian called Konovalov was with Ras Seyoum's army in the north; and the Cuban Alejandro del Valle was marching with Ras Mulugeta.

So far they had not achieved much. It was time for them to prove they could help Ethiopia stop the Italian invasion.

12

BOHEMIANS ON THE FRONTLINE

Adolf Parlesák and Vilém Breyer in the North, Late 1935

Adolf Parlesák wrapped a rough wool blanket tighter around himself to sweat out the fever and watched a wing of Italian aircraft fly high overhead. The Czech was so sick his teeth were chattering and his brain bouncing off the insides of his skull. He could imagine bombs falling from the planes and whistling down among the mountain peaks, the explosions blooming around him. The fever amplified his nerves like a gramophone horn.

Parlesák knew what it was like to be on the receiving end of Italian airpower: airstrikes had been hitting Ras Kassa's army for weeks. The first sign of modern warfare had arrived early in the morning of 3 November. Parlesák and Brayer were in their tent, a decent model with a carpet and celluloid windows. Parlesák was guiding a straight-edge razor around his jaw in a hand mirror when a servant ran up.

'The Italians are coming!'

'Don't be silly,' said Parlesák. 'The Italians are at least 200 kilometres away.'

He and Breyer were somewhere in the middle of 50,000 men, women, and children crammed into a field of tents. Campfire smoke rose around them like temple columns and everywhere was singing and marching and noise. New arrivals poured into the camp every day with their swords and antique rifles; wives trudged behind with blackened pots, spice bags, gourds of water, and screaming children.

They were up in the foothills of a mountain, the air chilly enough for Parlesák to wear a wool jumper under his uniform. He wondered how the Ethiopians could bear it in their thin cloth outfits. Parlesák had recently discovered a letter from home, received in Addis Ababa and forgotten, in which a Brno friend wondered how he could stand the African heat. His breath made icy clouds as he read it.

The servant pointed into the sky. A low droning noise could be heard far above. Parlesák rushed outside with shaving soap dripping from his face. Three Italian spotter aircraft were directly over the camp, glinting silver in the hard sunlight. Women began to scream. Soldiers grabbed their rifles and fired into the sky. One man pulled the trigger with his head turned away and could not believe when he missed.

'What a miracle!' he said in surprise.

The planes droned back to base. Ras Kassa ordered his troops to dig bomb shelters but got complaints and refusals. Digging was not work for soldiers.

'The Abyssinians hate work more than the plague,' thought Parlesák.

Ras Kassa gave up on manual labour and ordered everyone to take cover in the hills. The Italians airplanes never returned; Kassa's soldiers grumbled about spending hours squatting among the rocks. The army returned to camp, packed up, and moved higher into the mountains, walking horses and mules through the Alagi Pass with its sharp rocks that lodged in hooves and cut open bare feet. Tangled in the pass's occasional scraps of grass were rusty cartridges from nineteenth-century battles. Parlesák could hear the muffled sound of Italian airplanes bombing distant targets.

On 13 November the first Italian airstrike hit Ras Kassa's troops. Parlesák sheltered behind a boulder and watched bombs explode among screaming people, barking dogs, and stampeding horses. The few slit trenches built by the Ethiopians collapsed during the raid and buried alive the people using them for shelter.

Afterwards, unexploded bombs lay around the camp, slammed into the ground by the impact. Ras Kassa told his soldiers to avoid them but no one listened, convinced there must be money or gold inside that the ras wanted for himself. Through the night sporadic blasts lit up the camp as soldiers hammered open bomb casings with flat stones.

*

Haile Selassie had mobilised the country when the Italians invaded. The whole population trudged off to join one of the feudal armies. Ras Kassa, Ras Mulugeta, Ras Seyoum, and Ras Imru in the north; Ras Desta and Ras Nasibu defending the south; or one of the satellite forces orbiting them. Soldiers would receive one silver thaler a day from their chief. The official declaration was distributed:

> Everyone will now be mobilised and all boys old enough to carry a spear will be sent to Addis Ababa. Married men will take their wives to carry food and cook. Those without wives will take any women without a husband. Women with small babies need not go. The blind, those who cannot walk, or for any reason cannot carry a spear are exempted. Anyone found at home after receipt of this order will be hanged.

Not everyone wanted to fight. Farmers stayed home to defend their crops against hungry soldiers. When the inevitable firefights erupted, the rases blamed it on Italian spies and burned whole villages in retaliation. Survivors took to the plains with rifle and spear to become bandits.

Other Ethiopians openly collaborated with the Italians. As Ras Kassa's army moved north it rode through the lands of the Danakil and Galla peoples, some of them Muslims forcibly incorporated into Menelik's empire. Italy recruited those with the biggest grudges into a guerrilla army fighting against Christian rule. Galla tribesmen were known for castrating enemy warriors and sawing the breasts off women. They hung the dried trophies around their necks.

Kassa had a personal bodyguard of 200 soldiers riding with him. They wore faded khaki and ammunition belts around their chests and watched the hills for Galla snipers. They were prepared to die protecting their ras. Kassa spared twenty to protect Parlesák and Bayer. The guards were always late and could not understand why the Czechs got angry over something as trivial as time. But they earned their money holding back angry Ethiopians who assumed all whites supported Mussolini.

'White dogs invaded our country. Well, let's start with these here!'

Parlesák saw a depressed Greek businessman chained to a pillar in a hut, allegedly an Italian spy. He and Breyer tried to prove their loyalty by organising war games but the soldiers got angry when there were no real Italians to fight. The pair gave up and rejoined the human river flowing north. The journey was chaotic. Mountain passes clogged up and bridges jammed; overloaded mules refused to move and caused more chaos. Parlesák suggested creating a transport plan. Ras Kassa agreed but his courtiers were too full of mead to give the Czech any useful information.

'In another month we'll surely be in Asmara and there I will be able to offer you authentic Italian wine!' said one.

'Tell me how many soldiers Ras Kassa has.'

'How many? A lot. Enough that we can chase the Italians out and take Eritrea.'

'I know there's a lot of soldiers. But I need to know at least approximately how many so that I can assign individual groups to routes marches and build a plan.'

'The number of soldiers? God knows but I don't.'

An attempt to discover the number of heavy guns led to the proud display of a pile of junk at the back of a large tent, most of it broken bicycle parts. The Czech wrote out a rough transport plan which impressed Ras Kassa and no one followed. Parlesák's pessimism deepened when he watched soldiers practise their anti-aircraft tactics by blasting at eagles with machine guns. They couldn't hit a single bird.

Progress north would have been slow even with a transport plan. Tradition demanded Ras Kassa act as judge at every village he passed. The army ground to a halt whenever angry locals emerged from their huts to shout their grievances at each other. A neighbour was accused of using spells to kill a cow. Watching soldiers laughed and shouted their own comments.

'Your brain has turned to cow dung!'

'Where is your father?'

Ras Kassa sat though it all with a fixed smile on his face while naked boys with whisks flicked away flies. He gave judgment. The accused and accuser left in harmony, chatting like old friends. Kassa was harsher on anything involving his own men and ordered ten lashes with a hippopotamus skin whip when a group of soldiers looted a village and fought the inhabitants. Arcs of blood sprayed over spectators when the whip came down. The villagers who fought them off received fifteen lashes.

Religious festivals caused more delays. Kassa hosted hundreds of chiefs and gave them curry to scoop up in wedges of flatbread and mead to wash it down. The chiefs ate in relays, giving up their seats to waiting guests when bellies were full. Ras Kassa sat on a throne with his usual fixed smile. When the meal was over he would find a monastery and pray through five hours of chanted service among frescoes from the life of Saint George. Afterwards, the ras would organise another feast to honour the high priests.

When Kassa's army finally moved on it was a sea of falling tents, mules loaded, drums beating, trumpets sounding, men with umbrellas hurrying after their chiefs, women strapping babies across their backs, the clanging of cooking pots thrown into sacks. Ras Kassa would mount his horse with its gold bridle, surrounded by bodyguards and followed by a servant carrying his pewter stick with silver fittings, another carrying a fold-up canvas chair, a third his portable throne, a fourth the rolled-up strip of carpet the throne stood on. Then Kassa gave a signal and the army began to march.

Black swans in remote lakes up in the mountains had not learned to avoid humans. Parlesák grabbed one out of the water with his bare hands and passed it to servants for neck-wringing and the cooking pot. A soldier sidled up to Parlesák and Breyer while they were eating and offered to rent them his wife for a week. He was astonished they refused.

'You cannot go to war alone, without a woman! Who will help you if you're hurt? Who will dig your grave and bury you, if you're killed?'

The pair were the only whites around except the occasional courier sent by the Italians to persuade Ras Kassa to defect. A Swede called Nidstroem delivered his message and was immediately dragged off to Dessie as a prisoner. The soldiers around Parlesák and Breyer watched them suspiciously for days after. The Czechoslovaks felt increasingly isolated. Telephone calls could be made from the bigger towns they had passed, but no one answered. Radio connections were crackly and rare. The only news from the north was bad.

'... urgently and earnestly asks all sides for reinforcements! The Governor of Tigre is now hiding in the inaccessible Tembien regions and waits for the arrival of reinforcements ... An important pass ...'

Then a crackle and a hiss and silence.

*

After the airstrikes in early November Ras Kassa banned tent erection before dark and fires during the night. This fooled the Italian airplanes for a few days until the army marched into the camp of another chief unaware of the blackout order.

'The sea of fiery campfires looks like dots extended into infinity,' said Parlesák. 'They pepper the surrounding hillsides up to the peaks of distant mountains. Sometimes it looks like the world has suddenly flipped upside down, that under us is the starry sky and above our heads a country shrouded in darkness ...'

Italian planes came the next day. Parlesák and Breyer ran for cover. One plane came in so low it flew level with the cave mouth of Ras Kassa's headquarters halfway up the hillside. The Ethiopians fired into the fuselage as it passed, Kassa calmly pumping shots through his telescopic hunting rifle. The aircraft banked away, the engine shuddered, and it glided down into the valley below. A cry of victory rolled around the mountains. The plane's machine gunner held off a circle of rushing Ethiopians from his Perspex bubble, while the pilot jumped out and spun a stalled propeller. The engine caught and the plane took off. Ras Kassa's men howled in disappointment.

Through the night the sound of young warriors celebrating mixed with the noise of wounded men moaning in pain. Ras Kassa's army had one doctor, a shaman whose understanding of modern medicine covered only aspirin, quinine, and laxatives. Everything else got witchcraft and guesswork. Parlesák watched him operate on an injured man whose guts were spilling out. The shaman shoved a string of intestines back into the man's stomach with grubby hands and sewed up the wound. He looked baffled when Parlesák advised him to wash up next time.

The Czech stayed away from the witchdoctor when he came down sick with a fever. He was wrapped in a blanket and sweating the sickness out of his bones when Italian airplanes passed overhead on their way home from bombing Dessie. In his fever dream he wondered if they were coming for him.

Parlesák was too ill to care when news came in that the League of Nations had imposed sanctions against Italy. The peacekeepers in Geneva banned members supplying Mussolini with arms, ammunition, transport animals, raw chemicals, rubber, and implements of war; and enforced embargoes on loans, credit, and the importation of Italian goods. The arms ban also applied to Ethiopia. It was a gesture, nothing more. No big names in the League were going to take any real action against Italy: they either valued Mussolini as a barrier against the dangers of Nazi Germany or weren't hypocritical enough to overlook their own African colonies. Haile Selassie was publicly grateful and privately furious. Sanctions would do nothing to stop the Fascists.

It was Christmas before Parlesák's sickness passed. By that time he and Breyer had been joined by another Slav. Feodor Evgenievich Konovalov was a right-wing Russian soldier swapping one emperor for another. A tall and clean-shaven man in a rumpled khaki suit, he shared Parlesák and Breyer's tent and talked French with them as they marched towards the front line.

Konovalov had arrived in time to see the Italians rip up the Geneva Convention. Mussolini had declared war on the Red Cross.

13

PEACE TO MEN OF GOOD WILL

Feodor Evgenievich Konovalov in Northern Ethiopia, Christmas 1935

It wasn't much of a Christmas. Breyer strung together a bundle of hillside twigs into a mangy tree and set it on the folding table next to an oil cloth candle. The three Slavs sat in silence and stared into the flame. Outside the tent Amharic hymns lilted from one end of the camp to the other.

Tens of thousands of men, women, and children were celebrating the birth of Christ high in the northern mountains of Ethiopia. Breyer and Parlesák watched the smooth dance of the candle flame and thought of their families back in Czechoslovakia. Feodor Evgenievich Konovalov's mind was full of Russia.

He grew up in the Crimea, a sunny peninsula hanging between the Black Sea and the Sea of Azov. He remembered a youth full of vineyards and green coastline and fresh blue waves. A career in the military appealed and Konovalov joined up as an electrical engineer. Then the war came along and he discovered a love of flying in the Imperial Guards Squadron, eventually commanding a squadron. The Tsar sent him to London as part of Russia's last military mission. He came home to find Bolsheviks in power and the Royal Family executed in a provincial basement.

Konovalov joined the White Armies fighting Bolshevism but was smart enough to see the walrus-moustached reactionaries on his side were no match for revolution. He quit the monarchist ranks in 1919 and sailed for exile in Constantinople.

Somehow he found his way to Addis Ababa where a small colony of Russian exiles scraped a living. The Ethiopians sympathized with the White cause enough to have held a mass for Tsar Nicholas II in St George's Cathedral after his murder. Konovalov got an Ethiopian passport and a job in the Ministry of Public Works. The years passed in dusty suspended animation with a steady job and a house with hand-tinted photographs of the Tsar on the wall.

The only excitement was the occasional incompetent Bolshevik agent trying to infiltrate the Russian colony. In 1929 a Dr Gavrilov got deported for sleeping with someone's wife, advising locals not to get a second opinion on his diagnoses, and telling an undercover policeman he had ordered explosives from Bulgaria.

A few months before the Italians invaded, Haile Selassie decided to make use of Konovalov's military engineering skills and sent him to see Ras Seyoum, commander of Western Tigre. The Russian took a flight out to Mekele with one of Corriger's Ethiopian pilots and joined a mule caravan for a slow crawl to Adwa. Local morale was high; everyone remembered their victory over Italy forty years before.

'We have shed blood everywhere, ours and theirs,' said a warrior. 'When the peasants are working their land, they find human bones everywhere. Both sides lost many here, and to what purpose? This is our land. The Lord gave it to our forebears. Now these Italians want to come in. Forty years ago they came. You can hear their tanks and guns beyond the boundary. Let them do it. They will not have our land – our sacred, sweet land – as before, we will not give it to them.'

Ras Seyoum was a fifty-something aristocrat with popping eyes and a neat moustache and good manners. He sent the Russian on an inspection tour of the north. Konovalov found shallow trenches dug on the plains that exposed soldiers like butterflies on a pin. He told the local chiefs to move their positions back to the foothills of the mountains.

'These are the positions God himself created for you,' Konovalov said. 'You can see everything before you, and you remain unseen and under cover.'

'This is true,' said a chief. 'What do we do with these trenches below, which we made with such a cost of energy?'

'Let the Italians believe that our real positions are there,' said the Russian.

'And the big ditches – anti-tank ditches – are they good enough or should they be larger?'

'They are good.'

'What kind of war is this?' said another chief, suddenly angry. 'We always fight in the open field. What sort of war is this – fighting behind stones?'

Konovalov moved on and wondered if they would bother to dig the new positions. He found the same argumentative stubbornness across Tigre province. Months later he was in Adwa when the invasion began.

*

His houseboy had woken him at seven. It was a clear, bright day. From the balcony of his bedroom Konovalov could see nine white aircraft flying in from the north. Then the bombs started to fall. The next day he accompanied Ras Seyoum's men as they quit the town for nearby Mariam Shewitu. They could hear more bombs dropping on Adwa behind them.

Some Ethiopians stayed to fight but the Italians were advancing fast and couldn't be stopped. When the two sides clashed, Haile Selassie's men threw away their rifles and attacked with swords. They were mown down. Konovalov urged Seyoum to launch a counter-attack but the ras had different orders and fell back towards the mountains.

Seyoum's men rested in a wood where the sun burned holes in the tree canopy. Konovalov was arguing with the ras about the benefits of guerrilla warfare. Seyoum was unenthusiastic. Their conversation was getting intense when the Russian looked up to see soldiers around him staring angrily. Seyoum explained that his men couldn't tell the difference between Italians and Russians. All whites were the same. Konovalov dropped the argument. An airstrike hit the camp later that day. The whistling of dropped bombs, explosions, fire, screaming, dead bodies. Horses and mules broke their leads and galloped away.

The Russian was sent back to liaise with Ras Kassa's approaching army and met Parlesák and Breyer, who seemed happy to see another Slav. Soon Ras Mulugeta arrived in a nearby valley with his Mehal Sefari: 96,000 soldiers from the Ethiopian state army, supplemented by Belgian-trained Imperial Guard units with a handful of Swiss Oerlikon anti-aircraft guns. Konovalov went to investigate rumours that Mulugeta had a team of white advisers and doctors. He found no doctors and evidence of only one white soldier, a Cuban called Alejandro del Valle. An Ethiopian Red Cross ambulance crew led by Schuppler and Achmet was rumoured to be on its way but no one knew if it had received the orders yet.

There was some good news in the north. A few weeks back, Ras Imru's army had stopped Mussolini's men in a bloody battle at Dembeguina Pass where Fascist tank crews burned alive in their vehicles. Imru had pushed part of the Italian front back towards the Eritrean border before airstrikes stopped his men in late December. Now anyone in Ras Kassa's army with good eyes could see the tents of the Fascist camp as grey dots in the distance.

Ras Imru's counter-attack shocked the Italians. Some began to wish Mussolini had taken more seriously a peace deal offered by Britain and France in early December. The deal would have allowed Italy to keep occupied territory in exchange for a ceasefire. But the press found out and the public outcry cost some politicians their jobs. The war had to go on.

Konovalov sat with the two Czechoslovaks by their makeshift Christmas tree. Parlesák was staring deep into the candle flame:

In all of the world's churches and cathedrals this evening will sound a pious chant. Peace to men of good will. Yes, peace to men of good will. Who here, among these hundreds of thousands of jovial Abyssinians are not people of good will? Why, then, does it also not dawn for peace and calm? Just because a handful of Mussolini's Italian Fascists want to be famous. And they have succeeded, but not in the sense they intended. They will be remembered for eternity in history's book, written in bloody lettering, blood red from the thousands and millions of their countrymen and members of other nations whose death they caused.

,

The oil cloth candle flickered as it burned. In another part of the camp Seyoum, Mulugeta, and Kassa were discussing how to take advantage of Imru's success. Their men sung Christmas hymns outside. The trio agreed on a January attack that would encircle the Italian troops among the ravines of the Tembien district. They did not know that Marshal Pietro Badoglio, the mournfully weatherbeaten leader of the northern Fascist armies, had asked Mussolini for permission to use chemical weapons along the front. Badoglio would use any methods necessary to avoid losing this war.

*

Somewhere to the south, Brophil, Schuppler, Achmet, and Hickey wished each other the compliments of the season and speared sausages out of a tin. The Ethiopian Red Cross unit had stopped for Christmas dinner on its way to the mountains.

The journey had been a nightmare. They operated in the open air on a table crawling with ants. Locals crowded round to watch, jogging elbows and ignoring requests for help. No one was ever grateful for medical attention; the best the doctors ever got was smiling condescension. After one grim, blood-spattered day, Brophil lost his temper and told a gang of locals in lousy Amharic how much he hated them and wanted to leave the country. They grinned.

'The more we try to do for these people,' said Brophil, 'the more obstacles are put in our way.'

The ambulance's escort of Ethiopian soldiers spent their days scanning the horizon and stroking their rifles. Feral remnants of Gugsa's army were in the area. Brophil had been dismissive of Gugsa ('a poor, weak creature I understand') and his desertion to the Italians until an attack on 17 November left the Irishman's tent shredded with bullet holes.

'I'm still alive!' he wrote in his diary, more surprised than happy.

Others were less lucky. Ten soldiers got their skulls smashed in with rocks.

Now the Red Cross unit was spending Christmas safe in the territory of a tribe loyal to Addis Ababa. The chief had captured two of Gugsa's men and tied them up outside his tent. Whatever humanitarianism Brophil possessed had drained away after the attack and he asked why the men were still alive. The chief invited him to return when the torture session was over and watch the execution. The Irishman thanked him but the firing squad arrived early and he was bathing in a river with Schuppler when they heard the rifle volley.

'The whole thing was short and sweet,' he wrote in his diary, disappointed to have missed the shooting.

By 3 January the northern humidity had turned into a wet fog. The ambulance moved on and set up for surgery near Lake Hashenge, where the water was covered in a scrum of white birds. Three Italian airplanes appeared and circled the Red Cross flag. Schuppler and Achmet were operating on an injured woman when the bombs began to fall. Orderlies rolled her onto a stretcher and went for cover, Schuppler stitching her up as he ran.

'Not the best accompaniment to an enterprise demanding cool nerves and steady hands,' said Brophil.

Schuppler's outfit was not the first ambulance to be attacked. A Swedish Red Cross unit that arrived in November had already lost a medical orderly somewhere near Melkadida in the far south. Stockholm had done its best to discourage the unit by refusing finance but a Red Cross appeal to the public brought in 700,000 krona. A gang of devoutly Christian doctors signed up, along with haunted-looking blond pilot Count Carl Gustaf von Rosen who offered his plane as an air ambulance. Von Rosen was the black sheep of his aristocratic family. His father was a Nazi who carved swastikas all over the family castle; his aunt was married to Luftwaffe chief Hermann Göring.

On 30 December Italian planes hit the Swedish field hospital as it struggled along a muddy road. Twenty-eight patients were killed. Medical orderly Gunnar Lundström died when his jaw was blown off as he sat in the cab of a lorry reading the Bible. Red Cross chief Dr Fride Hylander was badly wounded. Von Rosen flew him to an Addis Ababa hospital. Rome refused to apologise and claimed Ethiopian troops used the Red Cross to mark their headquarters.

*

Up in Tembien no one seemed interested in prepping for the January assault. Konovalov watched Kassa's men go soft as they camped out by chilly gurgling rivers and let their women do all the work. The Russian spent his days walking round the camp, frowning and shaking his head. It was nothing like the icy discipline of Tsarist Russia.

'Ras Kassa was a level-headed, serious man, but his spirit was certainly not military-like,' thought Konovalov. 'Apart from this, he was extremely religious and therefore against all bloodshed. Ras Seyoum, a sensible, likable gentleman, a grand seigneur, and a responsible commander was not enthusiastic, with an unyielding attitude. They had spent their lives in the lap of plenty, and they felt at this time of their lives the hardships of a difficult campaign.'

On New Year's Day the camp packed up and moved out, leaving behind 200 typhoid sufferers. Italian aircraft attacked while Ras Kassa's men were climbing a mountain pass, bombs falling on packed mule trains and panicking men with nowhere to go. One plane got shot down by a lucky burst from an Oerlikon gun. The other planes circled overhead, pulping the crash site with their bombs. The Fascists did not want to be taken alive.

'About half an hour later,' said Parlesák, 'apparently satisfied with their executioner's work, the Italian airmen returned to Makale.'

The army was setting up camp again when Ras Kassa's son presented Parlesák and Breyer with a lump of metal and wires: a dismantled Italian bomb. They congratulated him. Their smiles froze when the young aristocrat explained he had hammered it open while sitting in the corner of his father's tent during the meeting of the three rases. A detonation would have wiped out the Ethiopian northern command.

Ras Kassa's soldiers remained cheerfully optimistic about the coming battle with the Italians. In Ras Mulugeta's camp a few kilometres to the south, one soldier was feeling less positive. Alejandro del Valle was a Cuban rich kid gone bad whose family owned half the island. He specialised in unsuccessful right-wing coups. Now he was fighting for Ethiopia.

Del Valle had seen a lot of torture, cruelty, and incompetence in the last weeks. He thought he might be on the wrong side.

14

OUR CUBAN FRIEND

Alejandro del Valle in Ras Mulugeta's Army, January 1936

Alejandro Ramón Narciso del Valle y Suero had a round face, glossy dark hair, and the self-confidence of a man who can rebel as much as he likes and still inherit millions. He came from money. His father had interests in banking and export, his mother was an heiress. Their combined bank accounts built the Palacio de Valle in the sun-soaked bay city of Cienfuegos on Cuba's southern coast. The Palacio was an overscaled villa tinted turquoise and ivory. Its architect had gone for a mix of Gothic and Moorish, with a drop of Empire style and a pair of sphinxes to guard the front door. Critics called it kitsch but the Del Valles didn't care.

Estate management and a family of eight turned out to be too much for Del Valle senior. In 1919 he dropped dead. Alejandro was twelve years old and the eldest son. Relatives sent him north to New York State's Poughkeepsie Military Academy where he spent his teenage years learning discipline on the parade ground. He became friends with a Mexican classmate whose father was an exiled general dreaming of coups and revenge. When the general took his son out of school and headed for the border, Del Valle joined them.

It was the teenager's first taste of a right-wing coup. Cheering peasants in villages as the general's forces advanced; scrappy firefights with better-armed government soldiers; coup forces melting away as the advance stalled; tense arguments among the remaining leaders; deserted villages during the retreat; scrambling toward the frontier as the coup collapsed. Del Valle got away in one piece but the adrenalin rush of adventure became an addiction.

'I would rather die while I'm alive than live as a corpse,' he told friends.

He joined the crew of a freighter and lived in a world of salt-laden, flesh-stripping wind, and sailors brawling in whorehouses. His family tracked him down and persuaded the runaway to attend Texas A&M University. He hit the books, studying Engineering and Agronomy to prepare for the management of family estates back in Cienfuegos, but spent his spare time learning to fly, getting involved with Freemasonry, and keeping up with right-wing contacts through South America.

Summer break 1932 saw Del Valle in Quito, capital of Ecuador. Right-winger Neptalí Bonifaz Ascázubi had been elected president but got blocked by liberal and leftist members of the government, who spread the lie he had been born in Peru. Bonifaz's backers included the Compactación Obrera Nacional (Consolidation of National Workers – CON), a movement with a strong fascist flavour funded by landowners but staffed by peasants and craftsmen. CON tried a coup that turned into civil war.

Del Valle had friends in CON and joined them for the fighting. He was wounded by machine-gun fire, arrested by government soldiers, and deported to Cuba. In Cienfuegos he read that CON had lost and Bonifaz given up the presidency. Another failed coup.

He got his first taste of success with extremists in his homeland. The ABC was an underground gang of middle-class young people with far-right views and a liking for paramilitary-style green shirts. The Abecedarios hated President Gerardo Machado, a silver-haired ex-military man who mixed liberalism with repression. Del Valle shared the hate and joined them.

He learned bomb making and became a domestic terrorist, dodging the secret police as he blew things up round Cienfuegos. His new friends were ruthless. They assassinated the President of the

Senate just to get Machado to attend his funeral; ABC activists had dug a tunnel to the crypt and packed it with explosives. Machado never showed and the terrorism continued until August 1933 when the army shook off its neutrality and overthrew the government.

The celebrations lasted only as long as it took everyone to work out that new strongman Fulgencio Batista would be worse than Machado. The ABC went back to their bombs but Batista had a better security apparatus than his predecessor. Del Valle escaped a firing squad thanks to some heavy bribes paid by his family. Relatives told him to leave Cuba and do some growing up. He settled in humid Miami.

In April of 1935 Del Valle's family received a ransom note. He had been kidnapped by Florida gangsters. The Del Valles were bundling cash into suitcases when Miami police found Alejandro enjoying himself at a nearby hotel, no gangsters in sight. They squeezed out a confession. Del Valle had faked the kidnapping to get money after his allowance was cut off.

'Cuban youth, reportedly heir to large fortune, admitted writing a kidnap note demanding $15,000 for his own return,' reported *The Daily Times*.

His family took the hint and sent Del Valle enough money to cover a trip to London. In the summer he booked into a room at the upmarket Park Lane Hotel. Over breakfast coffee one morning he read an article in the *Illustrated London News* about British soldiers volunteering to serve in Haile Selassie's army. Del Valle took a taxi to the Ethiopian embassy in Elm Park Gardens, Chelsea and got involved.

*

Ambassador Workneh Eshete was a seventy-one-year-old Ethiopian doctor with a neatly trimmed moustache, glasses, and a chilly stare. He had been brought up in India after a British soldier adopted him. Volunteers and would-be mercenaries had been wearing out the carpet in his embassy since Walwal.

'I have in my possession more than a thousand application forms from foreigners who want to join our forces,' he said to Del Valle. 'Fill in yours and we will take a look at it.'

Del Valle shook his head.

'I am offering my services now,' he said. 'If you agree, I am ready to ship immediately. Otherwise, I will return to America.'

Workneh looked at him like a scientist examining a slice of something unpleasant under the microscope. The Cuban would have got a polite handshake and a door slam like all the others but he had a pilot's licence. Two of the ambassador's sons were amateur pilots and had convinced their father that air power could beat the Italians. Workneh decided to risk the disapproval of Addis Abba and give Del Valle a chance.

No one back in Havana much cared about Ethiopia. Fascism interested Cuban intellectuals and the upper crust, but not enough for them to take sides. When the invasion began the government would unenthusiastically enforce League of Nations' sanctions and cut off sugar supplies to Italy. Only the island's 1,178-strong Italian community followed the war closely. The *Diario de La Marina* ran details of the latest battles while journalists like José Ignacio Rivero and Juan Luis Martin criticised sanctions ('why the rush?') and praised Italian foreign policy. They followed Rome's line that Ethiopians were uncivilised slavers who needed a humane European hand. Ordinary Cubans paid no attention. The continuing economic aftershocks of the depression were more important to them than wars in faraway places.

Del Valle came from too much money to worry about the economy. The day after his interview, Cuba's only Ethiopia-bound mercenary gave a flying demonstration at Croydon airfield. It impressed Workneh enough to offer a three-year contract at the rank of captain, sealed with an oath sworn on a bible and Lion of Judah flag. The ambassador arranged an Ethiopian passport for Del Valle to make travel easier. The Cuban spent the next few days getting a uniform run up by a London tailor and ordering a Mannlicher–Schönauer rifle with a supply of dum-dum bullets.

The journey to Addis Ababa took him via Port Said. Dealers pushed morphine, cocaine, and Spanish Fly; pimps offered up whores of all ages. It was a relief to get into the cleanness of the Red Sea to sunbathe, play poker with journalists like H. R. Knickerbocker, and watch the flying fish leap out of the water.

Del Valle arrived in Djibouti to find the French cracking down on foreigners entering Ethiopia. The customs officer was a lump of lard who spent his days lying in a hammock fanned by a Somali servant. He still managed to find the uniform in Del Valle's suitcase. The Ethiopian consul advised waiting a few days, then offering a bribe.

The Cuban killed time in the bars and had more luck than Hugh de Wet in finding girls. A local fixer arranged a visit to a murky native brothel with Knickerbocker and a Greek journalist. The Greek made the mistake of shining a torch into the face of his girl.

'It was leprous!' said Del Valle. 'From head to toe she was a living fistula.'

They didn't stay. A few days later a ten-franc note got him through customs and on board the *Chemin de fer franco-éthiopien*. The Ethiopian customs officers at Dewele were friendlier and their chief invited him for a meal in a house crawling with lice and a wife who sang out of tune.

Del Valle was glad to get back in the sweatbox train and make the puffing climb up the hillside towards Addis Ababa. He leaned out the window as they approached and watched a leopard chasing ostriches through the tall grass.

*

Army officers rescued Del Valle from the international scrum at Addis Ababa station and walked him to a room at the Majestic Hotel. It had a view of Haile Selassie's triumphal arch, a small-scale replica of the Arc de Triomphe built from wood and cardboard. The Cuban unpacked and hit the town.

The smart set did its drinking in a place called Mon-Cinéma that combined a film screen, a bar, and a gambling operation.

Del Valle settled in and spent his days with a whiskey and soda, talking French with Reul's mercenaries and English with Knickerbocker and the gang. He took an occasional stroll round Addis Ababa to find out more about the world of his new employers. Poor women were second-class citizens in Ethiopia, servants to their parents before marriage and a slave to their husbands after. Priests circumcised them as adolescents then sewed them up with golden thread, to be snipped open on the wedding night. Women who tried to follow their own paths ended as outcasts or prostitutes.

Del Valle sympathised but that didn't stop a critical approach to Ethiopian beauty standards. The Latin lover didn't much like what he saw of the locals. 'After the age of twenty the Ethiopian woman loses elasticity, grace, freshness,' he said. 'The breasts become enlarged and lose vigour, the belly bulges. The legs become muscular. The face fades, reflecting a premature senility.'

Men had it better in Ethiopia, unless they came from poor families who put them under the knife for a career supervising rich men's wives as a eunuch. The boys were buried up to their necks in a hole for three days after the cut. The family celebrated if they were dug out alive. 'I saw many of them,' said Del Valle. 'At first with horror, later disgust, finally almost tedium.'

*

After a few days Del Valle was called to an audience with Haile Selassie in the emperor's gloomy throne room. The carpets were red and grey, the walls painted dark brown. The Ethiopian leader liked to stare silently at his guests for a full minute before talking.

'Why do you want to defend Abyssinia,' Haile Selassie said finally, 'fighting alongside my soldiers against invaders of your own race?'

'Italy is a powerful country, one of the major warring powers,' said Del Valle. 'I was born in a small country. It irritates me that it seeks to conquer this land, against the opinion of the world'.

The emperor liked the answer so Del Valle got carried away and claimed he was fighting without pay and happy to die for Ethiopia. Neither was true. Then he tried his smooth Cuban charm on a young women helping with maps and papers. She turned out to be one of Haile Selassie's daughters. Del Valle quickly diverted the emperor's attention to military matters but a discussion on airpower revealed Workneh had been wrong about a pilot shortage. Corriger's air force didn't need anyone. Del Valle had the choice of going home or joining the army. He took the army.

Two weeks later he met Ras Mulugeta at the Ministry of War, a building in the palace compound buzzing with soldiers. Rain drummed on the windows. The ras was a giant old man with a white beard and aggressive eyes and a distrust of foreigners. He had killed hundreds of Italians at Adwa with a sword.

'The emperor has told me about you and says your help is sincere,' said Mulugeta. 'You will soon have a chance to prove it. I will go to the front with my troops to fight the Italians, white like you and the other ferengis. Do you want to join me as adjutant with a machine gun company?'

'I came to fight for Abyssinia,' said Del Valle. 'I do not fear death.'

The ras grunted and dismissed him. Del Valle hung around Addis Ababa waiting for further orders. When Italy invaded, a band of the Imperial Guard paraded through the streets playing the Ethiopian anthem. Mulugeta began mobilising his 96,000-strong army for the march north. The day before he moved out, Del Valle passed five convicts sitting calmly on the ground by the St George's cathedral hanging tree. They were playing a variant of checkers while waiting to die.

'They worry less about death than losing the game,' said Del Valle.

'They cannot prevent being hanged,' said the Ethiopian captain with him. 'But they can prevent the other man from winning the game.'

Del Valle paid to have them freed. He took the men as slaves, unconcerned most were murderers. Back at the hotel he was packing his bags when a white missionary called Smith appeared at the door and announced that fighting a war would cost Del Valle his soul. The Cuban kicked the man out of the room and told him to go to hell.

Getting to the front was a long round of setting tents, with campfires burning, meals swimming in spiced butter, sleeping among the snores of soldiers and snorts of horses, waking with the dawn, breaking camp, moving further north each day. Ras Mulugeta's army moved like a locust swarm, picking clean the land as it went. Sometimes the locals welcomed them, sometimes they stood in the doorways of their huts with angry eyes.

Near Dessie there was a firefight with an unseen enemy that left a few hundred dead. When the smoke cleared Mulugeta discovered the attackers were Haile Selassie loyalists under the command of Belgian Lieutenant Adelin de Fraipont. They had mistaken the Mulugeta army for bandits. De Fraipont apologised and beat his men.

In the town Del Valle met an Italian priest who spoke seven languages and was pretending to be a Frenchman to stay on with his mission. Mulugeta's men discovered his real nationality and hacked him to death. The army moved on towards the northern mountains, looting villages as it went. Near Kobo, Del Valle watched as a bandit gang captured in the countryside was tortured to death.

'The seven men were mutilated slowly: first ears; then hands; later, the tongue. Each blow of the sword, managed by the executioner, lopped off the anatomy of those captive wretches, and soon dying, legless and armless, they were just a head and deformed trunk, nothing moving except their dull eyes. And then the eyes were poked out by warriors' spears.'

The Cuban looked at the pile of dismembered corpses in a pool of blood and wondered if he had chosen the right side.

In the far north they climbed through mountains and plateaus, past cold empty lakes shining like black mirrors. Messengers arrived from Ras Kassa with requests to hurry. Italian bombers attacked. Del Valle's horse had its throat ripped open by shrapnel as it reared up among the tightly packed cavalry. When the planes flew off, Ras Mulugeta was furious the bombs had killed his favourite mule.

The army camped at Amba Aradam, a flat-top mountain riddled with caves and tunnels, four kilometres south of Ras Kassa's army. On Christmas Day, Mulugeta joined the other rases to plan the January attack in Tembien. They agreed that Mulugeta would stay with his men, blocking the Italian advance, while a combined force of Kassa and Seyoum cut through the Italian lines and encircled Badoglio's troops. It would be another Adwa.

Del Valle checked his machine guns and wondered about Ethiopia's chances against the modern weapons and massed divisions of the Italian army. Over in Ras Kassa's army, Parlesák and Breyer looked over their radio equipment while Konovalov remembered his years of military school. They all tried not to think about the coming battle.

Haile Selassie's foreigners would have been more pessimistic if they knew that any foreign right-winger with a working trigger finger had applied to join the Italian invasion. Irish, South Africans, Iraqis, Britons, Hungarians, French and others all wanted to be part of Mussolini's war. The fascist international was on the march.

PART III

WIN OR FALL

15

RAVAGING BAYONETS

The Rise and Fall of the Italian Foreign Legion, 1935–36

General Eoin O'Duffy looked like the kind of flabby-faced uncle who turned up at family gatherings full of crooked smiles and whisky and embarrassed everybody. His best days were behind him but the Irishman hadn't realised it yet.

Years ago there had been some steel behind the wet blue eyes and double chin. The general kicked the British out of Ireland as a member of the IRA, reformed the Irish police as head of the Garda Síochána, and shook up the Dublin establishment with his paramilitary Blueshirt organisation. A series of political reverses turned O'Duffy into a civilian and lost him control of Fine Gael, the party he helped create. The Blueshirts split and only a few thousand followed O'Duffy into his new adventure as head of the National Corporate Party.

The general had always been a man of the right but the NCP were unashamed fascists. They agitated for minimum wage, profit-sharing, and land redistribution, all wrapped in an anti-Semitic shell. NCP men leant muscle to farmers fighting off debt-collectors and marched through the streets brawling with leftists. O'Duffy made speeches from provincial balconies attacking democracy.

'Den Irske Mussolini,' said Norwegian newspaper *Hjemmet*. Norway didn't realise the Irish Mussolini was hanging on by his fingertips. Voters ignored him. Former colleagues attacked him.

His own followers were disturbed by rumours about O'Duffy's homosexuality. The general struggled to keep afterhours adventures in Dublin theatreland quiet. Irish fascists would not be happy following a man whose best friends were a gay couple known as 'Sodom and Begorrah'.

O'Duffy hoped to silence the gossip by pushing his way back into the spotlight with more extreme rhetoric. He threatened to re-unite Ireland by force. No one listened. He hinted at a coup d'état. The police could not be bothered to prosecute.

'A huge farce – there would appear to be little to fear from this movement,' said one Gardai report.

Then Ethiopia came along and O'Duffy was back in the headlines. A few weeks before the invasion he had offered to send a unit of 1,000 Irish volunteers to fight alongside Italy. The announcement was made among the speeches and jackboots at an international fascist conference in Montreux, Switzerland. Italian newspaper *Il Messagero* ran the story and O'Duffy returned home to a firestorm of controversy.

'After fifteen years in the political limelight O'Duffy has played his last card,' said the Marxist-Leninists of the Republican Congress. 'In turn Irish Republican, Imperialist Chief Thug and again professing Republican, he is now a hireling of Mussolini.'

Others pointed out the contradiction of a man who fought against British imperialism helping another nation colonise Ethiopia. The *Irish Times* made comments about Ireland's famous neutrality and linked the O'Duffy story to reports of the Italian Consul in Dublin urging expats to return home and join Mussolini's army. The general's more militant enemies promised to stop the Irish Legion getting to the battlefield.

'The dockers of Dublin would have something to say if it came to transporting O'Duffy's Blueshirts to Abyssinia,' said communist Sean Murray.

O'Duffy wrote letters to the press condemning slavery in Ethiopia, praising Mussolini, and smoothing down his project's rougher edges. He claimed to be acting only as a mail drop for

NCP volunteers who had spontaneously written to him, and announced that the Irish Legion idea would be talked over at the party's national executive meeting in late November. The invasion started before O'Duffy's cronies could sit down to vote. The Irish public sided with Haile Selassie and the Ethiopians, with a few exceptions in the Church who hoped Mussolini would make the world safer for Catholicism. The government in Dublin supported League of Nations sanctions against Italy.

The NCP protested sanctions with leaflets and marches and angry letters to newspapers. O'Duffy bought a large-scale map of Ethiopia to follow the fighting. With all the noise, only the most dedicated observer realised the general had quietly dropped the Irish Legion project. 'I do not think that Italy requires our physical support,' he said, 'but she would undoubtedly appreciate our moral support.'

By January 1936 Rome had received 3,500 applications from foreigners to join the invasion and at least five additional offers of national legions, including O'Duffy's effort. Thousands more foreigners applied directly to Italian embassies and consulates in their home countries. None of them could understand why Mussolini wasn't interested.

*

Up on the northern front the Italians had sent most war reporters home. They didn't want their retreat from Ras Imru in the newspapers. One of the last stories filed by Hungarian journalist Demeter Ödön concerned a guerrilla outfit encountered behind the lines. The Italian major in charge had an African foreign legion working for him.

'The most picturesque medley ever assembled in the Ethiopian mountains,' said Ödön. 'Rebel Tigre, Danakil hunters, Arab slave traders, lanky Somalis, grinning Galla tribesmen, who wore around their necks the dried genitals of the enemies they had killed.'

The gang was only a small fraction of the African troops fighting for Rome. Italy had over a million soldiers involved in the invasion and a large chunk of the manpower came from its colonies or elsewhere on the continent. In the frontlines were Eritrean soldiers in red fezes, Libyan infantry, white-turbanned mercenaries from Yemen and Somalia (which included Mohamed Siad Barre, future Somali dictator) and Ethiopians who rejected Haile Selassie's authority. Italian propaganda did its best to ignore the multicultural army. It pretended not to hear when African-American singer Josephine Baker, living in Paris, called for an army of black foreign volunteers to join the Italians and wipe out slavery in Ethiopia. Or when fallen UNIA hero Marcus Garvey claimed to be a black fascist.

'Mussolini copied fascism from me,' he said, 'but the Negro reactionaries sabotaged it.'

The newspapers in Rome preferred to call on international support from those who had 'not yet lost all sense of dignity of the white race.' Fascists, imperialists, and adventurers didn't need the encouragement. Applications to join the Italians forces had been pouring in for months.

Back on 3 August 1935 the *Ministero delle Colonie* (Ministry of the Colonies) asked Marshal Badoglio to look into the feasibility of creating a foreign legion for the projected southern front. France and Spain already had their legions. An Italian version would provide more manpower for Il Duce's African dream. The Ministry suggested the legion would need 225 officers, 269 NCOs, and 7,749 foreign troops, mostly infantry. Support services, such as artillery and communications, would need a further 178 officers, 134 NCOs and 2,270 Italian troops. The outfit would total around 10,000 men.

Badoglio was not impressed. Foreign units were always a problem, with higher desertion rates than natives and bigger disciplinary problems. More importantly, they could steal Badoglio's glory.

'Adwa was an Italian defeat,' he wrote to the Ministry, ignoring the colonial troops already in the ranks, 'to be avenged by Italian soldiers'

The *Ministero delle Colonie* dropped the idea but the *Ministero degli Affari Esteri* (Ministry of Foreign Affairs) had already taken an interest. The diplomats went directly to Mussolini with a sackful of application letters from foreign volunteers. A few came from women who wanted to be nurses, a few more from male engineers and mechanics, but most were men looking for the frontlines, motivated by ideology or money or an escape from bad pasts and worse legal problems. The Ministry broke down the figures: the biggest number of individual applications came from Romania (536), followed by Germany and France (345 and 315), with 280 from Yugoslavia, 189 from Hungary, 122 from Britain, 114 Czechoslovakia, and 105 each from Egypt and Poland. Individuals from another forty-six countries applied, including forty-five from the USA, twenty-two Russian exiles, five Iraqis, and two from Yemen. The true numbers were much higher. Rome counted only those who wrote directly or made it onto lists compiled by embassies.

In addition, fascist political groups offered to supply entire national units: 3,600 Hungarians, 1,500 Albanians, 1500 Bulgarians, O'Duffy's 1,000 Irishmen, 300 white South-Africans, and others.

Nationalities generally volunteered for Mussolini in lower numbers than for Haile Selassie, but there were exceptions. In June 1935, 400 Finns from Helsinki volunteered to fight for Ethiopia, even offering to pay their own expenses. The Ethiopians would not take them, using the excuse of a visa ban. At least 1,400 applied to the Italian embassy to fight for Mussolini the same month.

The average volunteer for Italy was young, unemployed, right-wing, and looking for adventure. Many applications included comments about white racial solidarity, a theme particularly popular among Germans, Britons, Poles, and men from South America. A majority of volunteers belonged to fascist or far-right movements like the Austrian *Heimwehr*; the Belgian *Legión nationale* (home to Reul and his men); the British Union of Fascists; Anton Mussert's *Nationaal-Socialistische Beweging* from Holland; France's *Action française* (Hilaire du Berrier was a member), *L'association des Croix de Feu, Jeunesses Patriotes*, and *Mouvement Franciste*; and the *Falange Española de las JONS* from Spain.

Berlin was backing Ethiopia, so the hundreds of German volunteers were marginalised figures hoping for a new life abroad. At least a quarter of those applications came from Jewish Germans, many of them doctors, looking to escape Nazi persecution. The rest were Freikorps veterans and Nazi Party members disillusioned by the Röhm purge of the previous year.

A Jewish Pole offered to create a Hebrew Legion, as did a Jewish Egyptian. Closer to home Professor Alessandro Stein, rabbi for the Italian coastal town of Abbazia (now Opatija in Croatia), offered a legion of Jewish soldiers from Germany and Poland if the volunteers were rewarded with land in Ethiopia or Palestine. Italy's lack of anti-Semitism endeared it to foreigners who preferred nationalism without pogroms. The most pro-invasion newspapers in Hungary were those published by the Az Est group, a media company owned by Frida Gombaszögi, a Jewish former actress.

'The Negus sent cannibals into battle,' ran a typical piece. 'Savage mobs, wrapped in lionskins demand furiously arms from the Negus. This is not a battle but a hunt of birds of prey.'

Even Jewish Hungarians at the liberal end of the scale supported Mussolini.

'The low-flying planes bring liberation,' wrote Tamás Kóbor. 'Let the bayonet do its ravaging task! The Italian is the only nation in the soul of which tenderness turns into battle.'

The foreign legion never happened. Mussolini listened to Badoglio and killed off the idea in late October 1935. Volunteers kept writing but received a polite rejection letter and a booklet defending the invasion. Ireland's General O'Duffy was one of many who pretended the decision not to go had been his own.

The Italian Foreign Legion project failed because it cost too much, put the spotlight on foreigners rather than Italians, and risked political infighting. More importantly, Rome had found a new source of manpower: the *Legione Parini dei fasci all'estero*, a 4,000-strong unit formed from Italians living abroad.

*

On 20 October 1935 the *SS Rex* sailed out of New York Harbour carrying 117 Italian-Americans on their way back to the mother country. A huge crowd cheered them off in a haze of cigarette smoke, tricolor flags, and patriotic songs. America's four-and-a half-million-strong Italian population was proud of its boys going to fight for the homeland. The US had 129 Italian-language newspapers. Eighty of them were pro-Mussolini.

Italian money funded propaganda and youth groups across America. Il Duce's photograph hung in churches and classrooms. A 700-strong crowd in Portland, Maine applauded when Mussolini was proclaimed 'a modern Columbus'. Over $14,000 was collected at another rally in Madison Square Gardens where women gave up their gold wedding rings.

The *SS Rex* was the first in a stream of ships taking volunteers across the Atlantic. Over 800 Americans would make the trip but the biggest group of volunteers – 3,670 according to the paperwork – came from South America, most drawn from the Italian communities of Brazil and Argentina.

The Ethiopia campaign was popular in South America. Italian-Brazilians lapped up propaganda sent from Rome. The *Società Dante Alighieri*, an openly Fascist outfit, organised public meetings to argue their side of the war. The Italian consulate in São Paulo bought outright the *União Jornalística Brasileira* news agency to place stories. Fascist propaganda films were screened for large audiences, 'provided they are not "men of colour".'

Not many men of colour would have been interested. Black Brazilians sympathised with Ethiopia and got into fistfights with Mussolini's partisans, as did Italian anti-fascists, who poured out propaganda leaflets stating their case.

'This insatiable octopus, sucking our blood daily,' read one, 'this cynical bosses' massacre of workers that has infected the Italian proletariat with the lure of joining the Duce's ridiculous imperialist adventure, that villain who has the courage to promise a full salary to those who allow themselves to be murderers of the Abyssinian people, while promising a pension for their widows.'

But that was a minority view among the 400,000 Brazilians who claimed Italian descent. A petition against the war circulated in Belo Horizonte, sixth largest city in Brazil and home to a significant

Italian community, managed only four signatures. Non-Italians like President Getúlio Vargas treated Italy's corporatism as a model. Members of the political elite made sure everyone knew they supported Fascism.

Peru's Italian population also got a big dose of propaganda, but the strongest medicine was reserved for the émigré millions in Argentina. Italians had been streaming into the land of pampas and gauchos since the nineteenth century and now Fascist organisations were all over the country. In December 1935 a petition supporting the Ethiopian invasion gathered nearly half a million signatures in Buenos Aires.

The *Associazione Patriottica Italiana* organised the shipping of food parcels, raised money, and acted as cheerleader for campaigns to donate wedding rings and jewellery. Other groups organised a boycott of British goods, triggering antifascist groups into buying British to make a point. The Italian Chamber of Commerce in Buenos Aires put together a fundraiser that delivered four gold bars to the Italian Embassy. The symbolism of the gesture made it into many South American newspapers.

By late January 1936 the Legione was forming up behind the lines down in Italian Somaliland. Its members practised marching, target shooting, and language lessons for those who had been overseas so long they'd forgotten their mother tongue. Many were sorry they would miss the fighting on the northern front.

The Slavic trio of Parlesák, Breyer, and Konovalov weren't going to miss anything. They were right in the middle of Ras Kassa's army as it advanced on the Italian front lines at a place called Warieu Pass. The Ethiopians intended to crush Mussolini's invasion or die trying.

16

BOHEMIAN ATTACK

Parlesák, Breyer, and Konovalov in the Ethiopian Counter-Attack, January 1936

No one could escape the lice. They crawled over testicles and through hair. They drank blood and laid eggs. Each louse was the size of a fat rice grain and looked like an albino spider that had swallowed a rain drop. Everyone in Ras Kassa's army was covered in them. Adolf Parlesák had got so used to lice he didn't notice himself scratching as he watched a column of Italian Blackshirts march towards the Ethiopian lines.

Ras Kassa's men were deep in Tembien district near the Warieu Pass. It was a land of rocks and dust and termite hills taller than a house. The army had set off just after the New Year when Ras Seyoum's men joined Kassa to create a 70,000-strong force of warriors, priests, warlords, women, and children. They hid in caves during an Italian airplane attack in a river valley; trudged up the sandy slopes of a mountain; ascended the peaks to view the Italian camp on the heights of Marbe-Shumearne; then captured some Eritrean troops watering their mules in a stream. The villages they passed through refused to sell them supplies. Italian aircraft had dropped propaganda leaflets threatening to destroy anyone who helped the Ethiopian forces.

'Our aircraft are fast as lightning. They will fly over your village and bomb your huts into the ground.'

Many locals played both sides, earning good money building roads for the Fascists one week and fighting with the emperor the next. Ras Kassa took advantage of the front line traffic for intelligence gathering. His most successful spy was an old man who tucked two unexploded bombs under his arms and told sentries he wanted a reward for returning these bits of metal fallen off an airplane. Panicky Italians waved him on and he strolled through camp after camp, memorising their locations.

By 8 January Kassa's army had made it to Abiy Addi, the capital of Tembien province. They rested then moved on to the mountains beyond, camping in the remains of a former Italian fortification at the foothills then moving up towards the summit the next day. Ras Kassa made his headquarters in a cave that had once been a church. His sentries could see Italian tents as an ocean of grey dots on the dusty plain ahead. Parlesák and Konovalov were inspecting the perimeter when they found a gang of men digging in an ancient cannon aimed at the Fascist positions.

'How are you going to hit the Italians,' asked Konovalov, 'when their camp is six kilometres away?'

The gun crew stopped digging and moved the cannon a few metres forward. The chief gunner showed Konovalov his technique: he looked down the barrel like a rifle and prayed. Parlesák left the Russian trying to explain how artillery worked and walked on scratching his lice bites. He met a group of Ethiopian soldiers bandaging bloody gunshot wounds. One of their comrades had been captured by Fascists but put on such a convincing act as a local villager that Blackshirts gave him coffee and let him go. Coffee was expensive in Ethiopia; the man told all his friends about the Italians' generosity. They dropped their rifles and headed for the enemy camp. A machine gun opened up on them.

'You know, we went to visit them, to drink coffee, and they started shooting at us' said a survivor to Parlesák. 'They're bastards, those Italians ...'

Later the camp came together for a religious service led by Ras Kassa's personal confessor. His strong, high voice drifted down the hillsides and across the camp. The soldiers answered him in one deep, echoing voice.

'We are fighting for a just cause! God knows ...'

'God knows ...'

'Italians want to grab the land! God knows ...'

'God knows ...'

'Grab your swords, grab the rifles and banish them! God help us ... help!'

'God help us ...'

Then applause. Parlesák, Breyer, and Konovalov joined in. Despite the noise, the Italians seemed unaware of the army infesting the mountains ahead of them. On 20 January Badoglio sent out the 2nd Eritrean Division and the 28th October Blackshirt Division to probe the terrain. Ras Kassa ordered the counter-offensive to begin.

'Every Abyssinian is a born soldier,' said Ras Kassa. 'When attacking, no power in the world will not stop him. Either win or fall!'

*

Parlesák watched the battle from Kassa's cave. Konovalov was on another hilltop with Ras Seyoum. They saw Ethiopian warriors flow down the mountainsides, white robes flapping against red ground, and into the Italian lines. Parlesák could see black bodies fall under machine-gun fire and those behind jumping the corpses as they ran forward. Italian bombers swooped low over the fighting.

The Blackshirts were surrounded in Warieu Pass. The Eritreans fell back to nearby Abaro Pass. The battle lasted all day and into the next. Waves of Ethiopians charged the Fascist positions. Three Italian tanks rumbled into the fighting but Ras Kassa's men climbed them and speared the crew through the hatches with long lances. Eritrean troops fighting for the Italians fired in the air and allowed the Ethiopians to pass through their positions, then deserted. Kassa's camp was full of red-fezzed Eritreans taking loyalty oaths to Haile Selassie.

More fighting, more airstrikes, more days and night of back and forth, capturing hilltops only to be pushed back then capturing them again, Italian forts overrun, close combat with swords dripping red in the sun. As Kassa's troops retreated at night each man shouted out his deeds and named the Ethiopian dead, firing a rifle into the air to drive away evil spirits. The shots continued all night, punctuating the crying of women left alone and children without a father. Soldiers returning to camp gave Konovalov a box of Italian cigarettes.

'Their camps are not like tents at all,' said one Ethiopian warrior. 'They are like good, solid houses. Inside they have many things, and here is one of them.'

He showed the Russian a mirror in a silver frame.

'Their strength is in their hands,' said another. 'When I tried to hit one with my saber, he took hold of my wrist and twisted it to try to make me drop my weapon. He would have succeeded if not for my comrade who finished him.'

Parlesák read through papers brought back from the Italian lines: a mother thanking her son for the money to pay the coal bill, a fiancée wishing her man back home, a creased and blood-stained military diary.

'At four o'clock in the morning Colonel Cecconi's artillery unit set out from the camp to put its guns, protected by heavy machine guns, into firing position on a nearby hill. The first group of black shirts left the camp soon after and proceeded to Abiy Addi ...'

Then the writing stopped. The Czech found long glass tubes containing brown liquid with writing that indicated use against chemical burns. Ethiopian soldiers tried to sell him loot, one claiming he had a litre bottle of Italian wine. Parlesák uncorked it to take a drink then jerked his mouth away at the last moment. The bottle was full of ink.

The Ethiopians nearly broke through the enemy positions. By the afternoon of 22 January Badoglio was begging for reinforcements to hold the line. He could barely keep the panic out of his official reports.

'Against the organised fire of our defending troops, their soldiers – many of them armed only with cold steel – attacked again and again, in compact phalanxes,' he said, 'pushing right up to our wire entanglements, which they tried to beat down with their curved scimitars.'

Losing the Weiru Pass would have cut the front in two and broken the back of the northern advance. But Badoglio got lucky. The Ethiopians preferred to loot Italian positions rather than press forward. Many abandoned the battle to bring plunder back to camp, heaping up watches, binoculars, shaving kits, and guns around their tents. They paraded for their women in Italian uniforms, all braided finery and insignia but too short in the arms and legs.

An Eritrean relief force under General Achille Vaccarisi, a solemn-looking man who waxed his moustache into points, arrived in time to rescue the Blackshirts at Warieu Pass. Italian airstrikes broke the wave of Ethiopian attacks. On the morning of 24 January Ras Kassa's army retreated for the last time, leaving 1,000 dead near the Italian lines. Back in the camp, Ethiopian women baked flatbread with paprika, salt, and honey; their men sat around laughing and bathing in the sun. Ras Kassa's army thought it had won.

Parlesák rolled the dial on his radio set and caught an Italian broadcast claiming victory. Badoglio had recovered from his panic and was already planning to restart the push southwards. Ras Mulugeta's army at Amba Aradam stood in the way.

*

A few days after the battle, Italian Caproni bombers dropped something into a neighbouring valley that threw up a yellow mist and the smell of mustard.

'Well, well,' said Breyer, 'they've given us a barrel of mustard and will certainly follow it up with a box of Prague sausages ...'

The first symptom of exposure to mustard gas was itchy red spots on the skin that turned into yellow blisters. Then the eyes began to burn and stream. Blood and snot dripped from the nose, stomach cramps caused vomiting and diarrhoea. The blisters slowly sealed up the throats of anyone caught at the centre of the attack. Most of those died within three to four days. Those further away could survive lesser exposure but were incapacitated for weeks.

Behind the lines, chugging north towards Ras Kassa's army, the ambulance carrying Schuppler, Ahmed, Brophil, and Hickey had already passed through villages of gas-blinded locals. Ethiopian shamans were treating the burns with wild honey poultices. Hickey had been gassed by the Germans in the trenches and told the shamans to concentrate on washing off chemical residue. Schuppler gave out painkillers. The ambulance moved further north each day, leaving the victims behind.

'Our patients may have lived or died,' said Brophil. 'We had no choice but to leave them to the mercy of providence and proceed on our way.'

Brophil was composing an angry telegram for Geneva about chemical warfare when Italian planes attacked again. He and Hickey lay behind the ambulance's tires, hearing bullets thunk into tins of worm powder. The Red Cross flag was shredded.

The crew tried to convince themselves that the Italians were not deliberately targeting medical crews. Nearer to the front, Brophil parked the ambulance under an overhanging rock and set out three Red Cross flags in a triangle. An Italian spotter plane flew overhead but Brophil attracted the attention of the pilot, pointed to the flags, and waved his arms in the wash-out signal. The pilot waved and left. His comrades were less chivalrous. The next day the roar of tri-motor planes woke the camp. Bombs dropped for forty-five minutes and two women died.

'The Red Cross emblem eventually held such an uncanny fascination for the Italians,' said Brophil, 'that I had to quit using it altogether.'

The Ethiopian Red Cross command recalled the Irishman to Addis Ababa and the ambulance rattled north without him. Ethiopia hoped a first-hand report from Brophil would get Geneva protesting. The International Red Cross had publicly condemned the use of poisonous gases in the First World War and campaigned for a 1925 treaty against their use.

This time the medical men seemed less enthusiastic. Red Cross president Max Huber lived in fear of Italy invading Switzerland, which had a significant Italian-speaking population. Swiss Foreign Minister Giuseppe Motta, a square-faced career politician, saw communism as the bigger problem. Neither man wanted to antagonise Mussolini. A speech about slavery given by the Italian representative to the League of Nations gave them the excuse to minimise support for Haile Selassie.

'The survival in Ethiopia of slavery and the similar institution named gebbar [serfdom] not only constitutes a horrible offence against civilization,' said the representative, 'and an open breach of the obligations by Article 23 of the covenant of the League of Nations but also represents a flagrant violation of the special obligations assumed by the Ethiopian government at the time of its admission to the League.'

Brophil knew that was all just smokescreen. He bypassed the Red Cross men and headed for the few pressmen who remained in-country. After the attack on Dessie all journalists had been escorted back to the capital and most had gone home, sick of strict censorship and news blackouts. Those who remained bar crawled with Du Berrier, De Wet, and Schmidt. The three pilots remained unemployed and blamed John Robinson for their failure to get into the air force.

Brophil cornered every newsman he could find and talked about mustard gas, Italian barbarism, and the inevitability of an Ethiopian victory. He had been nowhere near the recent battle at Weiru Pass but that didn't stop him claiming 15,000 Fascists died after being trapped in a valley for three weeks.

'They had no chance to come out alive,' he said confidently.

Haile Selassie was grateful for the Irishman's propaganda. He needed outside help more than ever. The Belgians and Czechoslovaks had cancelled arms sales; the League of Nations had given nothing more than sanctions; and the rest of the world seemed happy to watch Fascism eat his country. The emperor hoped that Imperial Japan or Nazi Germany would intervene in the war. Both nations were friends. Then a coup in Tokyo tightened the noose around Haile Selassie's neck.

On 28 February 1936 schoolboys in Hirohito's capital heard bugles blowing in the distance as they walked through a snowstorm on their way to class. For the rest of their lives, they would associate snow with revolution and betrayal and death.

17

BLACK DRAGONS AT THE BARRICADES

A Coup in Tokyo, 26 February 1936

Blood running down katana blades left red drip trails on the floor as the officers left the Minister of Finance's bedroom. They hacked him to death as he tried to sit up in the dark, tangled in his blankets. The minister's servants backed against the walls as the assassins headed for the front door.

'Excuse me for the inconvenience I have caused,' said one of the officers as he went out into the driving snow.

Another assassination squad in a different part of Tokyo gunned down General Watanabe Jōtarō, shaven-headed Inspector General of Military Education. A third gang hit the home of Viscount Saitō Makoto, Lord Keeper of the Privy Seal. They put forty-seven bullets in him and left the former battleship commander bleeding to death in his wife's arms.

The coup began at 2am on Wednesday 26 February 1936. Renegade officers assembled 1,400 sleepy-eyed troops near the emperor's palace in Tokyo and gave orders to occupy the city centre. Buildings were stormed and roads sealed off; machine guns poked their snouts through sandbag barricades. Assassination squads headed off to kill members of the government. The only opposition came from policemen who fought back attackers targeting Count Makino Nobuaki at a hot spring, buying the desiccated-looking cabinet minister enough time to escape. The attackers sent the building on fire in revenge and shot anyone who made it outside.

Rising sun flags went up around Tokyo with the words 'Revere the Emperor, Kill the Traitors' ideogrammed on their white fields. Putschists climbed the main police station and watched from the roof for the torch signal that would show the Royal Palace had been taken. Emperor Shōwa, better known to the world as Hirohito, was the key ingredient in their plan to turn Japan into an ultranationalist dictatorship.

The land of the rising sun was already a warrior state. Half its annual budget went on weapons. Military asceticism forced Japanese workers to use wooden pegs instead of nails because every scrap of metal went into tanks and airplanes and battleships. The police arrested young people for anything that hinted of self-indulgence: going to cinemas, drinking coffee, eating grilled potatoes from street vendors.

Civilians had little control over the army. The last prime minister who tried was shot to death by a gang of junior naval officers back in 1932. The Young Officers of the Army and Navy and Farmers' Death-Band had hoped to start a war with America by taking out his house guest Charlie Chaplin as well, but the film star was at a sumo match. The judge at the murder trial received 110,000 letters in the men's defence. Some were written in blood. Nine supporters chopped off their little fingers, pickled them, and sent the jar to the Ministry of War. No one was surprised when defence lawyer Sumioka Tomoyoshi managed to get light sentences for his clients. The right-wing had only contempt for Japanese democracy.

'Every single bullet must be charged with the Imperial Way and the end of every bayonet must have the National Virtue burnt into it,' said General Araki Sadao. 'If there are any who oppose the Imperial Way or the National Virtue, we shall give them an injection with this bullet and this bayonet.'

Araki was chief ideologue of a military faction known as Kōdōha (Imperial Way). It pushed anti-communism, ultranationalism, samurai spirit, and emperor-worship, with a light sprinkling of anti-capitalism that appealed to younger officers. Araki's rivals in Tōseiha (Control Faction) had more conservative support, saw America as the main enemy, liked technologically advanced weapons, and wanted to keep power in the hands of men old enough to know how to use it.

In early 1934 Araki was forced to resign after calling for war with Russia. The Tōseiha took advantage of his departure and spent the next two years purging Imperial Way supporters from the military. The final touch was ordering an army division loyal to Araki to a post far from Tokyo. A gang of the division's junior officers decided to strike before the relocation. On the snowblind morning of 26 February, Kōdōha supporters took over the city centre.

The group of putschists waiting on the police station roof finally climbed down. No signal had come from the palace. Emperor Hirohito's men had shut the gates against the coup and called in all army officers who remained loyal to the government.

*

Anyone who wanted a taste of the closest thing Japan had to a trashy read could pick up a magazine aimed at the country's female half. *Fujin Kurabu* (Women's Club) and *hufu no Tomo* (Housewives' Friend) were just the right side of salacious and the wrong side of decorous. Back in May 1933 readers browsing the gossip and recipes found a slice of real-life romance. An Ethiopian prince was looking for a Japanese wife.

The bride hunter was Araya Abeba, distant relative of Haile Selassie and minor functionary in the royal court. The stories described him as a light-skinned, monogamous, Christian prince. Some of it was true. *Fujin Kurabu* didn't mention that Araya's smooth baby face gave him a passing resemblance to an overgrown child, or that this undistinguished aristocrat could have got in big trouble back home for calling himself a prince.

'It has been my long-cherished ambition to marry a Japanese lady,' Araya told a reporter. 'Of all first-class nations, Japan has the strongest appeal.'

Ethiopia admired the land of the rising sun. Haile Selassie's constitution was modeled on the Japanese imperial version, and a gang of modernising intellectuals in Addis Ababa called themselves 'Japanisers'. They fetishised technology and scientific progress but could not accept a European vision of the future that rejected tradition. Japan offered an alternative path where military might and industry co-existed with tea ceremonies and samurai spirit, all beneath the benevolent gaze of Emperor Hirohito. Japaniser poet Blatta Gabra-Egziabher had done time in an Ethiopian prison for telling his readers the earth revolved around the sun. He could see the value of modernity. 'He who accepts it, fears no one/ He will become like Japan, strong in everything.'

The admiration cut both ways. Araya had picked up his enthusiasm for Japanese women while member of a diplomatic mission two years previously. One of the locals who ushered the mission through its tour was Sumioka Tomoyoshi, a double-chinned Tokyo lawyer with an interest in far-right politics and a side parting inching its way towards a comb-over. Sumioka was a busy man. He defended Charlie Chaplin's failed assassins, lectured ultranationalist groups, and ran the *Nippon Tsuran Kyoukaiearly* (Turanian Society of Japan), an outfit that claimed blood ties for Japan, Turkey, Hungary, Finland, and Ethiopia. The lawyer also had links to one of Kōdōha's most dangerous cheerleaders: the Black Dragon Society.

In the 1930s at least 600 Japanese far-right groups and secret societies lectured, plotted, and killed. Their 122,000 members worshipped the emperor and aimed to ditch the constitution for direct rule from the Chrysanthemum Throne. Groups like *Kokuryu-kai* (known to outsiders as the Black Dragon Society and insiders as the Amur River Society) thought the emperor had been led astray by liberals and the insufficiently patriotic. They saw the imperial household as the Romanovs of Japan, with the last days approaching and the crown ready to drop. The society would do anything to save the monarchy. *Kokuryu-kai* had been founded at the turn of the century by Uchida Ryōhei, a crew-cut martial artist with a droopy moustache. Over the years Uchida involved himself in spying and propaganda, and had recently hired a squad of Japanese prostitutes to squeeze information from Europeans they serviced in Manchuria. *Kokuryu-kai* was better organised than most similar groups. Its activities brought it close to the Kōdōha faction of the army. Many officers were impressed by the Black Dragon worldview, which combined Pan-Asianism with a more ambitious project for the alliance of all non-white peoples.

Sumioka played a small part in firming up the non-white side of the project. During the Ethiopian mission to Japan, he had become friends with Foreign Minister Blattengeta Heruy Welde Sellase. Together they pushed for trade between the two countries. After early promise the scheme went downhill and the economic links never amounted to more than a bankrupt Japanese dentist in Addis Ababa (no one paid their bills), a popular masseuse in the royal palace (she had a sideline in prostitution), and the misadventures of a loose-tongued Nagasaki businessman who was lucky to avoid jail for his creative approach to finance.

'We shall never have an important exchange of trade with Japan,' said Heruy sadly, 'for we have hardly anything that they can buy from us.'

The trade failure was worse news for Addis Ababa than Tokyo. Haile Selassie and Heruy looked for ways to revive links between the countries. Araya's desire for a Japanese wife had been kept quiet during the mission to avoid any scandal, but in early 1933 the emperor gave permission to take the idea seriously.

Araya had a Japanese friend in Addis Ababa called Shoji Yunosuke, a young right-wing journalist who had been exploring Ethiopia for the last year and was now packing up to go home. Heruy gave him a portrait of Haile Selassie for Sumioka and asked him to get Sumioka involved in the search for a suitable bride.

Sumioka was happy to help. At his suggestion, Shoji seeded stories about the marriage search in Japan's popular press. Twenty women came forward. Sumioka cabled their photographs and details to Addis Ababa.

The lucky girl was Kuroda Masako, twenty-three-year-old second daughter of Viscount Kuroda Hiroyuki of the Imperial Household's Forestry Bureau. Her father was a penniless aristocrat and the family lived in a small suburban Tokyo house. Kuroda was 5'3", spoke fluent English, knew nothing about her future husband, and had a face like an egg wearing lipstick.

'I understand that the people of Ethiopia are extremely interested in sports, and I believe that I shall be able to indulge my taste for athletics when I go there,' she said. 'Unfortunately I did not have the opportunity of meeting Prince Abeba when he visited Japan a few years ago, but I have firmly decided to go to his country and I am willing to put up with whatever circumstances come along.'

She had applied without telling her family but they accepted her decision after news of the marriage made them all celebrities. The union of a Japanese princess and an Ethiopian prince caught the country's romantic imagination.

'Fairyland Ethiopia Will Receive from Japan a Bride for the Royal Nephew,' ran a headline in *Fujin Kurabu*.

Others were less impressed. Addison Southard, America's representative in Ethiopia, pointed out that Araya lived on $50 a month and local living standards were nowhere near the fairyland Japanese aristocrats might expect. He was baffled that an Ethiopian man and Japanese woman had enough in common to try a relationship.

Araya wandered the streets of Addis Ababa with a book on Japanese architecture under his arm, looking for a site to build his future bride a house. Kuroda had already packed a trunk of Japanese dolls to keep her company. She decided to take some human companions and advertised for five girlfriends. So many applications flooded in the family had to move house.

Emperor Haile Selassie, King of Kings, the Elect of Zion, and the Conquering Lion of the Tribe of Judah and his pet dog, Bull, pictured in 1934. (LoC)

A residential street in Addis Ababa in the 1930s. (Martin Rikli Photographs, Special and Area Studies Collections, George A. Smathers Libraries, University of Florida, Gainesville, Florida)

Addis Ababa train station, 1935. (Martin Rikli Photographs, Special and Area Studies Collections, George A. Smathers Libraries, University of Florida, Gainesville, Florida)

A market in the city just before the Italian invasion. (Martin Rikli Photographs, Special and Area Studies Collections, George A. Smathers Libraries, University of Florida, Gainesville, Florida)

bove: Empress Menen Asfaw, wife of
Haile Selassie, photographed in 1933.
The empress-consort was patroness of
the Ethiopian Red Cross and founded the
Empress Menen School for Girls in Addis
Ababa. She was also a smart, discreet
adviser to her husband. (LoC)

ight: The ancient walled city of Harar,
where Haile Selassie and Menen Asfaw were
married. The inhabitants of the Muslim
enclave in southern Ethiopia were unhappy
about being ruled by a Christian emperor.
(LoC)

Left: A Dapper Hubert Julian, the Black Eagle of Harlem, on his way to New York by ocean liner after being expelled from Ethiopia, 1930. (Nationaal Archief)

Below: One of the few pictures of Austrian Nazi Dr Valentin Schuppler. He poses with the Ethiopian royal family and Red Cross personnel in Addis Ababa, autumn 1935. (Author's Collection)

British Author Evelyn Waugh, photographed by Carl Van Vechten in 1940. (LoC)

Belgian adviser Major Auguste Dothée (centre) with fellow Belgians and Ethiopian Imperial Guard officers, 1935. (Martin Rikli Photographs, Special and Area Studies Collections, George A. Smathers Libraries, University of Florida, Gainesville, Florida)

Major-General Eric Virgin (left), Swedish adviser to Haile Selassie, with Major Dothée in 1935. (Martin Rikli Photographs, Special and Area Studies Collections, George A. Smathers Libraries, University of Florida, Gainesville, Florida)

Hard-Drinking British mercenary pilot Hugh de Wet in Addis Ababa, late 1935. (Brian Bridgeman)

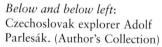

Left and far left: Hilaire du Berrier, an American pilot who posed as a French Count, in the late 1930s. (Author's Collection)

Below and below left: Czechoslovak explorer Adolf Parlesák. (Author's Collection)

Right: Ras Kassa, sad-eyed warlord of the Northern Front. (Wikimedia Commons)

Below left: Chicago pilot John Robinson (left) aka 'The Brown Condor' and French mechanic Yvan Demeaux, 1935. (Nationaal Archief)

Below right: Right-wing Cuban adventurer Alejandro del Valle in Ethiopia, 1935. (Author's Collection)

The Ethiopian Diplomatic Mission in Japan, 1931, with would-be bridegroom Araya Abeba (bottom right), Foreign Minister Heruy (centre), translator Daba Birru (second from left) and ultranationalist lawyer Sumioka Tomoyoshi. (LoC)

Turkish mercenary Vehip Pasha, defender of Ethiopia's southern front pictured in in his Ottoman army days. (Wikimedia Commons)

Addis Ababa's Germans protect their legation at the end of the war. (Martin Rikli Photographs, Special and Area Studies Collections, George A. Smathers Libraries, University of Florida, Gainesville, Florida)

Swedish instructor Captain Viking Tamm (left) photographed during the Winter War between Finland and the Soviets, tried to organise a last-ditch defence of Addis Ababa. (Wikimedia Commons)

Ethiopian troops line the road in Addis Ababa for some passing dignitary. (Martin Rikli Photographs, Special and Area Studies Collections, George A. Smathers Libraries, University of Florida, Gainesville, Florida)

The Ethiopian Red Cross opens its offices in Addis Ababa. (Martin Rikli Photographs, Special and Area Studies Collections, George A. Smathers Libraries, University of Florida, Gainesville, Florida)

Soap box oratory from Mussolini. The Italian dictator preaches his vision of a reborn Roman Empire. (LoC)

And perhaps a more extreme example of short-man syndrome; Austrian dictator Engelbert Dollfuß. A Nazi coup attempt against him would put Germany and Italy on opposing sides during the invasion of Ethiopia. (Author's Collection)

Above left and above right: Swedish aristocrat Count Carl Gustav von Rosen flew a Red Cross air ambulance across the Ethiopian battlefields. The picture on the left was taken in 1919 by Swedish portrait and court photographer Ferdinand Flodin. (Wikimedia commons)

Fairfield House, Newbridge, Bath, bought by Haile Selassie in 1937. He and his family would live there for five years. (Wikimedia commons)

Rodolfo Graziani (centre), commander of the southern front, who would become known as 'the butcher of Ethiopia'. His deep distrust of the Ethiopian Orthodox clergy would lead him to authorise the massacre of the monks of Debre Libanos and those pilgrims unfortunate enough to have arrived there on 21 May 1937 for the monastery's saint's day. He suspected the monks were complicit in an attempt on his life. (LoC)

Left: Italian cavalry showing off for the camera. (LoC)

Below left: Marshal Pietro Badoglio commanded Italian forces in the north and authorised the use of poison gas after a Christmas counter-attack by the Ethiopians. (Author's Collection)

Below right: Some historians have argued that the use of mustard gas had a negligible effect on the outcome of the war and that artillery was king, with airpower as its consort. Italy's modern artillery pieces outgunned anything used by Haile Selasie's troops; but the sheer volume of gas fired by the Italians must surely have has some effect, even if only psychological. (Author's Collection)

Haile Selassie's troops, here in traditional dress and in uniform, never wore boots. (LoC)

The emperor poses with a French Hotchkiss machine gun. (LoC)

Above: Ras Gugsa (centre, with scarf), the traitor who joined the Italians and sent his troops to ambush the emperor's armies in the north. (Author's Collection)

Below: Blackshirts in Makala, late 1935; one looks to be too young to be a drummer boy of the Napoleonic wars. (LoC)

Above: Blackshirts receive the sacrament from an Italian priest at Makala. (LoC)

Below: Ethiopian troops are blessed by an Orthodox priest before leaving Harar in November 1935. (Author's Collection)

Addis Ababa looted and burning at the end of the war. (LoC)

Crating up the Lion of Judah prior to shipping back to Italy. Italy plundered many symbols of independent Ethiopia and sent them back to Rome. (Wikimedia commons)

Ethiopian guerrilla fighters await the return of the emperor to his homeland. (LoC)

Sumioka, the Black Dragons, and a few Kōdōha celebrated the choice of bride with sake. Japan was edging a little closer to becoming leader of the non-white world.

*

Tokyo, February 1936. Everyday life in the capital continued while the soldiers barricaded the streets. Stalls sold hot potatoes. People held umbrellas against the snow. Workers hurried past by bicycle, car, and tram, in western suits and kimonos. The press ignored most of what was going on and referred to the men with guns as 'activist troops'. Politicians and officers ferried back and forth between the barricades and government buildings. Martial law was declared, but the rebels were put in charge of enforcing it. Across Tokyo, a lot of men in uniform burst into meeting rooms waving katanas and shouting demands.

The putschists were young fanatics of captain or below, marinated in samurai spirit. Many cheerfully admitted they were prepared, and even hoped, to die in the coup attempt. They demanded direct rule by the emperor under the warlike guidance of Kōdōha commanders. Details were blurry. Soldier spokesmen hadn't bothered to hone their demands, believing men like Araki would quickly step in and form a new government. Instead, Kōdōha leaders remained silently loyal to the establishment.

Morale on the barricades received a boost when Kita Ikki visited the day after the coup. Kita was a skinny, dark-moustached fifty-two-year-old who started off socialist and drifted to the extreme right. A member of the Black Dragons and other extremist groups, many saw him as the theorist of Japanese fascism. The coup had been planned by men who admired his writings, although he hadn't been asked to take part due to doubts over his occasional shows of disrespect to the emperor (a legacy of socialism) and bohemian private life, including a fortune-telling wife and an adopted Chinese son. Some soldiers found it hard to overlook his taste for Islam.

'The Japanese rising sun flag, after defeating England, reviving Turkey, making India independent, and China self-reliant,' said Kita, 'will shed the light of Heaven on all the people of the world. The coming again of Christ, prophesied all over the world, is actually the Japanese people's scripture and sword in the shape of Mohammed.'

Now Kita was on the barricades, wearing a Chinese robe, and telling soldiers that victory was close and the emperor supported them. The coup commanders believed him and slipped off their boots to celebrate in a tea house.

Kita was wrong. Hirohito wanted the putsch crushed. The slim thirty-five-year-old emperor of Japan was a living god who rarely interfaced with the real world. His suits didn't fit because tailors, not allowed to touch, had to guess his measurements. Hirohito usually left the decisions to his ministers; but the assassinations and attempt to occupy the palace had woken the dragon. Outside in the Tokyo snow, troops loyal to the emperor were closing in on the barricades.

*

Some Black Dragons wondered if it might have been different had the Araya wedding gone ahead. Uchida's vision of a united non-white world could have strengthened the Kōdōha position and made the coup unnecessary.

But marriage preparations had been called off at the end of 1934. Everyone involved, except the happy couple, had second thoughts. Addis Ababa got nervous after Baron Roman Procházka, former Austrian consul in Ethiopia, stirred up trouble with widely-publicised fantasies about Japanese colonization of Africa. Procházka had trouble getting the names straight but that was a minor detail to imperialists worried about Japan's creeping influence in Africa. Procházka airily declared:

Plans have been made for effecting mixed marriages between the eligible Japanese settlers (estimated at about 2,000 in number) and native Abyssinian women. This declared policy which is intended to produce a new race of leaders in the united revolt of the coloured peoples against the white races, was to have been inaugurated by the marriage of Princess Masako, a daughter of the Japanese prince Kurado [Kuroda], to the Ethiopian prince Lij Ayalé [Araya].

Italy picked up on the story and a Fascist newspaper wrote angrily about the 'kisses between the dark and the black by having a daughter of a Japanese peer married to an Ethiopian'. The backlash convinced Haile Selassie to kill the marriage. Araya was disappointed but obedient. A miserable Kuroda ran away from home for a while.

It was late the next year before anyone tried to resurrect the alliance between Ethiopia and Japan. On 1 August 1935 a meeting took place in a room at Addis Ababa's Majestic Hotel. Shoji Yunosuke, Iwabuchi Yoshikazu (another right-wing journalist), and Yamauchi Masao (an equally right-leaning businessman living in Addis Ababa) invited fifteen high-ranking Ethiopians, including Araya and Heruy, to discuss the situation. Shoji was keen to overturn Haile Selassie's belief that only the big European powers behind the League of Nations could stop Italy:

> Hitherto, Caucasian peoples have not regarded White and Coloured peoples as equal. Coloured peoples in Asia and Africa ... have been suffering for a long time under White oppression. In the Sino-Japanese War, Japan's counterattack on European powers lying behind China awakened the concept of independence among all Coloured peoples. As we now see the declining path of Western civilization, a strong wave of nationalistic movements is sweeping throughout the world including Asia, Africa, and South America ...

The three Japanese convinced their guests that Ethiopia should seek military support from their homeland. Later that month, Shoji and

Daba Birrou, an Ethiopian diplomat who had accompanied Heruy on his 1931 trip, made a trip to Tokyo. Shoji's newspaper *Osaka Mainichi* paid for a stateroom on the French liner *Atos II* and publicised the trip.

The pair arrived at Nagasaki in the middle of September. Birrou had brought sound movies of Haile Selassie for the Imperial family and an autographed photo of the emperor for Tōyama Mitsuru, eighty-year-old godfather figure to the Black Dragons and its predecessor movement *Genyōsha* (the Dark Ocean Society). Tōyama was an enemy of every government he encountered, including his own. Any Chinese, Indian, or Filipino dissidents visiting Tokyo always ended up at his Shibuya home.

Birrou was in Japan to ask the authorities for a major, captain, and lieutenant as military instructors; a crew of surgeons; fortifications engineers; four telecommunications engineers; two artillery instructors; one airplane sound locator instructor; teachers for young Ethiopians; medical supplies for 10,000 people and tents for a field hospital; artillery pieces, anti-aircraft guns, sub-machine-guns, automatic rifles, light tanks, and munitions; military telephones, tents, telescopes, and other tools for trenches. He had cash for the weapons and ammunition and the offer of Ethiopian coffee, hides, beeswax, and honey for everything else.

'Abyssinia is now menaced by foreign foes,' Birrou said, 'as Japan was some sixty years ago when she was about to open her doors to the outside world. Because the country is small, because the country is non-Caucasian, because it is weak, it must meet the foreign challenge. These things we non-white people are forced to endure.'

In Tokyo close to 2,000 members of the Black Dragons, *Aikoku Seinen Renmei* (the Patriotic Students Federation), *Kokusui Taishu-to Teishin-tai* (Nationalist Volunteer People's Party), the Ethiopia Support Society, Ethiopian Crisis Committee, the Showa Boy Scouts organisation, and other grouplets bouncing around the atomised nationalist scene, greeted the pair at Tokyo central railway station. They carried banners: 'Down With Italy!' and 'Rescue Ethiopia!'

There were tea ceremonies, respectful visits to shrines, and English-language talks by Birrou to enthusiastic but uncomprehending audiences packed into the Seiyoken restaurant, full of banzais and enough hand-shaking to sprain wrists. But the Japanese Foreign Ministry remained coolly distant. Birrou found himself splayed against a wall of glass, politely ignored by the powerful on the other side. The realisation crept in that all the right-wing journalists, former army officers and Pan-Asian *Kōdōha* fanatics he had met possessed no real influence.

The Tōseiha faction in the military had no intention of helping Ethiopia: its leaders preferred a pact with Rome. Their logic was simple. If Italy lost then Ethiopia's enemy was destroyed, if not then Mussolini would have proved himself a strong ally. The Japanese ambassador in Rome, pouchy-faced career diplomat Dr Sugimura Yotaro, assured the Italians that Japan would remain neutral in the event of a war.

Birrou stayed in Tokyo with his right-wing friends and watched cinema newsreels of Italy invading his country. The Ethiopian cause remained popular among the Japanese public. Tokyo newspapers and the Foreign Ministry in Addis Ababa were deluged with requests from Japanese volunteers to join the fighting. One request that made it to Addis Ababa was written in blood. Prominent black newspaper the *Chicago Defender* fantasised about Japanese volunteers 'tramping through African hinterlands to the aid of their darker brothers on the lofty plateaus of Ethiopia'. The Japanese government blocked most requests; distance and cost killed off the rest.

When a Japanese delegation opened in Addis Ababa in January 1936 Heruy tried to order weapons directly. They politely turned him down. Haile Selassie requested Japanese submarines sink Italian ships. Another polite refusal. Right-wing Japanese groups sent swords and bandages to Ethiopia in a symbolic gesture.

Symbolism was all they had. Bar Ethiopia in Tokyo banned Italian patrons. A patriotic society presented a fine antique samurai sword to Haile Selassie. A dish called Ethiopia Manjuu became popular: a brown steamed dumpling stuffed with azuki bean paste.

Then in late February, Kōdōha supporters launched their coup in Tokyo. Birrou and the Black Dragons followed it closely, wondering if a new government could help Ethiopia. By the fourth day of the coup, the public had been told to stay indoors. Trains and buses stopped running. Rebel banners and flags fluttered in the icy wind. Bursts of radio propaganda targeted the troops and a balloon floated over the city trailing a government banner.

'Your fathers, mothers, brothers, and sisters are weeping because you will become traitors.'

Hirohito ordered the putschists to surrender. Government soldiers took up positions facing the rebel barricades and cocked their rifles. For a moment civil war seemed possible in Tokyo centre. On Saturday 29 February the mutineers gave up and returned to barracks, depressed and disillusioned. Some committed harakiri: entrails slipping out over the blade of a tantō dagger as a companion's katana blurred towards the bowed neck. The leaders who stayed alive faced a court martial that jailed seventy and executed nineteen.

Any remaining Kōdōha supporters were forced out of the army and replaced by Tōseiha technocrats. Whatever slight hope the Black Dragons had for influencing Japanese foreign policy towards Ethiopia melted away like spring snow. Far-right ideologue Kita Ikka spent a year behind bars until his execution. As he stood against a wall waiting for the firing squad, a fellow condemned nationalist suggested they shout a final banzai for the emperor.

'I'd rather not,' said Kita.

In March 1936 Haile Selassie awarded Sumioka the Commander Class of the Order of Menelik. The Japanese lawyer wrote a letter of thanks, pledging support to the emperor and expressing his conviction that Italy could not win. By the time Sumioka sent his letter the northern front had collapsed, Haile Selassie's Minister of War was dead, and Cuban mercenary Alejandro del Valle was running for his life.

18

OUR CUBAN FRIEND
UNDER FIRE

The Death of Ras Mulugeta, 27 February 1936

Alejandro del Valle tied a grubby white rag to a stick and waved it over the top of the trench. The Eritreans stopped firing, cheered, and climbed wearily out of their positions to take the surrender. They were halfway across when Del Valle dropped the flag and told his men to shoot. The Eritreans died like rabbits in front of the farmer's gun.

It went against all the rules of war but the Cuban didn't care. They were dying up here on the mountain. The battle had been going on through the night, a snowglobe of shrapnel and bullets as wave after wave of Italians rushed them in the moonlight. The enemy had surrounded the mountain hours ago and cut off all retreat. Now flamethrower crews burned screaming men in caves and aircraft wheeled overhead through the night rain dropping mustard gas bombs. Del Valle got up high when the bombs cracked open but couldn't block wisps of yellow mist from his lungs. The front of the Cuban's uniform was stained with blood and spittle.

Amba Aradam was a flat tabletop of rock, the southern edge of which melted into the village of Antalo and the fertile Mehera plain. Until that morning Mulugeta's biggest problem had been keeping his 70,000 men fed. Cattle grazing on the plain provided beef and milk; locals bartered supplies in Antalo village. It was never enough. His warriors raided nearby settlements, looting farms and kidnapping women. Del Valle watched the Italians build positions in the foothills of the mountain while Ethiopian priests gave sermons to deaf ears about the evils of rape and theft.

The Cuban specialised in machine guns but Mulugeta had given him an artillery section with guns antique enough to have seen service at Adwa. They looked like oversized telescopes slung between cartwheels. A week earlier, the ras had ordered a test fire at the Italian lines.

'The shells are defective,' said Del Valle. 'If one of them falls, unexploded, in the enemy camp, the Italians will die laughing.'

'Ferengi, you have to shoot them,' said Mulugeta angrily. 'You are now responsible for that … That's an order.'

The Cuban dragged his guns into position near Amba Aradam's northern peak and faked some expertise by scribbling in a pad and looking meaningfully at the horizon. He had never directed artillery before. His crew loaded a shell. Del Valle sent up a quick prayer and pulled the firing cord. He was knocked to the ground in a cloud of peppery smoke and recoil as the shell screamed into the distance. Mulugeta grunted and went away. Later that day, a spy reported that the shell had killed three men in the Italian camp. The ras grudgingly congratulated Del Valle. The Cuban didn't say he had been aiming for a different target.

Del Valle left the mountain with his slaves and a group of soldiers to carry out diversionary raids down on the plain, hoping to distract the enemy from Mulugeta's troop buildup on Amba Aradam. He was picking his way through the tall grass when an Italian soldier stumbled up, plump and red-cheeked, fooled into thinking he had found his own lines by the sight of a white man. Del Valle's escort appeared and the Italian's face fell. He gave his name as Mocelli. Del Valle sent him back as a prisoner but knew the man would be murdered on the way. Mulugeta had no respect for captives or turncoats. A gang of Eritreans who tried to join his army were tortured for days and sent back to the Italian lines missing noses, hands, ears, tongues, lips, eyes, and carrying a note. 'This is what Mulugeta does to traitors.'

Ethiopians sometimes amused themselves by hacking their swords deep into a prisoner's neck and watching him run in panic, hands clamped over a spraying arterial wound that would bleed out in minutes. Any Italian units which made the mistake of surrendering during battle got hacked to death when they dropped their guns. Del Valle wondered again if he was on the right side. He tried to persuade the ras to stop, arguing war crimes made Ethiopia look bad to the League of Nations. 'For me the League of Nations and a dead hyena are the same thing,' said Mulugeta.

Perhaps Mulugeta was wiser than he seemed. Most of the dead were Africans serving with the Italians, or Ethiopians who had turned on their own government. No one in the League, Addis Ababa, or Rome seemed to care much about them.

Down on the plain Del Valle led an ambush against a truck convoy. His slaves shot the drivers out of their cabs and cut up Blackshirt guards with swords. Blood pools dried in the sun as they looted the trucks.

'We found 80,000 liras with a printed stamp saying "occupation army"; several maps and interesting documents, and a basket, which I appropriated in the distribution and contained a sparkling champagne, called Cinzano, five packs of Stella brand cigarettes, two pairs of handmade white woolen socks, and photography of a cute girl with the face of a Madonna, who signed the back Maria.'

He took the Cinzano and Maria back to the mountain, stopping in the foothills to go after a snow-white camel. The creature objected when Del Valle beat it with a stick and chased him and his slaves up a tree. They shot it dead. On the way back to Mulugeta's positions the Cuban found the corpses of men and horses lying near streams poisoned by the Italians. Higher up the mountain other men were thrashing in the mud; their bread had been laced with strychnine. Mulugeta's men burned down villages they held responsible and shamans dosed poison survivors with homemade medicine.

'Here's the formula,' Del Valle told friends. 'Each dose is composed as follows: thirty-three wild coffee beans and three wasps are taken and placed on an iron plate on the fire, until toasted. Add ashes, grind until pulverized and mix with wax and honey, then give in the form of pills.'

Poisoned food and water was only the first stage of Badoglio's plan to take the mountain. His troops were slowly encircling Mulugeta's position. The morning of 10 February began with an intense bombardment from 170 planes and 280 artillery pieces. A defiant Ras Mulugeta set up his throne in the open under a green umbrella with gold tassels. Within minutes the umbrella was hanging in shreds. Mulugeta and his men ran for the caves as shells smashed their panicking horses to pieces across the mountainside.

Eritrean troops climbed the slopes under cover of the bombardment but were beaten back. Italian tanks chugging up narrow paths were swarmed by Ethiopians and tipped into chasms, the crews inside screaming as they fell. By the second day the rain was falling hard. The temperature dropped and cold bit into the bones. Bitwoded Makonnen tried to break through the Italian lines from the plain; he was shot through the hips by machine-gun fire.

'Every day was a repetition of the previous one,' said Del Valle. 'Skirmishes, bombings, gunfire, fog, mud, and searchlights at night.'

Adolf Parlesák, on his way back to Dessie, diverted to the mountains but walked into a firefight with Dejazmach Gugsa's collaborators. A sudden air raid that churned up the ground and slapped bullets into boulders gave the Czech and his men a chance to disengage. They stumbled into a village; the residents thought Parlesák was Italian and immediately surrendered. When the confusion was resolved villagers told him stories of bandits robbing travellers, locals in blood feuds, collaboration with the enemy and no one sure of what was happening in the war. It was impossible to get up to Amba Aradam.

Parlesák returned to Ras Kassa, arriving on 21 February with the loss of two men. He told the ras that the Italians had completed their encirclement. Mulugeta's men were trapped on the mountain with no way out.

*

Del Valle wasn't the only white man helping Ras Mulugeta's army. Polish doctor Dr Stanisław Belau, an anxious tropical disease specialist from Warsaw, and his assistant, twenty-six-year-old former journalist Tadeusz Medyński, had set up a makeshift hospital in an Amba Aradam cave. Belau had been in Ethiopia running an SIM nursing home for the past few years, respected enough that Haile Selassie asked him to become a citizen. The doctor preferred to remain Polish but joined the Ethiopian Red Cross at the start of the war. Now he was in a damp cave on the front lines tending injured men moaning from gas burns and shrapnel wounds.

Another Red Cross foreigner was helping the Ethiopians back on the Mehera plain. Major Gerald Burgoyne ran a column of mules hauling the wounded back to a field hospital. The old reactionary had a white moustache and a face that had been set in a permanent expression of outrage ever since he witnessed a Christmas truce between British and German soldiers in the first year of the First World War. Burgoyne didn't believe in truces, shellshock, or pacifism. He had spent the years of peace foxhunting and snorting at the modern world, before shaving ten years off his age and heading for Ethiopia.

Burgoyne's capacity for outrage had already been pushed to the limit by Italian attacks on the Red Cross. On 15 January his mule column was resting north of Dessie. He had left the red flaps of his tent open to create a Red Cross flag and was chatting with a vet attached to the column when an Italian plane attacked.

'Your tent's gone,' said the vet.

'It had too,' Burgoyne wrote to his wife. 'A real good shot. The Eytie seeing the Red Cross put six big bombs carefully round it, the furthest 20 yards way – holes 15ft in diameter and four or five feet deep ... It was too evident that he deliberately bombed my tent ... Can't understand the idea.'

Afterwards Burgoyne sent a telegram to the Red Cross headquarters in Ethiopia. 'Wake up Geneva. It is evident that the Italians are making special targets of Red Crosses.'

During the encirclement of Amba Aradam, Burgoyne and his mule train moved up towards the mountain and found Bitwoded Makonnen badly wounded in a cave overlooking the River Buie. His attack had punched a narrow corridor through Italian lines but he was dying. Burgoyne dressed his wounds. Makonnen died the next day. After prayers the aristocrat's men decided to take his body home for burial hidden in a pair of war drums. They asked Burgoyne to cut their chief in half. The major found a bone saw among his equipment and got to work.

While Burgoyne was sawing, Dr Belau emerged from his cave on Amba Aradam and found everyone gone. A few hours earlier he had been haggling with Mulugeta over the price of mules while the ras gave orders for a break-out along the narrow path that had cost Bitwoded Makonnen his life. Belau refused to abandon his patients and demanded transport. Mulugeta offered mules but insisted the doctor pay for them. The Pole gave up in disgust and returned to his operating table. When he emerged, Mulugeta had pulled out with 4,000 of his men.

Italian troops swarmed over the mountain and cleared out the caves and crevices with hand grenades. Afterwards Blackshirts burned 8,000 corpses and human ash hung in the air for weeks. Belau and Medyński remained at their posts until Italian soldiers led them out at gunpoint. They endured days of beatings and mock execution squads before putting shaky signatures to letters supporting the invasion. Then a long sea trip to Naples, Belau's malaria returning during an involuntary stay in the city's drunk tank, before expulsion and the warning never to return to Africa.

Mulugeta's army fled south in chaotic retreat. Italian planes dropped forty tonnes of mustard gas on them in four days while local guerrillas picked off stragglers. The *Montreal Gazette* reported that Alejandro Del Valle had been captured by the Italians near Makale. Canada was misinformed. The Cuban was free and moving south, just surviving an attack by guerrillas who shot his mule out beneath him and charged in so close he took their skulls off at point-blank range with his revolver.

Major Burgoyne was elsewhere in the retreat. His mules carried Bitwoded Makonnen's bisected body sealed into two war drums until an Italian air strike smeared one mule across the road. The bitwoded's men scraped up their leader's lower half and buried it under a tree; the top got a more respectful resting place in the grounds of a nearby church. Burgoyne kept moving with the retreat. On 27 February he was walking down a road thick with corpses next to Tadesse Mulugeta, the ras's son, when Italian airplanes attacked again.

The two men had almost reached the shelter of a cypress grove when a bomb exploded between them. Both were blown to pieces. Mulugeta turned back when he heard the news and was last seen fighting off a guerrilla ambush. The minister of war's body was never recovered. His leaderless army kept plunging south.

Feodor Konovalov was standing in the chilly rock church of Ras Kassa's headquarters when he heard about the defeat.

'How could it have happened?' Konovalov thought. He answered his own question. 'The main cause was the unskilled generalship of our armies, their unpreparedness, and lack of training. The men, after all, were only peasants who had merely become "soldiers" because they had rifles thrust into their hands. They had no training whatever. With no schooling about what to do should the enemy attack, they immediately had to take their places on the battlefield. Old and tired, the ras found he was not the alert commander he should be, not being a military man by nature. Besides, he was unpopular among his troops.'

It was an ungenerous assessment but the war was at a tipping point. Mulugeta's defeat had peeled the northern front wide open. Only the armies of Ras Kassa and Ras Imru remained to fight the Italians. If they fell then the road to Addis Ababa was wide open.

19

BOHEMIANS ON THE RUN

The Collapse of Ras Kassa's Army,
Late February 1936

The Italian airstrike sliced off a thick slab of mountain and tumbled it down onto the women and children sheltering below. Adolf Parlesák and Feodor Konovalov huddled behind a pile of rocks on the other side of the pass and watched the impact. A brown dust cloud rose into the sky. They could hear screams over the noise of airplane motors and explosions. Konovalov shook his head.

'That's awful,' he said with tears in his eyes. 'This is terrible.'

Parlesák could barely find it in himself to care. He was a burnt-out case, exhausted, unwashed, lice-bitten, numb to any pain not his own.

At least 8,000 Ethiopians in Ras Kassa's army had died fighting the Italians so far. Each night warriors fired rifles to commemorate the departed and frighten off evil spirits; each day there were funeral processions through the camp. Everyone had dysentery, or typhoid, or something unidentified. Fly-crusted mule corpses rotted between tents until the stench got too bad and a team of Ethiopians dragged them to the camp's perimeter for the hyenas.

Breyer and Konovalov were tough enough to live with it but a few weeks back Parlesák had cracked and tried to quit. Ras Kassa reluctantly let him join a mule caravan headed for Haile Selassie's camp at Dessie.

All the Czech got was a grim round trip, helplessly watching typhoid sufferers die in a cave church turned into a first aid post, having his mule swapped for a knackered specimen by men he trusted, eating bread crawling with weevils, and making a diversion to break Mulugeta's siege that nearly killed him. But he managed to bathe for the first time in two months, plunging into an icy stream before returning to Kassa's camp in a worse state than he left it. There was no escape.

The good days were few. The Ethiopians shot down two Italian planes. In the wreckage of one they found the body of a joy-riding white woman tangled with the crew corpses. An eighty-mule caravan brought in 243,000 bullets to be distributed among the 50,000 soldiers still left in front line. Their comrades had died or deserted back home. The Ethiopian Red Cross ambulance of Schuppler, Achmet, and Hickey limped into camp. Irish doctor Marius Brophil was in Addis Ababa, where his main task seemed to be lying to the press about Italian advances on the northern front.

'He signed a statement, to be published soon, designed to show the Italian claims unreasonable,' reported an Associated Press correspondent prepared to run with Brophil's claims for the sake of Ethiopia.

Ras Kassa's soldiers had excavated some shallow caves for the wounded at the foot of a rock wall. The men lay outside, too weak to wave away the flies sucking at their wounds. Schuppler erected a tent and got to work treating patients. He amputated and stitched through the day, earning Parlesák's admiration for staying at his post as Italian bombs rained down.

'Why not mark the tent with a red cross?' Parlesák asked.

'It would just attract the Italian pilots,' said Schuppler gloomily, red to the wrists. 'They bomb all hospitals, tents, and buildings marked with a red cross … '

The ambulance crew and three Slavs were the only foreigners left on the northern front. Del Valle was fleeing south; Belau and Medyński were on their way to Italy; the few journalists still around had been corralled in Addis Ababa; the nearest Red

Cross unit was at Dessie; and the emperor's foreign advisers were nowhere near the frontlines. Parlesák reserved special contempt for Belgians and Swedes earning easy money as instructors.

'Countless European officers, who had joined the emperor's Abyssinian forces,' he said, 'remained idle in a safe base in Addis Ababa or in Dessie, a hundred kilometres behind the front.'

The Czech had no way of knowing the Swedes were doing their best to form up a new brigade in the capital. And Reul's Belgians had problems of their own. Haile Selassie had never found a proper use for their expertise. Three experienced Belgian soldiers were given the make-work job of censoring news reports in Addis Ababa; another was organising the city's police force. Relations between Belgians and locals were bad and getting worse.

The anti-foreigner sentiment was a side-effect of the growing realisation in Addis Ababa that Italy might win. Pilot John Robinson watched morale drop among courtiers who had started the war cheerfully optimistic that Fascist bombers could not crest the northern mountain peaks.

'The officials have begun to lose their boisterous idea about Ethiopia can beat the Italians at any time,' he wrote home. 'They realize now that they have been asleep for the last forty or more years. They are wondering who will save them from the Italians, instead of let the Italians come [so] that they could beat them.'

At the end of January 1936 Léopold Reul returned to Brussels, sick and needing an operation. Most of his fascists followed over the next few weeks. Haile Selassie could not persuade them to stay. Their pay was irregular, some were wounded or ill, and no one listened to them. Only a few remained: Captain Louis Norman in Dessie, De Fraipont and Bob Viseur in Addis Ababa, and Lieutenant Frère down south, now desperate to get away after seeing a group of Italian and Eritrean prisoners tortured to death by Desta. None of them had signed up for a shooting war. Their contracts were clear on that point.

'Never, during the conversations preceding the signature of the contract, nor in the minds of the other subalterns who went with me, nor in our contracts with the Ethiopian government, was there any question of war or of going to fight the Italians,' wrote Lieutenant Frère later. 'It was merely provided that, in case of war, there would be an increase of pay for the two field officers who might be attached to one or other General Staff.'

No one told the Italians. De Fraipont had been wounded in the Dessie bombing last year. Frère barely escaped alive in January when Ras Desta tried to invade Italian Somaliland but couldn't penetrate Graziani's defences. A Fascist counter-attack along the right bank of the River Juba sent Ethiopian troops into a retreating panic.

'Situation desperate,' Frère cabled to Addis Ababa. 'Telegraph my wife that everything is going well.'

Then he ran with everyone else.

*

Italian airplanes in the north switched from bombs to propaganda. Leaflets fluttered down claiming that Haile Selassie was dead and Ras Mulugeta defeated. Parlesák didn't believe the first and only accepted the second when survivors from Amba Aradam started trickling into Ras Kassa's camp.

After Mulugeta, other dominoes tumbled. Defeat at Chelikot-Antalo, near Mai Caich. Defeat at Adi Amheti where Dejazmach Makonnen Demissie was caught on horseback in the barbed wire and finished by machine guns. Stalemate for Ras Imru's army, squeezed out of the way by the Italian advance. Ras Kassa was the last thing stopping Mussolini's men driving south.

Italian troops began to surround Kassa's camp. Parlesák could see the lights of fresh enemy camps glittering at night to the south. The ras spent his days in a gloomy cave talking options with Seyoum and his chiefs. He had two canons of nineteenth century vintage, with twenty-seven rounds; a handful of light and heavy machine guns; a few Oerlikon anti-aircraft guns; ten to twenty rounds for each rifle. Many of his men had only spears. Kassa tried to convince himself his mountain positions were safe from direct attack or encirclement.

In the early hours of 27 February, the day of Ras Mulugeta's death, Italian mountaineers climbed the northern peak of the mountain and silently captured the Ethiopian positions. An attempt on the southern peak failed in a blaze of machine-gun fire. Badoglio gave the signal to attack. The first artillery shells fell while Kassa and Konovalov were in a cave church surrounded by ringing bells and chanting priests. Engines began droning overhead. They rushed out into the morning light to find rifle fire crackled at the perimeter and shrapnel chiming off rocks.

By the next day Ras Kassa's mountain was almost overrun. Counter-attacks held back the Italians but the frontline was crumbling. Parlesák and the others found Kassa sitting on his portable throne, the usual glacial calm turned to sullen misery.

'We have to retreat,' he said. 'But where? All roads south are occupied by Italian troops. We can only drive up the hills and then … Pack your things quickly and join the stream of troops.'

Konovalov tried to persuade the ras to abandon his positions and fall back towards Dessie. Kassa shook his head. His orders were to defend the mountain. The foreigners joined a mule caravan carrying Kassa's personal baggage with the Red Cross team tagging behind, and floated off in a human river of civilians and deserting soldiers.

Italian aircraft bombed them in a mountain pass, dust and shrapnel spraying as they ran for cover. Fifteen Ethiopians died and more went down as they fought their way out of the Italian encirclement. Men, women, and children jammed into pathways trying to escape. Mules collapsed from saddle bags too heavy with loot. The weak and slow got trampled.

When Italian planes came screaming in over a ravine, Parlesák and Breyer joined soldiers cramming themselves into caves high up in the cliff faces. Some Ethiopians refused to leave their possessions and were mashed by bombs that turned the path into a mulch of flesh, shattered wooden boxes, and pieces of leather satchel. Schuppler gave a quinine tablet to an Ethiopian with a mangled hand and the lie it would heal him in a week. The man believed every word.

They kept moving, leaving the wounded behind. Parlesák and the other foreigners were nearly killed by Ethiopian troops who thought they were Blackshirts. Embraces and apologies. Most of the horses died and even chiefs had to walk. The men back at Debra Amby held on, trying to delay the Italians, until Ras Kassa ordered the mountain abandoned and fled with his troops. Italian aircraft dropped flares to illuminate the retreating army for artillery spotters.

Days of forced marches followed. Breyer and Konovalov became too tired to carry on. Parlesák left them behind. He met Ras Kassa's sons who told him their father had escaped the Italians and taken a different route. They gave Parlesák a scoop of dirty water and a handful of grain. On the horizon a dust cloud signalled pursuing Italians. Breyer and Konovalov caught up again but soon collapsed. Parlesák abandoned them in the shade of a tree.

The Czech finally stumbled dirt-caked and crack-lipped into a damp cave occupied by Ras Kassa and his bodyguards. He fell asleep in the darkness and awoke to find his friends and Schuppler and Hickey present. Achmet had got separated in the retreat. The survival of the foreigners cheered up the gloomy ras who been convinced they were dead. He gave them horses and the army moved out, heading for Haile Selassie's camp.

The Italians hunted them. The journey was a nightmare of machine guns barking, wading through rivers waist-deep under fire, racing over a plain as mortar shells came whistling down and shaking the ground, leaping over the bodies of dead men, rocks baking under a killing sun, horses galloping through explosions. Men slept wherever they could. Parlesák's horse nuzzled him awake during the night, looking for protection from the howling hyenas out in the darkness.

By the middle of March they were trying to shake the Italians by trekking through the desert, forced to dig deep wells in parched riverbeds. Lips bled, skin flaked. The army moved silent as ghosts and threw themselves at any water they found. Parlesák stuck his head into a stream between a pair of horses, the three of them gulping down the muddy liquid.

Konovalov heard an old man talking late at night. 'There are the old books in most of our monasteries, preserved by the monks,' said the man. 'They prophesy many things – among others, that foreigners will enter our beloved country by force, and people will be unable to return to their homes for three whole years. The books say that in this time the Europeans will build all over the country. Buildings like those in Addis Ababa and good roads such as only they know how to construct. Then the peasants will return to their homes and become masters of these improvements. I had heard this prophecy before, but I did not believe then in its almost exact fulfilment.'

The Russian rolled over to sleep and wondered if the old man was right.

*

On 19 March Ras Kassa's army reached Korem, a village south of Lake Asang now home to Haile Selassie and his men. The emperor held court in a cave furnished with folding chairs, a cot, a sewing machine, and a carpet. Twin anti-aircraft guns guarded the entrance. The emperor was still and composed. He offered them a bowl of apples. Fresh uniforms replaced their rags. 'His words exuded confident calmness and admirable energy,' thought Parlesák.

He quizzed the whites about battles in the north and told them Ras Imru's army had finally disintegrated under Italian attack. Fascists had chased it through forests firebombed into sticks of charcoal. Airplanes tracked them. Desertions and death had left Imru with only 300 soldiers, all from his personal bodyguard. The front no longer existed.

Haile Selassie intended to move north and fight the Italians. Konovalov advised him to go south where enemy supply lines would be extended and weak. The emperor shook his head.

'But Your Majesty,' said the Russian, 'if your army ...'

'I know it would mean the end,' said the emperor.

Haile Selassie invited them to stay. He had 30,000 poorly armed soldiers with small reserves of ammunition, and few heavy weapons. The Italians knew his movements thanks to aerial surveillance and radio intercepts. Parlesák made a faltering excuse. So did the others. Only Konovalov decided to stay.

Haile Selassie gave a dignified smile and wished them luck on their trip back to Addis Ababa. He was getting used to being disappointed in foreigners. The League of Nations had let him down. Japan could not help. Now troops from Nazi Germany had reoccupied the Rhineland, a slab of smokestacks and river up against the French border.

He didn't discuss Germany with Parlesák and the others. They wouldn't have understood its importance to Ethiopia. Only the emperor knew that Adolf Hitler's Third Reich had once been a good friend.

20

NAZI ETHIOPIA

Adolf Hitler Withdraws the Hand of Friendship, 7 March 1936

The streets were carpeted with flowers when German soldiers marched through Cologne for the first time since the war. Crowds cheered the men in *feldgrau*. Catholic priests sprinkled Holy Water on passing tank columns. Twenty-five miles to the north, Düsseldorf was a forest of Nazi salutes and swastika flags. Down in the south-east, uniformed brass bands played in the squares of Mainz. The German military had entered the Rhineland.

The territory had been demilitarised at the end of the First World War to provide a firebreak for France in case the Germans got any fresh ideas about conquering Europe. Occupying Allied troops did their best to defeat opposition from the locals. Army veteran Albert Leo Schlageter became a martyr at twenty-eight when he was executed for derailing France-bound trains. Rhinelanders erected monuments and propped his photograph on their mantlepieces.

The Allies eventually went home having warned that any military activity in the area would meet an armed response. Their threat worked until the Nazis took power. On Saturday 7 March 1936 Hitler sent in nineteen infantry battalions. The Allied deterrent relied on co-operation between Britain, France, and Italy but the three powers had little in common after falling out over Ethiopia.

'I can tell you that for five days and five nights not one of us closed an eye,' said a German officer on the scene. 'We knew that if the French marched, we were done. We had no fortifications, and no army to match the French.'

France didn't march. Neither did Britain. Less than two years earlier Mussolini had forced the Nazis to back down over Austria, but this time made no effort to intervene. A complex web of alliances, pacts, and cold-blooded cost-benefit analysis lay behind the inaction. But to Haile Selassie the logic was simple: Fascist Italy had accepted the occupation in exchange for Germany supporting the invasion of his country. Another foreign nation had stabbed the emperor in the back. It shouldn't have been a surprise. Friendship between the Third Reich and Haile Selassie had been a succession of failed deals and diplomatic lies from the start.

*

On Christmas Eve 1934 the swastika flag was whipping in the wind over the German consulate in Addis Ababa. The Reich had been in Ethiopia since Emperor Menelik swapped a plot of dirt in his capital for embassy space down a leafy Berlin street near the River Spree. Not many of the German diplomats who had passed through the consulate over the years thought they got the best end of that deal.

Inside the consulate, newly arrived chargé d'affaires in Addis Ababa, war veteran and lawyer Willy Unverfehrt, was working late on a message to the Foreign Ministry in Berlin. He needed advice about a tricky diplomatic situation. Haile Selassie wanted to buy poison gas.

The use and manufacture of chemical and biological weapons was illegal under the 1925 Geneva Protocol. Adolf Hitler ignored the prohibition. He had a special artillery unit testing chemical weapons at Koenigsbrueck near the Czechoslovak border. Scientists worked on more powerful nerve agents in secret laboratories. Unverfehrt knew that selling gas to the Ethiopians would need approval at the highest level.

Earlier that day, the diplomat had gone to see the emperor at Little Gibbi, the new palace built as a modern counterblast to the unplanned sprawl of Menelik's old compound. Unverfehrt passed the sentry boxes painted in thick stripes of green, yellow, and red, walked up the gravel drive passing the hissing fountain and entered the airy building modelled on an English country house.

He had a hand-written letter for the emperor from Hitler. Haile Selassie read it and dismissed his interpreter. He didn't want any witnesses. Unverfehrt didn't know what his führer had written and was prepared to offer some bland-sounding diplomatic support about the recent confrontation at Walwal. Instead Haile Selassie asked him if the Third Reich could supply rifles, machine-guns, anti-tank guns, and aircraft. He also wanted poison gas.

Unverfehrt kicked the request up to Berlin. Nazi diplomats talked it over. It wasn't the first time Ethiopia had approached Germany for help. There had already been a few failed contacts, the earliest when an expatriate businessman went hunting for a military adviser.

*

Berlin wasn't the ideal location for a fifty-eight-year-old Ethiopian-German. Haile Selassie's emissary David Hall kept his head down and tried to pass for a swarthy Mediterranean type among the local stormtroopers. Official attitudes towards Nazi Germany's 20,000 strong black community ranged from violent persecution to contemptuous oversight.

Hall was a businessman with an alcoholic German father and aristocratic Ethiopian mother, born in Jaffa but doing business in Addis Abba. His company represented foreign firms and made good money from the Saint George Brewery. Two of his sisters ran a hotel in Harar popular with any journalists who managed a get pass for the southern front.

'Their Ethiopian blood gave them perfect easy manners,' said *Times* journalist George Steer, 'their German the quality of deliberate cleanness.'

Hall advised the Ethiopian Foreign Ministry in his spare time and did occasional back channel work on his business trips abroad. In early 1934 he was heading through the rattling trams and brown uniforms of Nazi Berlin to a meeting with a Major von Frauenholz. Haile Selassie wanted the major to become an adviser in Ethiopia and work alongside Major-General Virgin and the Belgians.

The recently retired Von Frauenholz liked the idea but was bureaucratic enough to check with the *Auswärtiges Amt* (German Foreign Office) for permission first. He got a negative reply. The diplomats saw too many problems in that kind of foreign entanglement. Von Frauenholz accepted the decision but asked for permission to take a strictly civilian role in the Ethiopian government. The *Auswärtiges Amt* agreed. Hall promised to ask Addis Ababa but something went wrong and the major never left Berlin.

The failure of the Von Frauenholz scheme didn't deter Haile Selassie. In late October 1934 he approached Unverfehrt's predecessor, Freiherr von Schoen, to discuss an agreement that would allow Ethiopia to buy German airplanes and weapons. This time the *Auswärtiges Amt* was intrigued but stodgier diplomats argued that western powers would not appreciate German involvement in Africa. Von Schoen stalled until Unverfehrt arrived, then dropped the situation in his lap.

On 24 December 1934 Unverfehrt visited Little Gibbi to give Hitler's handwritten reply to the emperor. Whatever the führer wrote is lost to history but it inspired Haile Selassie to request weapons and gas. Unverfehrt returned to the consulate and contacted Berlin for advice. The answer came back. He was to be polite, calm, and refuse any military help. Germany did not want to antagonise Mussolini.

Not everyone in Berlin agreed with staying neutral. The Third Reich was Social Darwinism in action, a crab barrel of overlapping interests and competition. On 7 January 1935 Haile Selassie had a visit from Major Hans Steffen, who combined his job as Ethiopian Consul General in Berlin with undercover work for Hermann Göring's *Reichsluftfahrtministerium* (Ministry of Aviation) and Alfred Rosenberg's *Außenpolitische Amt der NSDAP* (Foreign Policy Office of the Nazi Party).

Steffen had first visited Ethiopia back in 1928 as representative of his Berlin-based armament firm Steffen & Heyman, a two-man affair that exported weapons to Africa and the Middle East. He impressed Addis Ababa enough to be appointed Consul General for Germany and spent his time bouncing between the two countries.

During the January meeting he offered Haile Selassie eighty airplanes, anti-aircraft weapons, and a team of German technicians. He had official backing. Air force chief Göring, an overstuffed war hero with a morphine problem, had visions of setting up a Nazi air force for the Ethiopians. The Luftwaffe had been outlawed since the end of the war and Göring was looking for a place far from western eyes to get some experience for his pilots.

There was a problem. The emperor already had a German flyer at his side, and Göring's friends in Berlin didn't trust him. He and the *Reichsmarschall* had history together; but very different politics.

*

Ludwig Weber was a rat-faced pilot with slicked-back hair and gold teeth who had taught Hermann Göring to fly. Born in 1895 the son of a Freiburg tailor, Weber trained as an engineer before war interrupted his life. He was a talented flying instructor who knew what it was like to shoot down the enemy (two kills) and be shot down himself. Göring learned enough from Weber to knock twenty-two aircraft out of the air and take over Manfred von Richthofen's squadron when the Red Baron was killed.

The two men had lost touch by the end of the war. Göring joined the Nazi party while his former instructor showed an entrepreneurial streak and formed a company with his brother to build cars and motorcycles. Weber loved speed enough to become a professional motorcycle racer in days off from the workshop. But the company failed and in 1928 Weber joined the Junkers airplane manufacturers as a pilot.

He ended up in Ethiopia because the Junkers plane bought by Haile Selassie in 1930 had crashed a year later. The company sent Weber out to repair it. It was a long job but the quiet German impressed Haile Selassie, who asked him to stay on. Weber agreed.

The career change may have been triggered by a taste for adventure, but some people in Berlin thought the pilot was worried by the rise of Adolf Hitler. Weber was closemouthed enough that not even family knew his politics but rumours circulated he had belonged to the *Kommunistische Partei Deutschlands* (German Communist Party – KPD). If true, his homeland had become a dangerous place.

In Addis Ababa, Weber talked up plans to build a thirty-plane Ethiopian air force using German engineers. Pierre Corriger objected but was sidelined by Haile Selassie, who wanted to buy some independence from the French. Weber's plans reached important ears in Berlin and inspired Göring to piggyback on his old instructor and send in Steffen. Göring even tried to bring Weber on board, although it was never clear how much the former KPD man was willing to collaborate.

It all went wrong for a mess of reasons: rumours ranged from Italian protests, to Hitler slapping down his rogue subordinate, to the legalisation of the Luftwaffe on 26 February 1935, which allowed pilot training out in the open. Another factor may have been Weber's claim he could build the Ethiopian air force for two-thirds the cost estimated by Berlin. When the *Reichsluftfahrtministerium* officially quit on the idea in May 1935, it claimed only that Weber 'lacked sufficient professional knowledge' to create an air force.

The collapse of the plan didn't stop Steffen pitching a new offer to Addis Ababa before he left at the end of the March: 'young, strong persons in the mould of good sergeants' who would settle in Ethiopia and train young locals into *Hitlerjugend* (Hitler Youth) style organisations. The *Auswärtiges Amt* approved the incredible scheme but the *Reichsministerium für Volksaufklärung und Propaganda* (Ministry of Propaganda) shut down the plan, worried about the political fallout of transplanting Nazi paramilitary organisations into Ethiopia.

Weber stayed on in Addis Ababa as pilot and engineer. Despite his dreams of building an air fleet he would only construct one plane (the *Ethiopia I*) from a kit ordered in Europe. When the war began Weber made a single flight with Haile Selassie and spent the rest of his time flying messages to outlying commanders. In March 1936 he made a last trip to Debre Marqos, bringing back three rebel leaders who had plotted against the emperor. Aggressive locals surrounded Weber's plane as the chained men climbed on board. The situation threatened to turn into a riot. The German took off without waiting for the armed guards to board and spent most of the flight looking nervously over his shoulder at the prisoners. The three men sat silent through the flight. They were hanged from the tree opposite St. George's cathedral.

*

Haile Selassie refused to give up on the Nazis. In July 1935 businessman David Hall turned up at another Berlin to flat to talk with Kurt Prüfer, former German representative in Addis Ababa. Hall wanted a credit note of three million reichmarks to buy weapons and equipment. This time Hitler agreed. Weapons had their serial numbers filed off, and were shipped to Ethiopia.

Hall succeeded where others had failed by emphasising that Haile Selassie and Hitler had a common enemy in Italy. National Socialism and Fascism were not seen as synonymous. Britain, France, and the Soviet Union saw Fascism as a buffer against Hitler's National Socialist state and Mussolini was happy enough to play along by blocking the Dollfuß coup. Equally, Hitler could see the benefits of turning Ethiopia into a quagmire that would weaken Italy's efforts to protect Austria. A long war would also distract the eyes of the world from the Rhineland, which the Nazis had plans to reoccupy.

Money was loaned, weapons sent, and German cinemagoers enjoyed a propaganda film called *Abessinien von Heute – Blickpunkt der Welt* (Abyssinia Today – Focal Point of the World), made by Swiss photographer and fascist sympathiser Martin Rikli. The film praised Haile Selassie as a model of modernity and mocked Mussolini. Censors banned it in Austria, Hungary, and Italy.

Haile Selassie's African-American supporters would have been horrified if they knew about his relations with the Nazis. But they shouldn't have been surprised. Ethiopia' ideological lines were a tangled mess. At the same time Addis Ababa was reaching out to Berlin, Fascism's arch enemies in the Soviet Union were giving discreet support to the invasion. Although a member of the League of Nations, the USSR continued to supply Mussolini's nation with food (91 per cent of Italy's oats), coal, and oil. Marxist-Leninists had no problem opposing a patriarchal emperor, boosting an ally against Nazi Germany, and disrupting Japanese empire-building. When news got out, the National Association for the Advancement of Colored People (NAACP) angrily cabled Soviet Foreign Minister Maxim Litvinov.

'Does your anti-imperialism stop at black nations?'

They got no reply.

'Russia is showing increasingly a tendency to dump the Negro overboard whenever Russia's interest in the Negro conflicts with Russia's interests,' said a disgruntled NAACP official.

Communists round the world continued to pump out propaganda against the invasion but avoided anything more practical. The Italian Communist Party, in Paris exile, limited itself to imploring anyone thinking of joining the invasion to think again.

'Keep away from Africa!' said one leaflet. 'Don't shoot your brothers, the Ethiopian people. Embrace the Ethiopians as your brothers. Turn your guns against the Fascist leaders, assassins and robbers.'

No one listened. Back in Berlin, Hall got another credit note for 1.2million reichmarks of weapons. Foreign Minister Konstantin Freiherr von Neurath, a smooth sixty-three-year-old salt and pepper type saved from being handsome by extra weight around the jowls, disagreed with Hitler's policy and did his best to stop the order being filled. The *Waffenamt* (German Weapons Office) dodged the minister's opposition by not bothering to notify him when it shipped 6,000 rifles, 600 machine guns, and twelve 3.7cm Pak 35/36 anti-tank weapons that looked like sawn-off castle turrets on wheels.

German support ended abruptly on 22 September 1935 when Ulrich von Hassell, the aristocratic German ambassador in Rome, informed Hitler that Italy would lose if it invaded

Ethiopia. The führer now began to worry that a defeat would lead to the collapse of the Fascist regime and rise of a communist government. By November 1935, a policy of neutrality had been officially adopted. Weapon sales to both Ethiopia and Italy were banned, and German propaganda began supporting the invasion. Berlin ignored Major Steffen when he suggested a mutual assistance pact with Ethiopia.

No efforts were made to stop materials already ordered or recall instructors who had gone with them. The Austrian Captain Rudolf Brunner arrived in Addis Ababa on 5 November with some machine guns. A last shipment of German wheeled anti-tank guns arrived at the start of 1936 accompanied by a young German called Lieutenant Herman Masser, who had served in the Reichswehr. He joined the Swedes near Addis Ababa to train the Imperial Guard on the guns.

Nazi Germany's official policy quickly slipped from neutrality to openly cheerleading the invasion. Mussolini showed his gratitude by withdrawing Italian troops from the border with Austria. On 6 January 1936 Mussolini told Von Hassell he had no objection to Austria coming under Germany's control. The ambassador would later joke that Haile Selassie deserved a statue in Berlin for his role in bringing Italy and Germany closer together.

Unaware they had been sold out, the Austrians remained enthusiastic about Mussolini's adventures in Africa. An editorial appeared in the government-owned *Wiener Zeitung* newspaper among the business announcements and obituaries.

'Mussolini is a leader who is not a hypocrite,' it said, 'but openly acknowledges Italy's hunger for territories and sources of wealth.'

Haile Selassie still hoped for more Nazi support. In January 1936 David Hall again approached Prüfer, this time looking for training planes and unfilled hand grenades. The deal never happened. The reoccupation of the Rhineland on 7 March 1936 showed why Prüfer had been playing for time.

Haile Selassie's last hope for international support had gone under. The emperor would have to save Ethiopia by himself. If the country united behind him, he might still have a chance.

21

TRADITION, HONOUR, PATRIARCHY

Haile Selassie at Maychew, 31 March 1936

When the Galla bandits switched sides during the fighting, Konovalov knew it was all over. Haile Selassie's courtiers had been bribing them for a week before the battle, handing over black satin cloaks and fifteen dollars a man. There were honeyed words of trust and respect from both sides. Then the Galla went back to hills with their gifts and their unreadable faces and took up positions. The plain spread out beneath them, with the Italians up at Lake Ashangi and Ethiopians in the mountains near Maychew.

Konovalov knew the Galla couldn't be trusted but Haile Selassie refused to listen. He needed all the manpower he could get. The armies of Ras Kassa and Seyoum had been dribbling into the camp at Korem for the last week. Everywhere was campfires, horses, tents, and movement. Other chiefs were marching their men across the country to join the emperor's forces. Everyone knew it was the last chance to stop the Italians.

The Russian had stayed on when the other foreigners hitched a ride to Dessie with the British Red Cross ambulance unit. Haile Selassie asked him for a military map of the terrain. Konovalov and three Ethiopian graduates of France's St-Cyr military academy lay flat on a bed of pebbles in the mountains and sketched the Fascist positions below.

'The entrenchments of their first lines were visible and something else behind them among the bushes,' said Konovalov. 'It looked as though their observation posts and artillery were on the high mountain of Amba Bohora. To the north-east, behind the first line of mountains and before the descending plain, mingled with the Ayeby Desert, we could see movement.'

A stream of vehicles and mules plugged into the rear of the camp. Men buzzed around neat lines of tents. Artillery was dug in and sighted.

'It was obvious the enemy was planning some manoeuvre and they were aware of our presence not far from their camp. I thought they could easily see the emperor's camp from the air.'

Konovalov went back to the emperor and found him sitting in an easy chair in the royal cave. There was wine and apples and calmness. Haile Selassie seemed more interested in discussing lost battles in Tembien, casting subtle blame on his commanders. His thoughts eventually focused on the present and he ordered the Russian to write up a plan of attack. Outside the cave, Ethiopian warriors hid themselves under the lush greenery of the mountain when Italian planes droned overhead.

Konovalov wrote out a plan for an immediate attack. Haile Selassie countered: his chiefs would not attack without more men; reinforcements and a 75mm artillery piece were on the way; perhaps they should wait. Konovalov nodded, knowing that argument was not an option.

On 23 March, Fascist airplanes bombed an Ethiopian open-air Mass. Haile Selassie stepped outside the cave to watch airplanes scream past, tipping metal canisters onto the mountainside.

'Ils sont très braves, ces pilots,' he said.

The next day the emperor went to meet with the local Galla, known to be sympathetic to the Italians. He spread money and charisma around, then headed uphill to study the Italian camp through binoculars. Cactus juice glistened in the sun like broken glass. Across the plain white men were building defences and bunkers. The Fascists knew a battle was coming. They couldn't understand why it hadn't already happened. Neither could Konovalov, shading the emperor with a sun umbrella.

Haile Selassie decided to attack on 28 March, then delayed when his chiefs pleaded for more time to organise their armies. The next day a military council had to be cancelled when overexcited soldiers fired into the air when the emperor appeared and would not stop. Haile Selassie went back to his cave.

The last reinforcements arrived. The chiefs finally agreed a plan The army would march together towards the front line then split into three sections: Ras Seyoum's 4,000 men would cross the Maychew river and head for the heart of the enemy lines; Ras Kassa's 12,000 men would attack the south-western defences; Ras Getachew Abate's 10,000 including the Imperial Guard, would attack the Italians in the east. A fourth group would launch a diversionary attack on Amba Bohora mountain. Konovalov got command of a small artillery section.

The attack would begin on Tuesday 31 March. It was St George's Day, the patron saint of Ethiopia. Konovalov chain-smoked Italian cigarettes and wondered if he should have left with Parlesák and the rest.

*

The Czech explorer was being bounced around the passenger seat of a Red Cross lorry on its way to Dessie. A man called Smith was at the wheel, a fortysomething British adventurer who spoke a fistful of foreign languages and had recently returned from South America's Chaco War. He and Parlesák had both travelled in southern China. They talked about the region's square churches, the food, the culture. Smith drove with one hand on the wheel and the other on a bottle of whisky.

The driver caught Parlesák up with the latest news about foreigners in Ethiopia. Carl von Rosen and John Robinson had passed this way a few weeks ago after their airplanes got destroyed during a 17 March raid on Korem. The Swede tried to save his plane by uncovering its Red Cross markings. The Italians didn't care. A bomb hit the petrol tank and blew up the plane; Robinson's airplane was already molten metal.

Von Rosen was in Korem to pick up a Dutch doctor called Van Schelven. Ethiopian soldiers had recently found the medic lying half dead on a stretcher in a guerrilla camp. He had been one of two doctors and fifty Ethiopian guards in an ambulance convoy sent up north by the Dutch Red Cross. It drove straight into an ambush in the Raya Azebo region, where Christian locals had sided with the Italians.

One doctor got away and made back it to Korem. Van Schelven was shot in the chest. The Dutchman lay on the ground watching blood bubble up through the bullet hole while rebels slit the throats of his guards. He managed to crawl into the bushes when the rebels started castrating the corpses. They dragged him out. Van Schelven thought he was dead but the Azebo liked doctors and took him to a filthy hospital with their own wounded. Ethiopian soldiers found him when they overran the camp.

Von Rosen's plane was a charred wreck so he commandeered a car and drove Van Schelven to Dessie. The doctor groaned every time the wheels went over a pothole. John Robinson took the same route a little later. The Brown Condor had spent the war running taxi missions to Dessie and Korem, dodging Italian fighters and mustard gas. He tried some recruiting on the side, writing to pilot friends back home in November 1935 with the offer of jobs in Ethiopia. The Challengers were enthusiastic but couldn't get passports.

The Royal Ethiopian Air Force had grown steadily through the war, reaching twenty-four planes by early 1936. Local pilots included Asfaw Ali, Tesfa Mikaël, and Bahru Kaba, who had studied in France. Expatriates joined them, like the Martin brothers, sons of the Ethiopian ambassador in London. Robinson could have hired De Wet, Du Berrier, or Schmidt but refused because of their barfly reputations. Hugh de Wet had made things worse by drunkenly gatecrashing an airplane sale to complain about the price. Even in the desperate spring of 1936, Robinson preferred to reach out to contacts in Britain for more pilots than consider the trio in Addis Ababa.

Britain was fertile territory, obsessed with the Ethiopian war. Rival propagandists slugged it out in the public arena. Pro-Ethiopian pamphlets like *Abyssinia: The Essential Facts in the Dispute and an Answer to the Question 'Ought We to Support Sanctions?'* from *The New Statesman* went toe-to-toe with Italy's *The Last Stronghold of Slavery: What Abyssinia Is*. The Italians circulated newsreels so full of bombing and death that opponents showed them at anti-war rallies. Haile Selassie supporters demanded armed intervention but memories of slaughter in the First World War were too fresh for the British government, a coalition affair dominated by the Conservative Party. It refused to do anything more than enforce League of Nations sanctions.

Robinson's advert for Fokker pilots appeared in April's edition of British magazine *Flight*. It was all too late by then. Anyone writing in got no reply. The Italians controlled the skies, the Ethiopian air force was on its knees, and the Brown Condor was making his own escape plans.

Back on the road to Dessie, Smith took another swig of whiskey and asked if Parlesák would go back to the frontline. The Czech shook his head. The war was over for him.

*

The Battle of Maychew began at 05:45 on 31 March 1936. Ethiopian troops crouched in their positions watching the enemy as the sun came up. Some mumbled prayers, some fondled rifle bolts. On the other side of the lines, Italian confidence was high. Futurist art leader Filippo Tommaso Marinetti believed a superior breed of Italian had been born in Ethiopia.

'War brings out the heroism of man,' said Marinetti, 'along with discipline, initiative, intelligence, and the spirit of comradeship. In civilian life I knew people who were insignificant and insipid.

Later, when I met those same people at the front, I discovered these people had literally become like Nietzsche's superhuman. They were cleansed by war, which had helped them to overcome their moral weakness, anxieties and those things psychologists call complexes.' These Italian supermen relished fighting.

'To be brutally frank,' said Marinetti, 'I can tell you that there is nothing better than to fight for Italy in Abyssinia.'

The sun was glowing through the hills when Konovalov's line of cannons opened fire and Ethiopians charged across the plain. Ras Getachew's men hacked their way through the eastern end of the Italian lines until the attack clogged up around a fortified position in a burned-out chief's compound on top of a hill. Getachew had been moving too fast to bring heavy machine guns and his men ran at the compound walls with swords and rifles. The Italian defenders dropped grenades on them from above.

Ras Seyoum's men punched into the centre of the Italian lines and pushed the enemy back across the Maychew River. Ras Kassa's men advanced more slowly against thick ranks of enemy but broke through the first defensive positions. The diversion group seized Amba Bohora but did not dig any defensive positions. Italian reinforcements pushed them back down the mountain.

A second Ethiopian wave flowed across the plain and crashed on the Italian positions. Fascist bombers were already in the air, raining death from above. Fighter planes skimmed the ground and machine-gunned scrums of Ethiopians running for cover. Haile Selassie sent a third wave against the crumbling Italian centre. It got close enough for the Imperial Guard to use their bayonets. But the line held when the commander of an overrun unit called down artillery fire on his own position.

The Galla, in their brown cloth kilts, had spent the battle watching from their hillside positions. They chose their side and came running out of the hillsides. They attacked Haile Selassie's troops. Konovalov saw them as he stalked up and down his cannon line directing fire and knew this was the end.

A final assault all along the front faltered as it grew dark. By the evening most Ethiopians had retreated back towards Korem. They had been fighting for thirteen hours. The emperor had been with them in the front line. Konovalov found him with the reserves lying exhausted in a quiet ravine, tired but grinning.

'I am happy we managed to attack the Italians,' Haile Selassie said. 'It was essential to our honour, but I never had any hope that we could vanquish them by one blow and reoccupy Debarre, Amba-Alage, and so on.'

It rained that night and men gave up on sleep to tell each other war stories. The next morning the emperor ordered a fresh attack. Konovalov clambered up through the mountain ravines to his artillery positions in the dawn light.

'En route, I thought about our situation, feeling that our attack had not risen to expectations. We had not ousted the Italians, and our soldiers had occupied only one portion of their lines. Could we have done more?'

The sun crept over the battlefield and Konovalov could see the Ethiopians had abandoned any positions won the day before. It began to rain more heavily. He watched Italian reinforcements moving into their lines. The Russian came down the mountain to report and found Haile Selassie in conference with his unhappy-looking rases. Konovalov suggested retreating and reassembling for a later attack. The rases agreed and offered other excuses. They refused to fight any more. It was a polite, respectful mutiny. The emperor's face sagged a little and some of the light went out in his eyes. At dinner that evening Haile Selassie looked so depressed that Konovalov handed over his medallion of St George.

'Your Majesty, all this will pass,' he said. 'You will see that everything will be as it was. Almighty God will not permit this unfairness. Here is the image of Saint George, which saved my life during the time of the First World War. Allow me to give it to Your Majesty, with my blessing.'

Haile Selassie kissed it and put it in his pocket.

The next day the Ethiopians walked away from the battlefield, the emperor's army calving like an iceberg as it went. Men went back to their villages and warlords to distant provinces. The emperor took a detour to pray at the square, cross-shaped rock churches of Lalibela, carved out of the hillside. A mob of soldiers looted his possessions when he was gone.

'Clearly, this was the swan song of the old, traditional, patriarchal Ethiopia,' thought Konovalov. 'In its life and organisation, Ethiopia lacked two essential things – study and training. The gap was too wide between it and European progress in intellect and culture. Ethiopia could not bridge this gap at once, nor could it hold out in a collision with a highly industrialised European power despite patriotic ardour and heroic resistance.'

Haile Selassie rejoined what was left of his army and trudged towards the capital. The northern front had collapsed. The only resistance left in Ethiopia lay in the south where all that stood between Addis Ababa and Italian Somaliland were demoralised troops, a few unnerved warlords, disloyal Muslim locals, and a trench network built by a bad-tempered Turk from the days of the Ottoman Empire. It would be a miracle if the south lasted long enough for the emperor to make it back to his palace.

PART IV

BETWEEN THE FIRING SQUAD AND THE THRONE

22

THE TURKISH DEFENCE

General Mehmet Vehip Pasha on the Southern Front, April 1936

It used to be Constantinople, a city built by fourth-century Roman engineers on a blade of land stabbing into the Bosporus. Towering stone walls faced inland and water protected the rest. The Hagia Sophia cathedral in the city centre celebrated Rome's embrace of Christianity. An iron chain across the straits kept out enemy fleets.

The city survived the fall of Rome's western heartlands and lived on as capital of the new Byzantine Empire, an aftertaste of Roman life spiced with the east. Its cobblestone streets saw centuries of religious schisms, marauding crusaders, and hooligans rioting every time their favourite charioteer lost at the Hippodrome.

In the fifteenth century Sultan Mehmed II's troops came over the walls and ended Byzantium. The Ottoman Caliphate settled in its place and converted the Hagia Sophia into a mosque.

All things fall and 500 years later Mustafa Kemal Atatürk carved modern Turkey from the Ottoman corpse after the First World War. The capital moved to Ankara and the old Byzantine metropolis was renamed and left to rot. By May 1936 Istanbul was a backwater of headscarfed women haggling in the souks, fifteenth century cannon balls rusty in the long grass, and men outside cafés reading newspaper stories about the war in Ethiopia.

Mussolini expected support from Turkey thanks to a 1928 treaty and his warmly expressed admiration for Atatürk. Instead, Ankara cosied up to the League of Nations. The Turks took the sting out of the betrayal by opposing military sanctions, but enforced all the others.

Istanbul's café readers skipped the Italo-Turkish diplomacy and ate up reports about the adventures of a native son in Ethiopia. Many in the old capital remained nostalgic for the days of the Caliphate. They were fascinated by a short, fat, fifty-eight-year-old general who made his reputation back when the Ottomans ruled territory that stretched from Mecca to the Black Sea.

His name was Mehmet Vehip Pasha. The government in Ankara didn't approve of his presence on Ethiopia's southern front, claiming the general was 'an implacable enemy of Atatürk' with no connection to Turkey. Vehip agreed.

*

The southern front was dusty scrubland and blue sky, home to some of the country's toughest warlords. At the start of the year, Haile Selassie had sent them pushing forward to invade Italian Somaliland and drive Mussolini's men into the sea.

The advance collapsed when Graziani went on the offensive. Dejaz Beiene Merid was badly wounded and his troops fled. Ras Nasibu sent panicky radio messages to the emperor which the Italians intercepted and exploited. Ras Desta's forces were bombed to a halt near the River Juba and retreated with 3,000 casualties. Desta's reputation died with his defeat. Addis Ababa had to drop leaflets by airplane begging troops to obey their ras. The Belgian Lieutenant Frère, advising Desta, barely escaped with his life. He had a row with the ras in the aftermath and was soon back in Addis Ababa on his own, having either quit or been expelled.

The front had stabilised by the end of the spring. Vehip Pasha seemed confident. The Turk had built what he claimed was an unbreakable defensive line across the south of Ethiopia. Observers weren't so sure.

Vehip's road to the southern front started in early June 1935 when an Ethiopian delegation visited his home in Port Said, Egypt. The former Ottoman general had been born in Yanya (present-day Ioannina in Greece), a humid and rainy city then part of the Caliphate. His father was Yanya's mayor. Vehip preferred a military career to politics: fighting the Italians across Libya in 1911; desperate clashes with Greeks around the forts of Bizani in the Balkan wars; defending Gallipoli during the First World War, where he lost an important command because he refused to serve under a German; and fighting Russians on the Eastern Front.

Vehip returned to Constantinople in defeat after the First World War. An attempt to enter politics led to arrest and jail time for misuse of office. It was a murky case with the prosecution driven by Atatürk, a former subordinate at Gallipoli, who blamed Vehip for talking too much about the mass murder of Armenians during the war. The general escaped to Italy and joined anti-Atatürk opposition groups around Enver Pasha, another Ottoman loyalist. Enver's men took help from anyone who could help, including Britain and Bolshevik Russia. Moscow enlisted Enver to put down a Muslim rebellion in Central Asia, but religion won over politics and he switched sides to be killed in an August 1922 cavalry charge.

Enver's death knocked the fight out of the rebels and Vehip Pasha quit politics to drift around Europe. He picked up a Romanian passport when Ankara voided his Turkish citizenship. By the mid-1930s the general was in Egypt helping reorganise King Farouk's army.

The Ethiopian cause was big news in Cairo. The Italians tried to push their angle with well-funded propaganda, including books like *Al-Habasha aw Ithyubya, fi munqalab minta'rikhiaha* (Ethiopia at a Turning Point in Her History) by Egypt-based Lebanese writer Bulus Mas'ad. It painted Ethiopia as a savage anti-Islamic country that needed civilising. Haile Selassie's supporters counter-blasted with lawyer Muhammad Lutfi Guma's *Bayna al-asad al-Ifriqi wal-nimr al-Itali* (Between the African Lion and the Italian Tiger). The author was a promoter of Easternism, an ideology popular among a slice of Egyptian intellectuals that promoted solidarity among all eastern civilisations and opposed western imperialism. Egypt's newspapers took the Ethiopian side, running flattering pieces about Haile Selassie in the run up to the war.

'May God help you blacken with shame the faces of the descendants of Nero,' said Cairo's *Ahar Sa'a*, 'and whiten the faces of the people of Ethiopia.'

'The builder of modern Ethiopia,' said *The Egyptian Gazette*, 'a successful reformer, a genius, a phenomenon, a leader and a brain far greater than any other Ethiopian of the time.'

Nabil Ismail Daud, a member of the royal family, started a recruitment campaign for a volunteer military unit. He offered six Egyptian pounds a month, with more for elite troops. It was big news until reporters discovered only a few volunteers had come forward and Daud had no money to pay them. The king shut down the project. Daud would eventually get to Addis Ababa with six followers for a short fact-finding trip.

Someone at the Ethiopian embassy in Port Said was intrigued by the idea of help from Egypt. In the summer of 1935 diplomats approached Vehip Pasha with an offer to join the emperor's team of foreign advisers. He accepted. The Turkish government quickly disassociated itself from the general, spreading rumours Vehip made his money from opium and cocaine, and emphasising it had no control over him.

'Vehip Pasha is a man who left Turkey at the start of the National Struggle and entered into a thousand adventures,' said a magazine close to the government. 'His actions serve only to further the ambitions of other countries, and many years ago he lost his Turkish citizenship.'

The general didn't care what Ankara thought. He reached Ethiopia in the summer of 1935 and found a country rusted to a halt by tradition and hierarchy. Then altitude sickness hit him hard. He spent his first few months in bed at an Addis Ababa villa drafting a report for Haile Selassie, full of generic advice (make peace with Italy or prepare for an attack on all fronts) and mild criticism of the modernisation programme brought in by foreign advisers. Privately, he was contemptuous of the Belgian effort.

'For some reason, they didn't have a battalion despite working for two years,' Vehip said. 'Not even a company.'

The report was politely received, and ignored. The general considered returning to Egypt but changed his mind and invited some anti-Atatürk friends to join him. One letter went out to Çerkes Ethem, a guerrilla leader based in Jordan who had lost his Turkish citizenship for criticising the new regime. Vehip asked him to bring his expertise in warfare to Ethiopia. Ethem liked the idea but was too sick to travel.

The general wrote more letters. Fifty-three-year-old Kâzım Karabekir, a retired military hero writing his memoirs in Ankara after falling out with Atatürk badly enough to do some jail time, announced he and three friends would head for Ethiopia. The Turkish government stopped them leaving the country.

Only two of the rebel Turks contacted by Vehip made it to the battlefield, both arriving after the invasion began. Their murky nationalities and loyalty to a forgotten empire helped them fly under the League of Nations radar; their Muslim faith eased their way past xenophobic locals. The Ethiopian empire had many Islamic citizens. Some didn't like taking orders from Christians.

*

The walled city of Harar in the south was the fourth holiest city in Islam. Evelyn Waugh visited in the weeks before the invasion and found merchants selling bullets by the handful out of sacks in the main square, but little enthusiasm for fighting Italy. The sheikhs in Harar decided Waugh was a secret agent and gave him a message for London: they wanted the Ethiopian Muslim south annexed into British territory. Their people were sick of persecution and over-taxation by the Christians. The sheikhs ignored Waugh's denial of any government connections and told sly stories about how Haile Selassie had ordered them to pray for victory in the mosques, but hadn't specified whose victory. Waugh wrote for the *Evening Standard*:

[The empire] was taken by conquest a generation ago. The Emperor Menelik succeeded to a small hill kingdom and made himself master of a vast population differing absolutely from himself and his own people in race, religion and history. It was taken bloodily and is held, so far as it is held at all, by force of arms.

Fascism held a fascination for Muslim intellectuals whose loyalty compass spun under the magnetism of artificial states, ancient kingdoms, ethnic groups, and the call of Islam. Books and broadcasts aimed at the Islamic world painted Mussolini as a liberator for Muslims, and Haile Selassie as a barbarous Christian who oppressed followers of the Koran. 'The usurper, the tyrant, the oppressor of Islam,' said *Al-Waqit* newspaper of Aleppo.

Lebanese Emir Shakib Arslan, who had watched the Ottoman Empire fall and thought Italian help could build a new caliphate, broadcast radio propaganda supporting the invasion. Arabic newspaper *Jama Islamiah* came down hard on the Italian side, publicising Fascist claims about independence for Muslim parts of Ethiopia. Not everyone believed the propaganda.

'Ethiopia is an ancient Christian nation and therefore should be helped by other Christian nations,' said Emir Abdullah Ibn Husayn of Transjordan, a British protectorate. 'The Ethiopians have a special place in the hearts of all Muslims and Arabs, as they protected Islam its early days and deserve the sympathy of us all in the present struggle'.

Pro-Ethiopian feelings were also found in Arab newspapers like *Filastin* of Jaffa, *Al-Tariq* of Baghdad, and *Al-Qabas* of Damascus.

'I am ready now in 1935 to sacrifice my life for Ethiopia,' wrote exiled Syrian nationalist leader Dr Abd al-Rahman Shahbandar, 'the same as I was ready to do so in 1925 for Syria.'

Muslims who supported Haile Selassie pointed out that the Ethiopians were linked to the Habesha, an ancient Christian people who helped the Prophet Muhammad and earned themselves exemption from Jihad.

'Leave the Abyssinians alone, while they leave you alone,' was a hadith attributed to the Prophet.

On the other side, many in the Italian Catholic hierarchy saw the invasion as a Christian crusade. Cardinal Ildefonso Schuster of Milan talked about bearing the cross in triumph over the Ethiopian plains. Monsignor Cole, Bishop of Nocera in Umbria, called the invasion 'just and holy'. The Bishop of San Minito declared himself ready to melt down church plate to fund the war.

The only person in the hierarchy who didn't support the invasion was the man at the top. Pope Pius XI had been involved in some behind-the-scenes diplomacy with France and Britain before the invasion to arrange a peace deal. The talks were slow and Mussolini sent in the tanks before anything could be accomplished. Once the fighting began the Pontiff kept quiet, afraid a failure in Africa would lead to the anti-clerical left taking power. Only those closest to him knew his true feelings.

'Going and taking something out of someone else's safe,' he said. 'A war which is only a war of conquest would be clearly an unjust war ...'

*

Vehip Pasha's two colleagues arrived shortly after the Italian invasion began. Farouk Bey was an angular fiftysomething with a moustache, receding chin, and a talent for administration. He had been an intelligence officer in Palestine during the war, then the Turkish military attaché in Athens. He quit after arguing with Atatürk. Farouk Bey kept his thoughts to himself, beat Ethiopians who stepped out of line with a swagger stick, and buried himself in paperwork and logistics.

Fellow officer Muhammed Tãrik Bey el-Ifriki was a more colourful character. Italian spies first noticed him in November 1935 marching a 100-strong group of men through Djibouti. He had taught them to cheer Haile Selassie and Vehip Pasha, and curse imperialism. Tãrik Bey liked to tell journalists his group were a foreign legion of Ethiopian, Sudanese, and Arab specialists ('all of them know what to do, how to handle machine-guns, wireless, telephones, mines') but the spies said the men were Ethiopian expatriates heading back to fight.

Tãrik Bey was born in Nigeria ('he has characteristic negroid physiognomy,' said the spies, 'with transverse scars on his cheeks') and ended up an Ottoman army officer after a series of adventures that began with being sold by his parents. After the disintegration of the Caliphate he had switched his allegiance to anti-colonial causes in Africa.

His homeland, under British rule, was enthusiastically pro-Ethiopia. Namdi Azikiwe's *West African Pilot* newspaper kept readers up-to-date on the war. The more radical Nigerian Youth Movement linked aid for Ethiopia with demands for independence from Britain. In the nearby Gold Coast black intellectuals designated the first week of November 1935 as Ethiopia Week and held rallies, meetings, and collections.

Down in white-run South Africa the *South African Opinion*, popular among African readers, was strongly anti-Italian. Black dock workers went on strike in Cape Town and Durban rather than unload ships flying the Italian flag. By the summer of 1935 at least twenty black-run organisations opposing Mussolini had sprung up. 'Hands off Abyssinia!' they chanted on marches.

South Africa's white veteran politician, Jan Smuts, a long, sun-beaten face under a goatee and thinning white hair, had opposed Mussolini's invasion from the start. He cared little for Haile Selassie but thought a defeat would stir up trouble between white and black elsewhere in Africa. Smuts was alarmed when 6,000 African men applied to the Ministry of Native Affairs to fight in Ethiopia. Amakolwa tribal chief Walter Kumalo threatened to raise a bigger tribal army.

'Kumalo said he could raise a picked regiment of Zulus who would face anything,' reported a journalist. 'He is uncertain, however, how to make the offer, and thinks he had better write to the Negus [emperor].'

Smuts' racism and Haile Selassie's reluctance to take foreigners killed off the South African volunteer idea. Tãrik Bey was the only foreigner born in Sub-Saharan Africa known to have volunteered for Ethiopia.

He had trained in Turkish and German war colleges, spoke a spread of different languages, and saw action at Gallipoli and the

Sinai and the Caucasus during the war. When the shooting stopped Tãrik Bey moved to Syria and acted as bodyguard for head of state Ahmad Nami. The emir of Transjordan poached him, but British officials made life difficult so Tãrik Bey returned to Syria, where he studied engineering and cartography. He was overseeing public works projects round Damascus when Vehip Pasha's letter arrived.

Farouk Bey and Tãrik Bey joined Vehip on the southern front. Their leader was advising Ras Nasibu and constructing defences in the low mountains south of Dagghabur. The Ottomans clashed with the Belgian duo Debois and Witmeur, two serious men who wore shorts, complained about the heat, and regarded themselves as the dejaz's official advisers. 'There were lawyers, there were shopkeepers, there were comedians,' said Farouk Bey.

Relations got worse when Nasibu appointed Vehip as his chief-of-staff two days before the Italians invaded. Vehip Pasha formed a General Staff but refused to let the Belgians join, unhappy they earned more money than him. Debois and Witmeur left for Addis Ababa, mocking Vehip Pasha's fortifications as they left. 'The defences thought up by the Turkish general are in the realm of high fantasy.'

Vehip preferred to claim they ran away when Italian bombs fell on Jijiga. He carried on with the construction of twelve miles of trenches across the southern plain. 'An African Verdun,' he said proudly.

The positions had no parapets, no water supplies, no fire steps or radio communication, no barbed wire or gun emplacements. Vehip liked to pose on the trench top looking masterfully at the scrubland to the south.

'Out there will be the grave of Italian Fascism,' he said. 'When the Italian native troops hear of ME they will desert.'

In the late spring of 1936 observers were less confident a middle-aged Ottoman could hold off Italy. Badoglio was swinging down from the north like a hammer. Graziani was the anvil in the south. Dessie was under siege from local guerrillas, no one knew what had happened to Haile Selassie, and foreigners were fleeing the capital like rats.

23

A LITTLE SCRAP

The Fall of Dessie and Collapse of the Southern Front, 12–14 April 1936

Arnold Wienholt had written down the Amharic phrases he needed to deal with Ethiopians.

'This is an order.'

'Pay attention.'

'Speak the truth.'

'Bring clean water.'

He needn't have bothered. No one listened to him. Dessie was a chaotic mess of soldiers, civilians, Red Cross teams, journalists, and locals doubling prices in the market. Bandit attacks made it impossible to reach the frontline and risky getting back to the capital. Nothing in town worked and no one had any idea what was happening.

Wienholt knew he could get Dessie running like clockwork if only people would listen to him. Put up defensive positions. Send out scouts. Adopt guerrilla warfare. The raw-boned fifty-eight-year-old Australian with cropped hair and dark goatee had been a war hero, farmer, big game hunter, senator, and booster for the British Empire. He was used to being obeyed. Nobody listened.

The man who saw himself as one of nature's leaders wasn't much good at communicating. A withdrawn man with few friends and a family who never felt they really knew him, Wienholt believed in a hierarchy that made social niceties unnecessary. Everyone from King Edward VIII down to a Maasai cattle herder knew their role and duties. Some people gave orders and other people took them. It was simple. The Ethiopians should understand that.

Wienholt had arrived in Djibouti at the end of November 1935 posing as a journalist for Brisbane's *Courier Mail*. Australia had a big appetite for stories about the war. Most people sympathised with Haile Selassie. There were public meetings in town halls, pamphlets, and donations to the Red Cross. It helped that the eucalyptus trees around Addis Ababa and the horses of the Imperial Guard were both imported from Australia.

A small but significant slice of Catholics took the other side. Journalist and radio broadcaster Denys Jackson called Ethiopians 'slave riding barbarians'. Archbishop of Brisbane James Duhig told the audience at a Convent School event that Mussolini's actions reflected the settlement of their own country.

'Australia was as black as Abyssinia is now.'

The Italian immigrant population supported the invasion. Businessman Filippo Maria Bianchi was behind the pro-Mussolini *Il Giornale Italiano* newspaper. He volunteered to serve in Ethiopia but never left Melbourne, preferring to win hearts and minds with Australia's first Italian cookbook. Bianchi convinced himself that recipes for 'Curried Spaghetti' would bring readers to Mussolini's side.

The Australian government favoured Haile Selassie but registered the intensity of Catholic and far-right feeling. The Minister for External Affairs lost his job trying to walk a tightrope between the two sides by talking up Ethiopia but opposing sanctions. His replacement refused to make the same mistake and endorsed the League of Nations.

Arnold Wienholt's own pro-Ethiopia enthusiasm came from his conservatism. He despised the League as international meddlers but understood the anger felt by Britain's African subjects at the invasion. Fighting for Haile Selassie would strengthen the empire's white rule, keep Mediterranean types in their place, and provide action for an old soldier who still felt tough as leather. Wienholt left behind a wife and daughter and headed for Djibouti.

After the usual waiting and bribery he got the train to Addis Ababa and was in the Hotel de France by Christmas Eve. He had bought with him an Australian-style saddle and dreams of heroic cavalry charges but was disappointed to discover the Ethiopians had no interest in foreign volunteers. He joined the Ethiopian Red Cross as a transport officer to get closer to the front line.

Wienholt reached Dessie in mid-March with twelve mules, a crowd of helpers, and orders to contact Schuppler's ambulance crew. Bandits and guerrillas were swarming further north and all roads to the frontline were cut off. The Australian stabled his mules and went to talk to Haile Selassie's son Asfa Wossen, now in charge of the town. Wienholt had lots of ideas about military tactics and the importance of buying up cattle behind the lines. The crown prince gave him a strained smile and ignored everything he said. Wienholt blamed the prince's Belgian adviser, Louis Norman, a friend of Reul who had fought the Germans in central Africa back in the last war.

The only friend Wienholt had in town was Diogenes Dalendzas, a Greek who had been living in Addis Ababa when he joined the Ethiopian Red Cross. Dalendzas' homeland endorsed the League's sanctions to get back at Italy for occupying the Dodecanese islands before the First World War. A man from Athens called Verssos Verghis claimed to have recruited thousands for a volunteer legion to help Haile Selassie. If true, nothing came of it. Other Greek military men living in exile after the failed coup of March 1935 volunteered directly to Addis Ababa. The Ethiopians had no funds or interest in taking them, especially when they discovered the coup had been a republican effort against the monarchy.

A few weeks later Wienholt and Dalendzas saw exhausted Ethiopian soldiers start pouring into Dessie, fleeing defeat in the north. The British Red Cross unit rolled into town on 9 April with Parlesák, Schuppler, and the other foreigners. Wienholt cornered

Schuppler to ask if he could get through to the front. The Austrian told him the frontlines no longer existed.

Hickey joined the conversation with news the Ethiopians would be pulling back to the capital soon. He warned Wienholt not to expect the locals to tell him when they left. The Australian started sleeping in his clothes with a rifle by the bed.

*

The whole town was on the move three days later. Trucks, cars, civilians, hobbling soldiers wearing captured and blood-stained Italian regimental scarves. The Belgian Norman, red-faced and stressed, paced around town advising all Europeans to evacuate south. Wienholt observed:

> There were thousands upon thousands of mules, pack horses and donkeys. Big chiefs riding their fast pacing mules with scores of running riflemen around and behind them, smaller chiefs with smaller bodyguards; here and there numbers of high-class women riding on mules and accompanied by various personal escorts; many other women on foot, often more or less loaded ... young boys of not more than twelve or fourteen years, often carrying modern rifles and covered with bandoliers ... The whole force [seemed to be] following some Ethiopian Pied Piper.

The evacuation order had come from the crown prince. His father had lost the battle at Maychew, an enemy column was marching closer, and reports had come in of locals planning to kidnap him for an Italian ransom. He quit Dessie and headed for the capital. Norman directed the evacuation but the Belgian's nerves were fraying. Guerrillas had fired at his house during the night.

Journalist George Steer arrived at Dessie in the middle of the retreat and found his lorry fighting its way upstream through a river of fleeing Ethiopians. The South African-born Steer had dark hair, mournful eyes, and a passing resemblance to Charlie Chaplin. In the back of the lorry was a cargo of gas masks homemade from gauze bandages and soda by Lady Barton, wife of the British Minister at Addis Ababa. The newsman expected to get a few stories out of his enthusiastic welcome. Instead, he found himself ignored as the town flowed around him in a desperate race to escape the Italians. Steer was driving through the centre of Dessie when Captain Norman finally snapped and ran up to the lorry. 'Take me away this evening!' he said. 'Save my life!'

Norman loaded his kit and a supply of tinned food into the back of the lorry. Worried about the suspension, an unsympathetic Steer threw most of it back in the dirt and clambered onto the cab roof with a Mauser rifle. They joined the evacuation south to Addis Ababa. Dutch Red Cross ambulances rolled down the road ahead of them. Steer could hear missionaries in another lorry singing hymns while guerrillas snapped off shots at them from the hills.

Up ahead, Parlesák, Breyer, and the rest were with the British Red Cross convoy snaking along the narrow hillside roads. One lorry tipped over the road edge, its Somali driver barely leaping out in time; another had to be abandoned when the engine died. Parlesák nearly had his skull blown off when an Ethiopian soldier sitting behind him twitched his trigger finger as they bumped along the Imperial Highway towards the capital.

Things got worse when Azebo tribesmen tried an ambush from higher ground. Sniper bullets starred the convoy's windscreens and Dr Melly ordered everyone to take defensive positions. The driver Smith drained his bottle of whisky and climbed up the hillside to where tribesmen stood watching. There was a discussion in bastard Amharic, then he punched two of the guerrillas in the face and came back.

'Let's go. They're more afraid of us than we are of them.'

He uncorked another bottle of whisky. Later he gave Parlesák the real story: Smith had told the Azebo he had a magic weapon that would kill all of them. They believed him after he knocked two of their leaders unconscious.

The Azebo had regrouped by the time the rest of the exodus passed. Wienholt had to fight his way through. He tried to stay in Dessie when the evacuation began, hoping to drive north and link up with Haile Selassie, but by the afternoon the town was empty and guerrillas were creeping in like hyenas.

Wienholt left Dessie on horseback with the town burning behind him. Bandits were already looting. He joined the retreat and tried to organise a rearguard to protect the slowest convoy members, mostly women and children. He couldn't find anyone who would listen to him. He and Dalendzas took the fight to the guerrillas, firing back with their rifles when shots came down from the hillsides. During one attack Dalendzas took over a light machine gun and sprayed the attackers' position, the bullets sparking over the hillside. The Greek got a wound in the leg during the fighting. Wienholt barely noticed, happy to be sniping the tops off bandit skulls.

'The little scrap seemed to buck one up wonderfully,' said the Australian, 'one had at last found something real to take part in.'

The convoy moved on, the rain started to fall, and lorries pushed through the mud past roadsides littered with abandoned cars. Then eucalyptus trees and clear sunlight and the outskirts of Addis Ababa. Wienholt reached the capital on 28 April. The news there was bad. The southern front had fallen. The Ottoman Verdun had only lasted four days.

*

One of the few outsiders who had seen Vehip's trench system up close was American *Time* journalist Laurence Stallings, a sleepy-eyed and one-legged war veteran with a taste for pacifism. He didn't like Fascism but couldn't find much love in his heart for Africans either.

'A poetic genius of immense verbal power,' wrote George Steer, 'with the dislike of the Confederate States for coloured men.'

His prejudice extended to Turks. Stallings met Vehip early in the war and was unimpressed by the overweight mercenary in a tall woolskin hat and uniform of the Imperial Guard. The general was calling himself 'The Hero of Gallipoli'; Stallings preferred 'Old Eagle Beak'.

'Glad to see you here in Harar,' said Vehip Pasha. 'If you visit me later at advance headquarters, bring plenty of medicine for yourself. You will have fever.'

They visited the defences further south, Vehip pointing out the thorn bushes and low-slung hills of the south. The general seemed happier talking about the battles at Gallipoli, claiming that lack of water, not bullets, had defeated the British ('Yes, with 250,000 men the English could conquer Ethiopia slowly but absolutely') and would also defeat the Italians.

'Why do you ask me such things as details of Ethiopian defence? Water will defeat the Italians for me. I have to do nothing.'

Stallings, who knew the Italians were digging wells, went back to Addis Ababa convinced Vehip's defences would not stand against a serious attack. In April 1936 he was proved right. Italian forces led by Colonel Frusci and General Agostini moved forward. Planes smashed Jijiga to rubble, almost hitting a Finnish Red Cross unit and sending an Egyptian Red Crescent unit running for cover. The Egyptians had already lost their Dr Sawy to dysentery, then seen his body go up in flames when the plane taking it home, flown by British Red Cross pilot Charles Hayter, clipped a eucalyptus tree on takeoff.

On 14 April the Ethiopians launched a desperate counter-attack. Hand-to-hand combat pushed the Italians back but the Fascists had already started to encircle the Ethiopian advance. Dejaz Abebe and Dejaz Makonnen saw the trap closing and pulled out, abandoning their barely used German anti-tank guns. Within a week the Italians were rolling up the southern front.

Haile Selassie's men retreated to Sasabench where the Ottomans had built their defensive line. Despite Vehip Pasha's boasting, the defences fell to the Italians in four days. There was little resistance. The Ethiopian leaders had already fled, accompanied by the Ottomans, and the troops they left behind surrendered when artillery mashed up the trenches. On 30 April Graziani's troops drove through flat plains of white mimosa into Dagghabur, capital of Ogaden.

Up in the capital, talk alternated between resistance and catatonic depression. Most of Haile Selassie's foreigners were making plans to leave the country. Some had already gone. John Robinson had taken the train to Djibouti when his contract finished. And Hugh de Wet had been kicked out of Ethiopia after an incident with a girl, a Belgian, and a lot of alcohol.

24

SABOTEURS AND SPIES

Expulsion and Collaboration among the Foreigners, Spring 1936

She was dark-eyed and Greek and had an elegant way of perching on a barstool. Hugh de Wet drank whiskey and admired her legs. The big-nosed Belgian at her side chatted in French, ordered more drinks, and lit her cigarette. Eventually he headed to the toilets. Du Wet strolled over and took his place.

It wasn't a smart move to steal a Belgian mercenary's girl. Hilaire du Berrier would have known that but these days the American kept his distance when De Wet was working on an all-day drunk. The pair had finally given up on their mercenary air squadron and taken to part-time journalism work, swapping ideas and sharing leads on stories. De Wet was good company when sober. But alcohol changed the 'pukka English gentleman', as Du Berrier saw him, into a more aggressive character. Not long ago Du Berrier had tried to drag his friend out of an Addis Ababa bar. De Wet pulled a revolver. The American kept his distance after that.

So there was no one around that evening in March 1936 to tell De Wet he shouldn't antagonise Bob Viseur over a Greek girl. Fifty drinkers were lined up at the long bar, drinking and talking over the noise of the gramophone. Viseur was chatting up the girl. When he left for the toilet, De Wet took his seat and turned on the English charm, telling her she deserved more respect than the Belgian had been giving her. Viseur returned and told De Wet to leave.

'Who are you?' drawled De Wet.

The Belgian slapped De Wet's face.

'That is who I am,' he said.

De Wet clicked his heels.

'You will hear from me Monsieur le Capitaine.'

They arranged to fight a duel. News spread around town. Du Berrier shuttled between the pair trying to get an apology from his friend and forgiveness from Viseur. But the heat and alcohol and stress of the Italians rolling closer each day had got to everyone. Both men wanted pistols at twenty paces.

The day before the duel exasperated Ethiopian courtiers stepped in. They hadn't forgiven the drunken Englishman for the trouble he caused over an airplane sale six months earlier.

*

Back in October 1935 a thirty-seven-year-old Parisian called René Drouillet arrived in a brand new Beechcraft B17L aeroplane. Drouillet had a toothy grin and a naval background that he quit to join the air force. He flew observation missions over Morocco during the Rif rebellion. There were a few crashes, some insubordination and AWOL. Drouillet and the Aéronautique Militaire went their separate ways.

In 1928 he turned air mercenary and flew a plane to Afghanistan to help the emir battle anti-western rebels. Drouillet landed on a rough air strip, praised the emir, and discovered he had landed among the rebels. He spent ten uncomfortable days as a hostage before the French embassy sprung him.

Drouillet got a taste of the quiet life as a postal pilot and a training instructor. In 1935 adventure came knocking again when Greek General Nikolaos Plastiras, exiled in Cannes, organised a coup to stop the restoration of the monarchy in his homeland. Drouillet was hired to fly him to Greece. At the last minute the general decided a train would be safer. The coup plotters failed to overthrow the government and Drouillet never got paid.

In the autumn of 1935 the Frenchman was testing the new Beechcraft Model 17, a sleek stagger-winged biplane (the lower wing farther forward than the upper) aimed at the luxury end of the market. Its American manufacturers hoped Drouillet could kick-start sales in Europe. The Frenchman had just read about Haile Selassie impulsively buying a Percival Gull monoplane flown in by British pilot Charles French, originally chartered by the *Daily Telegraph* to transport film out to Djibouti. Drouillet suggested flying a Beechcraft to Ethiopia and selling it to the government. The manufacturers liked the idea and Drouillet touched down at Addis Ababa in late October. The emperor liked the plane and had no problem with the price tag: $12,000.

Hugh De Wet was outraged when he heard about the deal. He told drinking buddies that no plane was worth that much and went off to stop the sale. Du Berrier tried to intervene but the Englishman shook him off and headed for the four sheds and overgrown grass runways that made up the airstrip at Akaki, all of it overlooked by a freshly built model prison. De Wet was drunk, as usual, and an incoherent argument led to nothing except embarrassment. Guards escorted him away. Haile Selassie bought the Beechcraft and asked Drouillet to stick around Addis Ababa. He had a job for him.

The Ethiopians allowed De Wet to stay in Addis Ababa in case they needed more pilots but the duel drained away the last of their patience. Armed guards loaded him on the next train to Djibouti. Du Berrier waved goodbye at the station. De Wet arrived penniless in London and went to stay with his sisters. His father shook his head. Another of his son's plans had ended in failure.

*

The Ethiopians never trusted the foreigners hanging around Addis Ababa. They expelled some when the war began and kept a careful eye on the rest, watching for spies and saboteurs. Paranoia ramped up as the Italians drove deeper into the country. On 20 February 1936 newspapers ran stories that a plot to murder the emperor had been discovered. Someone had tampered with the controls of his private plane and put sand in the engine.

'Only a skilled hand could have damaged the imperial plane in a manner so certain to lead to disaster and yet difficult to discover,' said *The Montreal Gazette*.

The obvious candidate was a foreigner working in the air force. The Royal Court had been suspicious of pilots after Hubert Julian went rogue back in America. The Italian consulate in Paris paid his trip home, seeing propaganda advantage in the Black Eagle's disillusionment with Ethiopia. Figures from £250 to $60,000 were talked about in the African-American press. The money also funded a lecture tour across America but Julian got so bitter and audiences so rowdy that the Italians officially distanced themselves from him.

Someone sabotaging the plane sounded convincing but Haile Selassie had only flown a few flights in the early days of the war. He preferred his transport to have four wheels. The assassination plot, if it ever existed, was misinformed and misdirected.

There were more accusations of espionage the following month. Vincent Schmidt got into a row with Babichev about being shut out of the air force; the argument turned bitter and Babichev accused him of spying for the Italians. Schmidt had to leave Ethiopia. The American wasn't a spy but didn't want to end up like Count Maurice de Roquefeuil du Bousquet, a Frenchman who had arrived in the 1920s to work a mica concession a few miles out of Jijiga. He brought a wife, some slaves, and a few lion cubs. As war crept closer locals noticed a gang of Somalis visiting the house at strange hours. Soldiers grabbed one leaving the house and found undeveloped film of lorries and transport routes. In early September 1935 they arrested the count. No one wanted to talk about happened to him.

Other spies were smart enough not to get caught. A thin-faced Soviet pressman with shifty-eyes and a monocle, Lieutenant-Colonel Boris Zeitlin had been an infantry officer in the Latvian army and a circus ringmaster when times got tough. 'A wild rider, sniper, flier, and juggler', he was in Ethiopia directing the documentary *Abyssinia*. Zeitlin did double-duty as a Soviet spy; his information may have passed through Moscow to the Italians. He had a third, even more squalid side. In 1937 the Soviets sent him to the gulag for abusing underage girls.

Another reporter used his larger-than-life persona to deflect suspicion. Harun al-Rashid Bey aka Wilhelm Hintersatz had a shaved head, a duelling scar, and a fondness for tall astrakhan hats. He earned the iron cross as a German colonel assisting the Ottoman Empire during the war and converted to Islam. He served in a Freikorps unit during the post-war left-wing uprisings in Germany and had some contact with Enver Pasha in the Caucasus. No one suspected Al-Rashid Bey was passing information back to Italy under cover of reporting for a Turkish newspaper. The authorities were distracted by his wife (young, blonde, attentive), smart car, and chauffeur called Fritz.

Addis Ababa managed to catch one enemy agent. Adolf Parlesák heard about a Syrian called Nasr employed in a transport division of the army. Soldiers claimed to have discovered a secret radio he used to communicate with the Italians.

Among all the paranoia and double-crossing, one plot aimed at Haile Selassie seems to have actually existed. The Italians had an agent lined up to kidnap the emperor and fly him into enemy territory. It was the same man Hugh de Wet suspected of trying to overcharge the Ethiopians for a Beechcraft Model 17.

*

When the pipe split and started spraying oil over the cockpit windows, René Drouillet was flying over Italy on his way to Addis Ababa as unofficial head of the Royal Ethiopian Air Force.

Paris had recalled Paul Corriger back on 15 November. The Frenchman resigned as air force chief and left for Djibouti at the end of the month. Mechanics Thierry Maignal and Yvan Demeaux, both seconded by Paris, remained loyal to the Ethiopian cause and quit the Armée de l'Air to stay on. Maignal eventually left Addis

Ababa on 20 January but Demeaux, a trim Frenchman with a few patches of hair still clinging to his head, remained in Addis Ababa with his wife and young daughter.

Drouillet was already in country when Corriger left. He flew the emperor on a brief inspection tour of the southern front and was competent enough to be offered a position as new head of the air force. Drouillet liked the idea but the French ambassador complained. Haile Selassie made Drouillet his Conseiller de l'Air (Air Adviser) instead, the same job with a different title. Misha Babichev became the air force's official face.

The Frenchman's first move was to increase the size of the air force. He headed off to America to buy more planes, hoping to dodge League of Nations sanctions. The Ethiopians were sharp enough to insist Drouillet use the cash from the Beechcraft sale, and promised to reimburse him. By 22 February Drouillet was back in France at an airfield near Le Havre. A new Beechcraft B17R airplane lay in pieces across a hanger while a greasy local mechanic tried to fit it together. Drouillet had done a deal with his old friends at the aircraft company and picked up the plane for exactly $12,000, a figure that made some courtiers in Addis Ababa suspicious.

They would never get a chance to question him. A few days later Drouillet landed the plane at Villacoublay airbase and was arrested. Officially charged with flying an unlicensed foreign aircraft, newsmen thought the American government had leant on Paris, unhappy Drouillet had breached an agreement not to export the plane to Ethiopia. The Beechcraft B17R was impounded.

On 25 April the pilot got permission to check the plane's engine. While French officials were examining the outside of the airplane, Drouillet started the engine, rolled down the runway, and took off for Ethiopia.

He was heading into a desperate situation. The frontlines had fallen and the Italians were closing in on Addis Ababa. *The Chicago Defender* was reduced to running photographs of a tired looking John Robinson over fantasy stories that he was leading a squadron of bombers to stop the enemy by blowing up mountains in the north.

'Military experts gasped at the audacity of the plan,' said the *Defender*, 'many calling it as strategic and feasible a maneuver as was the trick Hannibal of Carthage played on the ancient Romans by lining the hills with oxen, carrying lighted torches.'

By the time the story ran, Robinson had left Ethiopia. His contract was almost finished; he was exhausted, having put in 728 hours of flying; and Ethiopia was collapsing. The Brown Condor steamed out of Addis Ababa on the *Chemin de fer franco-éthiopien* at the end of April, accompanying John Meade, military attaché of the US embassy. Robinson departed so quickly he left a house full of expensive gifts accumulated from the courtiers and aristocrats of Haile Selassie's court.

Drouillet continued flying into the eye of the storm until engine trouble forced him down at Centocelli, Rome, on 28 April. Fascist soldiers forced him off the plane. The director of the Ethiopian air force had fallen into the hands of the Fascists.

Drouillet's lawyer Jean-Charles Legrand arrived, persuaded the Italians not to shoot his client, and somehow wrangled a personal interview between Drouillet and Mussolini. Both men kept quiet about the talk but a confidential Italian memo noted that Drouillet had offered to kidnap Haile Selassie and fly him to Asmara, capital of Italian Eritrea. The pilot expected to be paid for it. Il Duce agreed.

On 9 May 1936 Drouillet was allowed back in his Beechcraft. He returned to Villacoublay where he was arrested and bailed, eventually getting a lecture from the judge and a 300 franc fine.

No one knows whether Drouillet was serious in his kidnap plan. He made no attempt to fly to Africa and the whole episode may just have been some fast talking to get out of jail. Or he might have realised the kidnapping was pointless. By the time the Italians let him go Haile Selassie had fled his empire and the Fascist boot was on the Ethiopian neck.

25

SWEDISH DIE-HARDS

Viking Tamm Tries to Save Addis Ababa, Late April 1936

Captain Viking Tamm knew things were getting desperate when the Ethiopians started taking prisoners. He and his men had ground to a halt in Debre Berhan, a dust cloud of churches and markets built where the old trade routes came together north-east of the capital. Tamm was on his way to stop the Italians. Everyone else in Ethiopia was going the other way.

Remnants of Haile Selassie's armies were flowing through the town, hungry and leaderless and desperate. They shook their rifles at Tamm when he tried to stop them and kept moving south towards Addis Ababa. Journalists leaned out the windows of passing lorries to shout that the northern front had collapsed.

Tamm wanted to push on and fight the Italians but his drivers, a gang of Indians hired in the capital, refused to move. They had got his men to Debre Berhan but abandoned their lorries when they saw the chaos and retreating armies. The Swede appealed to their patriotism. The Indians showed him their British passports. He pulled out his wallet and started negotiating.

He broke off talks when Lij Legesse Gabremariam drove by with a group of loyalists, some guns, and five Italian prisoners. Tamm hailed him down, surprised to see the white men. In battle, Ethiopians rarely took prisoners, hacking apart anyone who tried to surrender. Adolf Parlesák claimed they did not understand that a dropped rifle and raised hands meant an enemy wanted to give up. Other observers weren't so understanding. Only twelve Italians prisoners would survive the war, compared to several thousand Ethiopians held by Mussolini's men. No one remembered any captured Africans fighting for Italy being kept alive.

Now, with the enemy closing in, Haile Selassie's men needed all the bargaining power they could get. Gabremariam was taking the Italians to Addis Ababa as hostages. Tamm asked if the lij could spare any drivers. Gabremariam shook his head impatiently. Tamm asked if he could spare his canons. Gabremariam and his men drove off without answering.

Tamm's Indian drivers finally agreed to drive on after some tough bargaining that filled their wallets. The convoy headed up to Ad Termaber, a pass 75 miles south of Dessie where 300 peasants squatted in trenches waiting for the enemy.

Ad Termaber looked defensible on the map. The reality was a twenty-five mile long gash in the earth under the command of a bureaucrat called Tsehafe Taezaz Haile who paced around with a nervous look on his face and shoe leather slit open to relieve his bunions. The only way to communicate with the capital was a telephone back at Debre Berhan. The local village chief had locked himself in his house and refused to come out.

Tsehafe Taezaz Haile briefed Tamm on the situation. Badoglio was seventy-five miles away at Dessie waiting for engineers to ready the Imperial Highway for his 'Colonna de ferrea volonta' (column of the iron will), an armoured snake of tanks and trucks flanked by columns of Eritrean troops. Ad Termaber was the last place the Italian advance could be stopped before it reached the capital.

Tamm and his men began to dig positions. Tsehafe Taezaz Haile disappeared on an inspection tour. After a few hours it became obvious he wasn't coming back. Tamm was now in charge of the last defensive line in the country. Ethiopians elsewhere were taking measures to secure their futures. On 30 April, Ras Seyoum sent a message to the Italians.

'I have done my duty. What are your terms?'

*

Back in Addis Ababa, 800 men of the newly formed Patriotic Organisation were lined up in St George's cathedral swearing an oath never to betray Ethiopia. Another seventy men had been hired by acting mayor Blatta Takele Wolde Hawariat to spread morale-boosting rumours around the city's brothels. More government money paid for an anonymous Canadian to run a guerrilla training camp west of the city.

None of the journalists who had returned to see the fall of Addis Ababa knew anything about the Canadian. He was happy to keep it that way, one of a handful of foreign volunteers who dodged the journalistic radar, like an Assyrian who trained infantry in the west before the war, and Captain Wittlin from Switzerland who commanded an Oerlikon anti-aircraft battery among the yellow rocks of Awash. All three worked hard at keeping a low profile.

No one was even sure if the Assyrian and Wittlin were still in the country. Foreigners, civilian and military, had been packing their bags for weeks. Belgian mercenaries Frère, Viseur, and Norman had already taken the train for Djibouti, where a disillusioned Frère cornered some Italian representatives with stories about Ethiopian war crimes and suspicions Desta had murdered Lieutenant Cambier. Only De Fraipont remained. Embassy staff began sandbagging their doorways. The mosquito whine of panic increased to a roar in late April when Italian planes flew low over Addis Ababa. They dropped leaflets and tricolore flags. Locals were instructed to fly a flag from every house as a sign of surrender.

Rumours spread that the Fascists would be in Addis Ababa within days. Soldiers arriving from northern and southern fronts milled through the streets and built a tent city near the Imperial Palace. De Fraipont tried to organise them but no one wanted to take orders any more. Bandits were seen at the outskirts of the city, sniffing at the collapsing Ethiopian state. The houses of Europeans who had fled to Djibouti were burgled. Foreigners began moving into the embassy compounds.

Lieutenants Bouveng and Thornburn, the remnants of Viking Tamm's Swedish team, remained at the training camp just outside

Addis Ababa with the German Lieutenant Masser. The brigade they had been organising was finally ready: 870 NCOs, 4,100 men, 117 mules, 1,298 pack mules, and officered by cadets. It looked impressive from a distance but close up the men were too old or young, many from tribes who didn't speak Amharic. Orders were given in sign language. The brigade had antique rifles and only got those because Viking Tamm had gone to see government ministers back on 17 April and demanded weapons. They asked his opinion on the war.

'It was with a feeling of great satisfaction,' he said, 'that I told them what I felt.'

The ministers promised guns if Tamm would take the brigade out to Ad Termaber and stop the Italian advance. There was a moment of hesitation, then he agreed. Tamm insisted on getting vehicles, weapons, and money first. It took two days for crates of guns and sixteen trucks to turn up at the camp. No money. Tamm loaded up a battlegroup and drove into Addis Ababa where his cold Swedish fury and the men's machine guns persuaded Makonnen Habte-Wold Ababa to hand over $30,000 from the treasury. Truck suspensions groaned under the 840 kilos of cash.

Tamm's battlegroup left the city on the evening of 22 April and headed north to Debre Berhan. Bouveng and Thornburn had orders to form the remaining brigaders into two more battlegroups and join him.

*

What was heroic in Addis Ababa looked like stupidity in the bleached sunlight of Ad Termaber. Forty-five of Tamm's men deserted in three days. Locals had told them 100 Italian lorries were heading their way. Tamm wasted hours driving back and forth to Debre Berhan, trying to get Addis Ababa on a crackling telephone line. Bouveng and Thornburn still hadn't arrived.

The Swede left Lij Ayde and Kifle Nasibu in charge of the brigade and drove back to the capital. Eighty miles from the pass, Tamm drove past some Ethiopian guards on perimeter patrol. He didn't realise they were part of Bouveng's battlegroup marching to the front; or that Thornburn's group had not even left the training camp. Further on, Tamm encountered Dr Melly's British Red Cross ambulance unit heading north and advised them to turn back.

On 29 April Tamm found a town with a working telegraph and contacted the crown prince in Addis Ababa. He asked for the air force to locate Bouveng and order him to the pass. A pilot took off from the capital's airfield and managed to locate the Swede and his men. He dropped the orders from 5,000 feet and raced back home. Bouveng never got them but, typical of the confusion in Ethiopia's shrinking territory, was already heading for Ad Termaber.

The Italians attacked the pass before he got there. It was all over quickly. The local villagers switched sides and led Fascists up the hillside's twisting mule paths. One brigade officer and fifty men were killed in a sharp firefight before the Ethiopians quit their positions and drove away. On the way back to Addis Ababa they encountered Bouveng and told him it was all over. Everyone headed for the capital, passing through Debra Behan on 30 April. A white flag was flying over the town. The locals gave them hostile looks.

*

'They are prepared to die for you,' said Blatta Takele as he paraded 800 chanting men of the Patriotic Association in front of the emperor.

'They shout like this with your machine guns behind them,' said Haile Selassie. 'But none would fight for us.'

The emperor was a broken man. His country was lost and his warlords weary and defeated. The only resistance came from Blatta

Takele who had strongarmed the emperor into agreeing to move the capital to Gore in the south-west. A few lorryloads of government papers had set off for the last redoubt, accompanied by De Fraipont.

The Australian Wienholt got himself involved and bustled around Addis Ababa advising any Ethiopian he met about the benefits of guerrilla warfare. He was happy and excited, loading his rifle and saddling pack mules, until a government official advised him to take the next train to Djibouti. The emperor had changed his mind. He wasn't moving to Gore. Haile Selassie would sail for Europe and plead his case at the League of Nations.

Blatta Takele paraded his 800 men for the emperor, a plea to remain with the subsonic note of threat. It led to more council meetings, indecisive and pointless. The emperor was determined to leave.

Ministers asked Tamm to defend the city. He refused and immediately withdrew his fellow Swedes from Ethiopian service. He and Bouveng spent the night in the capital with the rain hammering down on the tin roof of their hotel and the sound of rifle fire from somewhere in the distance. The next day Thornburn turned up with the remaining cadets and Lieutenant Masser. Tamm told the soldiers he was no longer their commander. No one blamed him.

'This is the end of Ethiopia,' said one cadet. 'This is thanks to our own chiefs. Go, God bless you. Save yourselves.'

Masser decided to keep on fighting, refusing to believe the situation was as desperate as Tamm claimed. Soon after, the German received orders to take his anti-tank guns to the city limits only to find all the ammunition was on a truck halfway to Gore. He went back to the training ground with the cadets.

Early in the morning of Saturday 2 May a train steamed out of Addis Ababa station carrying the emperor's wife and children, their courtiers, thirty aides and family members, ten tons of personal baggage, dozens of cases of liquor, and one hundred steel boxes containing gold bars and silver Maria Theresa thalers, plus a yapping, tangled furball of lap dogs on leads. In the bustle and panic no one realised the emperor hadn't been seen at the railway station.

Haile Selassie and his bodyguards had ridden secretly out of the city that morning. They joined the train at its first stop in Akaki, ten miles away. The emperor didn't want his people to see him leave, especially when there were rumours Blatta Takele would shoot up the train rather than see it go. Haile Selassie left behind Ras Imru as regent and Bitwoded Wolde Tsaddik as president of the provisional government in Gore. Blatta Takele and other die-hards could not believe their emperor had gone.

'My country,' said a stunned Blatta Takale. 'There is no one left to defend your cause.'

*

Adolf Parlesák was dreaming of fighting on the northern front and woke up to find the rifle fire was real. The Czech was staying in a small Greek hotel in the centre of Addis Ababa. He looked out the window and saw a car overloaded with Ethiopians soldiers peeling down the road, guns firing at nothing. The emperor had left and order was breaking down. Parlesák packed his bags and headed outside to hail a passing taxi. The driver slowed but wouldn't stop.

'The government is gone!' he shouted out the window. 'Today many people will die!'

Parlesák could hear shooting in the distance and see thin trees of smoke building in the air over distant districts of the city. Crowds were drifting around the market places, sullen but expectant, waiting for something. The Czech walked briskly to the station, two locals earning good money carrying his luggage. The railway offices were barricaded and sandbagged. French troops from Somalia formed a fence of rifles and bayonets around the platform. The last train was leaving Addis Ababa.

Among the chaos of foreigners, ministers and aristocrats fighting to get into the carriages were Tamm, Bouveng, and Thornburn, calmly negotiating with the station master for a private train.

A heavy bribe worked. Parlesák attached himself to the Swedes in time to hear about a carriage waiting for them at the next substation. The four men forced their way onto the crammed *Chemin de fer franco-éthiopien*. The Australian Wienholt was already wedged into a corner seat in a dark depression, convinced the emperor had personally destroyed his chance at a heroic last stand in Gore.

The train pulled out of Addis Ababa at 8am. Parlesák and the Swedes disembarked outside the city. The train steamed off for the border, picking up Vehip Pasha and his men at Diredawa on the way. Parlesák and the Swedes discovered their private train had already left. They spent a day in the rain at the substation discussing their options.

Shortly after dusk a locomotive and a single carriage spiked with machine guns pulled up at the platform. It had been commandeered at Addis Ababa station by four Ethiopian pilots. They had spent the day fighting their way across the city trying to find a working airplane but discovered the last one left had been flown out by Babichev when they reached the air field. Parlesák and the Swedes climbed aboard the carriage.

They found Babichev in Awash, looking for petrol to refuel the plane. He told them looting had begun in Addis Ababa. The train rolled on towards the border with French Somaliland, the train driver stopping at every station to phone ahead and check the Italians hadn't overrun the line. At the last stop they picked up a Greek trader and his wife who burst into the carriage full of sweaty panic and tears. They had been held at swordpoint by bandits.

'We wait until the train passes,' said the bandit leader, 'then we kill them.'

Parlesák saw il tricolore flapping over the head of an African soldier in a white uniform, and rows of neat European houses. French Somaliland. Safety. Miles away to the west, Addis Ababa was burning.

26

MARCH OF THE IRON WILL

The End of Ethiopia, 5 May 1936

George Steer's tyres crunched over strips of film lying unspooled in the street. No one would be watching the submarine and adultery flic *Hell Below* at Mon Ciné bar tonight. Looters had wrecked the place and stolen its alcohol, chairs, and the photographs of film stars pinned to the walls.

Addis Ababa was falling apart. The morning after the emperor's train steamed for Djibouti, his twenty-nine-year-old American legal adviser John Spencer looked sleepily out of the window and saw snow lying in thick drifts outside. It took the Harvard man a few seconds to realise the road to the station was clogged with white feathers. Mobs looting abandoned houses had slashed open hundreds of pillows and mattresses.

'The chief of police, whom I knew, came up to me in a frenzy declaring that a revolution had broken out after the departure of the emperor and that even the police were killing each other,' said Spencer. 'As though to emphasise the truth of his remarks, a machine-gun chattered nearby. The British consul, Hope-Gill, came up at that point, pleading with the chief of police to take matters in hand and exert some authority. 'The poor man was too excited even to hear him.'

Rumours raced round town that the emperor had ordered his belongings distributed among the people. Crowds looted the palace and carried off tapestries, carpets, thrones, light bulbs. Someone opened the jails. The armouries were looted. Blatta Takele rode through the streets setting fire to buildings, determined to leave nothing for the Italians.

John Spencer headed for the American legation compound. Other Americans followed him, including Hilaire du Berrier who had stayed to the end working for the tabloid sensationalists at London's Central News Agency. Drunk Ethiopian soldiers staggered along the road outside the legation in stolen top hats. They sold champagne to passersby for a few copper coins a bottle and fired their rifles every time a vehicle passed. The post office was on fire.

George Steer drove through the chaos on a rescue mission. His journalist fiancée Margarita de Herrero y Hassett of Paris' *Le Journal* was half-Spanish and one of the few female reporters around. She had a flat in the centre of town and Steer was on a mission to bring her back to the safety of the British legation compound. The print of *Hell Below* crackled under his tyres. A woman in a bowler hat carrying a knife zig-zagged drunkenly down the other side of the street.

Steer found Margarita hiding in her flat while a servant beat a burglar out the door with the flat of his sword. Pilot Ludwig Weber turned up with three German mechanics, all heading for their own legation, and helped load De Herrero's cases into the car. Everyone piled in and Steer drove off, weaving around the body of an old Armenian lying among the broken glass of his shop window with a rope around his feet and a bullet in the head. Cut telephone wire hung from poles. Someone was firing a machine-gun from the roof of Keverkov's tobacco monopoly. An old Greek woman jumped onto Steer's running board clutching an icon. She had been at Smyrna when it burned in 1922 and was having traumatic flashbacks. She pushed the icon in Steer's face. 'The Virgin in the picture looked at us, in beautiful robes, oval-faced, bland and still.'

Weber and his mechanics jumped out near the swastika flag cracking in the wind over the German legation. Steer carried on to the gates of the British compound and found Sikh soldiers and barbed wire. Inside it looked like a refugee camp. Nearly 1,800 people were sleeping in tents or on verandas. The legation jail cell had been turned into a store room.

Another 2,000 people were in the French legation with more scattered around the smaller embassies. Hindu and Arab shopkeepers stayed in town to save their businesses. They shot anyone who tried to break in, with occasional ceasefires when looters scurried up and tried to sell them handfuls of bullets for cash.

*

Steer was back on the streets later in the day looking for stories. As he drove past the German legation, Weber and the three engineers emerged dragging their belongings in a trunk. They had spent the morning under the swastika flag with a scrum of expatriate Germans, including Lieutenant Herman Masser. Weber couldn't stomach any more National Socialism. He thought he knew the location of a flyable airplane. Steer agreed to drive them.

The looters had solidified into mobs that rumbled through the streets, smashing their way into houses and attacking foreigners. Feodor Konovalov stayed indoors with the doors bolted and watched through the window.

The Russian had arrived back in Addis Ababa after a long retreat from Maychew with the emperor's army. He had been bombed from the sky, tried to help soldiers with faces pulped by shrapnel, fought off bandits who robbed him in a cave ('I gave them a little rough treatment'), and trudged the miles to the capital. The army disintegrated on the way, with soldiers looting villages and stealing from each other. Peasants ambushed them from the fields.

'Where are your soldiers?' Konovalov asked a chief.

'What do you mean by soldiers?' the man said. 'Today there are no more soldiers: they are all brigands, for whom we no longer exist.'

During the retreat, the Russian saw a young boy with a Belgian automatic rifle in one hand and a hippopotamus skin shield in the other. It seemed to sum up the war. Now Konovalov watched from his home as the bodies piled up. He had no legation to help him. If the Ethiopians didn't kill him, the Fascists would.

Weber had no intention of hanging around to discover his fate. He directed the car to a wooden stockade outside the city. Inside was a Junkers W 33c, a single-engine transport plane. Maps and a flight suit had been stolen but everything else worked. One of the German engineers was spinning the propeller when a gang of Imperial Guard soldiers strode up and blocked the runway. Weber appeared in the Junkers doorway wearing his red Luftwaffe cap from the war.

'Open the doors,' he said. 'I am the government.'

The German engineer out front let go of the propeller and pointed his rifle at soldiers. There was a moment of silence and calculation, then the guardsmen dropped to their knees, kissed the ground in front of the airplane wheels, and ran off. Weber got back in the cockpit to work switches and flick dials with his fingernails. The propeller caught and the Junkers rolled down the runway and wobbled off into the Ethiopian sky. It would crash-land in Sudan.

Steer stayed on the ground. He was getting married later that day in the British legation. White flags waved from most of the houses as he drove back into the city.

*

Cornelius Van Hemert Engert had an egg-shaped head, round glasses, and a worried expression. The American legation was under attack and his wife Sara refused to leave the front room. She sat knitting in a corner while bullets slapped into the walls. Two Ethiopian servants had already been shot in a well-organised attempt to rush the gates. Snipers fired at the windows whenever someone turned on a light or twitched a curtain. Du Berrier stood by the flapping curtains and fired back. Engert was on the radio trying to get a message to the British legation. He needed urgent help but every message had to go via Washington.

'Both Legations had their own radios, but these were attuned to communicate with their respective capitals and not with each other,' said Cordell Hull, American Secretary of State. 'Consequently, Engert radioed his message to me. I had it telephoned to the American Embassy in London, which communicated it to the British Foreign Office, which, in turn, radioed it to their Legation in Addis Ababa – all within the space of a few hours.'

Engert wanted the legation's women and children evacuated. Sir Sidney Barton agreed but the British had problems of their own. A mob was attacking the outer walls and putting shots through the windows. Sikh soldiers hosed down anyone who got close with a Lewis gun.

Out back George Steer had just married Margarita de Herrero. Her boots were muddy and Steer drunk. When the mob attacked he staggered off to defend the gates with a rifle and a white carnation in his buttonhole. Steer was so drunk he had to sit in a chair to shoot. In the middle of the firefight a taxi drew up and a group of robbers dodged the bullets to try and sell their loot back to its original owners.

When the attack was beaten off a convoy of Sikh soldiers from the 14th Punjab Regiment drove out to help the Americans. They turned up outside the legation and scared off the snipers by peering at the street over the circular ammunition pans of their Lewis guns. Engert's civilians crept out of the building and clambered into a lorry, then spent the trip paralysed with fear by a war correspondent's pet cheetah that lay curled up in the truck bed.

Du Berrier, Spencer, and some of the men stayed behind. Sara Engert refused to leave her husband. Bullets began smacking into the building soon after the Sikhs drove off.

Looters elsewhere in the city hit the Ethiopian Red Cross building. Dollar bills, bandages, and wads of postage stamps littered the street outside. The only real medical care in Addis Abba was now provided by the British Red Cross under Dr Melly, which had taken over the Empress School, a rare modern building in the centre of the city. When the shooting began four doctors went out in shifts to collect the wounded and bring them back to a blood-spattered upstairs classroom where Schuppler and Dr Empey operated fast, throwing amputated hands and feet out of the window.

Schuppler carried out forty-five operations on Saturday 2 May, more the next day, and sixty-five on Monday. Colonel Llewelyn sat in the school's entrance pointing his rifle at anyone who passed the main gates too slowly. Frank De Halpert, a sixtysomething in a homburg and raincoat with a rifle on his shoulder ('tall, handsome, and grey-haired in his IRA get up,' remembered an observer), could barely keep his vicious temper on a leash whenever a looter waved a gun in his direction. The molten fury of his rage seemed to deter them from trying anything.

The anger did not protect his boss. Dr Melly got shot when a drunk leaned into the car, pushed a revolver into his chest, and pulled the trigger. De Halpert went to shoot looters in revenge but the dying Melly stopped him. 'They don't know what they're doing,' he said. 'Don't cause more bloodshed than there is.'

Melly was not the only dead medic. The Stadins, who had provided medical care alongside Schuppler in Dessie back during the bombing raid last year, had turned up in Addis Ababa to get more supplies. The amiable Mrs Stadin was killed by a stray bullet that came through the wall while she was sleeping.

*

By Tuesday 5 May the American legation could not hold out any longer. Engert made another radio call. A fresh convoy of Sikh soldiers fought their way through the streets to evacuate Du Berrier and the rest. Engert bribed some Ethiopian staff with 100 Maria Theresa thalers each to stay behind and look after the legation.

'I had just thirty minutes to decide what to take with me from my home which I might never see again,' said Sara Engert, 'and in the excitement I made some pretty odd decisions. I took, for instance, the needles with which I was knitting a skirt for my little girl. But I left my grandmother's silver spoons on the dining room table.'

The siege of the embassy was the last surge of violence. By late afternoon Addis Ababa grew quiet. The sound of revving engines could be heard in the distance, then vehicles appeared on the horizon. Konovalov watched as Marshal Badoglio's *Colonna de ferrea volonta* got closer.

'The column advanced slowly. Many military motorcycles equipped with light machine-guns began to occupy bridges, crossroads, and other points of the town. The young, sunburned Italian soldiers cramming the lorries entered the town singing, uplifted by the conquest of this old African Empire. The Fascist war machine, which had organised this capture, had promised them a happy future in the vast and rich Ethiopian lands.'

Over 25,000 Italian soldiers in 2,000 tanks and lorries, flanked by Eritreans with flowers in their rifles, oozed into town, an oil slick of black shirts. Addis Abba was silent. The British legation emptied out and people stood on the street to watch the column pass. A few clapped politely until Fascists hissed the Union flag fluttering over the compound.

'There was nothing spectacular about it – no shouting, no excitement, no cheering crowds, not the slightest ceremony,' said Herbert Matthews, a *New York Times* man riding with the Italians. 'Yet it was one of the great moments of modern history, and it lacked no genuine element of drama and color. The setting was an imperial capital in ruins – buildings still burning, the stinking dead still lying about the streets, gutted houses and stores gaping blackly and emptily at us as we drove by.'

Some Ethiopians raised their arms in the Fascist salute.

*

Around forty foreigners directly helped the Ethiopian war effort: Reul's eleven Belgians, Tamm's four Swedes (one of the original team left when the fighting began), at least five French (all pilots or engineers), five Germans (three of them engineers in the air force), Vehip's three Ottomans, two Czechoslovaks, a Syrian and an Assyrian, and individuals from America, Armenia, Austria, Canada, Russia, the Swiss soldier Wittlin, Hubert Julian of Trinidad, and a Romanian member of the air force ground crew.

That number can be boosted to over a hundred by adding foreigners who joined the Ethiopian Red Cross, from doctors Schuppler and Achmet to unqualified adventurers like Burgoyne or Wienholt; and those, like Eric Virgin, Pierre Corriger, or the Belgian military missions of Dothée and Polet, who helped train the Ethiopians before the war.

Three of the core forty volunteers were black (Julian, Robinson, Tãrik Bey el-Ifriki), with perhaps four from the Middle East or Turkey (Vehip Pasha, Farouk Bey, Nasr the Syrian, an Assyrian): a total of around 16 per cent. The rest of Haile Selassie's mercenaries were white. Many of those were on the far right.

Reul's eleven men were fascists, Brunner from Austria was a Nazi, Del Valle a fascist sympathiser, and Konovalov would later show support for far-right causes. That's 28 per cent of Haile Selassie's foreign volunteers who supported fascist or Nazi ideas, a higher figure if you include failed volunteers like Du Berrier and De Wet, add in ex-Reichswehr man Herman Masser who likely had his mission approved by Berlin, and allow Hubert Julian to be genuine in his support for Italy once he left the battlefield. Most others were conservatives. Tamm and his Swedes were anti-communist while Vehip Pasha remained loyal to a Caliphate that had no time for democracy.

Only Weber, and possibly the three German mechanics he hired, were on the left (forming a maximum of 8 per cent), and even those political views are more rumour than fact. African-American pilot John Robinson was no friend of Fascism and racism but his actual politics are unknown.

It was a strange foreign legion to support a black emperor against a Fascist invasion: majority white and leaning heavily to the right. Perhaps some of the far-righters having backgrounds in *Action française* organisations had made them sympathetic to a monarchy under attack (although the leadership of *Action française* in Paris didn't think that way); perhaps the fascists saw both Haile Selassie and Mussolini as dictators with an interest in empire-building. An argument could be made that the emperor outranked King Victor Emmanuel III, Italy's nominal head of state. But most likely, adventure and money trumped any political ideology.

Ethiopia's motives in accepting them are harder to parse. Men like Brunner might have seemed safe hires because of Nazi Germany's opposition to Mussolini. But Reul's team had an admiration for Italian Fascism that made them a significant security risk. Perhaps the easiest explanation is that the contemptuously xenophobic Ethiopians had no interest in the opinions of foreigners. Ferengi were ferengi, to be used or ignored as necessary.

The Ethiopian Red Cross mirrored the mercenaries' political spread with far-right (Schuppler), conservative (Burgoyne and Wienholt), and apolitical (Hickey) types found driving ambulances and stitching up patients. Regardless of beliefs, Red Cross units from all countries took serious casualties. At least three doctors died, along with a significant number of attendants and transport officers. No mercenaries were killed in the conflict, although Cambier of the official Belgian mission apparently died of natural causes and De Fraipont was injured in the Dessie bombing.

There were may have been more volunteers. Somalis, other Africans, and Arabs from the Middle East criss-crossed the border for trade and travel before the war, while many Indians and Greeks ran businesses in Ethiopia, and a few African-American expats worked farms. Some may have taken part in the war, even if no one bothered to write about them. Foreigners who avoided the press and kept quiet in the aftermath could still be unknown today. The Italians were rumoured to have executed a fellow countryman from Fiume who had been helping the Ethiopians, although this may have been a garbled version of the Sergio Costante story, a soldier who deserted the Italian ranks two week before the war and worked as a car mechanic in Addis Ababa. The Red Cross believed he was killed by Ethiopians while trying to reach Djibouti in May 1936.

If deserters are accepted as foreign volunteers, then several thousand Eritreans and others quit the Italian ranks during the war, with at least fifty loyal enough to serve Ethiopia's provisional government at Gore after the fall of Addis Ababa and another 1,600 fighting on as late as the summer of 1936 with Ras Desta's guerrillas. Fearing Italian retribution, they did their best to hide from history.

*

The more paranoid of Mussolini's military men spent the war afraid a global anti-Fascist army would materialise in Ethiopia. Italian spies chased down reports of international brigades organised by Masonic lodges in Beziers or leftists recruiting a mercenary army in Paris. None of it was true. The complexities of the situation – emperors versus dictators, blacks versus whites – discouraged the left from taking action. Any recruitment ideas that threatened to take off were grounded by funding and transportation problems or opposition from the Soviet Union, the left wing's lodestar and discreet ally of Mussolini.

In any case, the Ethiopians did not want foreign manpower. They had plenty of their own and xenophobia to spare. Any rogue elements who thought about importing large numbers of outsiders would have found their plans blocked by Haile Selassie's desire not to antagonise the League of Nations; a lack of money to pay and equip the newcomers; and many foreign nations, especially those with colonies or large non-white populations, preventing their citizens from travelling to Ethiopia.

The only foreigners welcome in Addis Ababa were small numbers of specialised military instructors who had arrived before the war. The Belgians, Swedes, and multinational crew of pilots were part of a race against time to form a modern army out of the Ethiopian feudal system. The war came too soon, leaving no one too impressed by what the instructors achieved. Even the Imperial Guard only looked impressive on the parade ground.

'From the moment they had passed out of the care of their Belgian instructors they had lost the appearance of regular troops,' said Konovalov. 'Not once did I see them conform to any military discipline, or even in ordinary ranks.'

The other foreigners who joined the fighting tended to be isolated adventurers who took advantage of personal contacts and obscure homelands to slip through the cracks. For all their enthusiasm, men like Konovalov, Del Valle, Parlesák, and Breyer were very small cogs in the Ethiopian war machine.

The Italians had far more foreigners fighting in their ranks, with tens of thousands of colonial troops from Eritrea and Somaliland, along with Ethiopian rebels. Several thousand men of Italian descent from across the world also signed up for the invasion. Mussolini gave grandiloquent speeches of thanks but made little use of them.

The war experienced by 700 Italians from Argentina was typical. Recruited by a priest called Onorato Amendola di Tebaldi, a thirty-four-year-old former war correspondent in the Chaco War and son of a dead Italian general, they would be held behind the lines for most of the fighting and only see action in April 1936 mopping up the last Ethiopian resistance. During the war at least 5,000 Italians, 10,000 of their African soldiers, and somewhere around a quarter of a million Ethiopians died. Only nine Argentine-Italians would be killed.

Italy's African-born troops made a significant contribution to victory and paid for it with lives and limbs but other foreign fighters in Ethiopia played a role either insignificant or symbolic. It made no difference whether they fought for the Ethiopian throne or Mussolini's dreams of a reborn Roman empire.

AFTERMATH

Haile Selassie, 1936–2000

On 16 February 1992, they found Haile Selassie's bones buried under a concrete slab in a toilet. A group of royalists had got permission from the newly installed transitional government of Ethiopia to spend a long weekend digging up the grounds of the palace. The corpses of fifty murdered officials appeared the first day. The diggers had no luck with the emperor until late on Sunday when a former courtier came forward. He guided them to the bathroom of a private office where the remains of Haile Selassie had been hidden by the Marxists who overthrew him eighteen years previously.

The royalists gave more respectful treatment. They laid out the royal bones in a coffin, draped over a velvet maroon shawl trimmed with gold brocade, and displayed the polished wooden box in the crypt of the Bhata Church. Haile Selassie's photograph looked down on the scene. The transitional authorities carefully undercut any nostalgia for the dead emperor by quarantining the coffin in the crypt's closet under a coat rack.

Ethiopia had been through revolution, Marxist dictatorship, civil war, genocide, and famine. Huge hammer and sickle banners still hung on Addis Ababa's main roads. Now the Marxists were in jail or on the run and the new government was trying to work out the future of Ethiopia.

'To some degree, all of us are in the dark about how to fashion a collective identity as Ethiopians,' said Samuel Assefa, special

assistant to the president of Addis Ababa University. 'For me, a
shared identity is an achievement. It is not something ready-made.'

The transitional government still blamed Haile Selassie for
the poverty and feudalism, ignorance and mysticism that had
triggered the Marxist takeover. Ministers rejected calls for a state
funeral. The royalists refused to bury their lost leader without
one. The emperor's bones would stay in the crypt closet for
another eighteen years. Even in death, Haile Selassie wielded a
kind of power.

The emperor's life had been full of controversy and reversals of
fortune since he sailed out of Djibouti in May 1936 on his way
to European exile. Not many would have put money on him ever
seeing Ethiopia again. On the way up the gangplank of the British
warship taking him to safety, he stopped to mutter a few words
to the courtiers gathered on the dock. Parlesák, the Swedes, and
Vehip Pasha were among them. The mood was bleak and weary.
The Turk muttered about how the war could never have been won.

'Ethiopia cannot be controlled,' he said. 'I had come to a war
and found defeat.'

The emperor thanked them for their efforts and wrapped himself
tight in his cloak as he walked up the gangplank. The naval guns
on HMS *Enterprise* boomed out a royal salute.

Two months later Haile Selassie was in Geneva addressing the
League of Nations. He talked about collective security and begged
for action against the Fascist occupation of his country. Italian
journalists booed him from the visitor's gallery. Romanian Foreign
Minister Nicolae Titulescu jumped to his feet, furious at the breach
of protocol. 'À la porte les sauvages!' Throw out those savages.

The next day, Jewish Slovak journalist and actor Stephan Lux
shot himself on the floor of the League debating chamber. Lux
wanted to draw attention to German militarism and anti-Semitism.
He died in hospital, leaving behind letters to senior politicians about
world peace. Both Lux and Haile Selassie would be disappointed.

*

Gore was a rainy bit of nothing close to the border with Anglo-Egyptian Sudan. Ras Imru was doing his best to keep up the fight but locals wanted him gone and Italian troops were closing in. Imru's men were already thinning out and drifting back home. They knew a lost cause when they saw one. Among the die-hards was a single white face. Belgian mercenary Adelin de Fraipont had discovered a love of Ethiopia somewhere in the chaos of the last year. He refused to leave with the rest of Reul's men and stayed on to organise provisional government troops. Imru was grateful. The other foreigners who made it to Gore had not stuck around.

Carl von Rosen and Marius Brophil turned up in June, flying in from Amsterdam on a mission to locate a Swedish Red Cross unit gone missing in the chaos. Von Rosen had flown fifty-five rescue missions during the war and airlifted eighty-one wounded to Red Cross bases. Brophil had enough appetite for adventure left to tag along for a final mission; there were rumours he has been asked to collect information by British intelligence.

Their first sight of Gore was cloaked in a fog bank. The engine was spluttering when Von Rosen spotted a flat strip of land near a ravine. They came in steep, with Brophil rolling petrol cans up the aisle to weigh down the rear landing gear and praying it would stop them bouncing into the abyss. Then the plane was on the ground with propellers still spinning and Ethiopian soldiers appeared in the doorway holding bottles of champagne looted back in Addis Ababa.

Ras Imru had no news about the Swedes. The pair hunted the ambulance from the air until Italy sent a message to Cairo's Swedish embassy threatening to bomb Gore if its pilots saw Von Rosen again. The diplomats passed on the threat, along with the news that the ambulance unit was reported to have made it across the border to Kenya. Ras Imru gave the pair a dignified goodbye and they made a grim August flight home, full of malaria, food poisoning, and dysentery.

Alejandro del Valle had already been and gone. He retreated from the northern front with everyone else and rolled into Addis Ababa to find chaos and looting. The Cuban camped near the

Ministry of War and tried to organise some defences but got no further than a few trenches. No one was in the mood to listen to a foreigner. The only diversion was a water diviner who claimed to be able to find anything with his forked stick. The sceptical Cuban buried his Swiss watch and watched with pleasure as the man wasted five hours before admitting he couldn't find it. Neither could Del Valle. He still hadn't dug it up when orders came in to leave for Gore before the Italians arrived.

The Cuban took a battlegroup of eighteen men, including his slaves, and set off for the west. Soon it was lush jungle with screaming packs of baboons, dense greenery, and sleepy lions who barely bothered to raise their heads when men passed. Del Valle's men burned any village they encountered and didn't bother to justify their destruction. There was a diversion to rescue a family of German missionaries from bandits, who killed several soldiers and the missionary husband; another diversion to see the cave of the Queen of Sheba, a damp hole full of mouldy human bones.

In Gore, Del Valle realised the fight was over when he heard about the emperor's departure and fall of Addis Ababa. He volunteered to take Frau Müller and her children over the border into Anglo-Egyptian Sudan. Ras Imru gave the Cuban an escort but had no illusions they would return. There was a final splash of blood when the group passed through Shankala territory and a soldier called Muna ran off with one of the local women.

'A day later we found them dead. The woman had her belly cut open. And inside, as a macabre filler, was the head of the unhappy Muna that the Shankalas had separated from his trunk.'

On the banks of the White Nile in Sudan they found Malakal, where the British consul put them on boats to the capital. They slipped down the river watching half-submerged hippos snorting from the water. In Khartoum they got fresh clothes and clean rooms with baths. Del Valle freed his slaves and advised them to join the other soldiers enlisting in the British army. Frau Müller and her children went off to mourn their loss. Del Valle headed north to the Mediterranean.

He hit Europe to hear that Gore had fallen to the Italians. Ras Imru abandoned the town at the end of October 1936 and the Fascists occupied it the next month. The *ras* was captured at the end of the year but De Fraipont escaped and spent the next two years struggling back to Belgium with Mussolini's men on his trail every step of the way.

Ethiopian resistance degenerated into isolated guerrilla warfare, assassinations, and bloody reprisals. Pragmatists collaborated with the country's new rulers. Ras Seyoum got a senior post in the administration. Ras Getachew received 7,000 lire a month for his services. Daba Birrou returned from Japan to accept an Italian passport in a lightning storm of flash bulbs. By that time the Japanese nationalist scene had forgotten all about Ethiopia and turned its focus towards imperial expansion into China.

A few of Haile Selassie's foreign legion hung on in occupied Addis Ababa. French engineer Demeaux and his family hid in the French legation during the chaos at the end of the war. The Italians arrested Demeaux when he ventured out to check his house, but grudgingly released him after French diplomatic pressure. Hilaire Du Berrier was filing stories about the new regime when his name appeared on a list of mercenaries. He escaped Italian custody and made it to Djibouti.

Konovalov expected to be arrested at any moment but the Italians ignored him, which fuelled conspiracy theories among Haile Selassie loyalists that he had been a double agent. His Tsarist background and Ethiopian passport may have saved him. He spent his days writing a memoir of the war.

Other foreign volunteers were already back home. In America, the Brown Condor and the Black Eagle were getting very different kinds of publicity.

*

A scrum of cheering African-Americans carried John Robinson off his liner at the Port of New York. The Brown Condor was dressed for the occasion in a tan sweater with embroidered Ethiopian lion, khaki trousers, and a pith helmet. He was hoisted into someone's shoulders and paraded around the port area while the crowd cheered. Harlem was determined to find something to celebrate after the defeat of Haile Selassie.

The news from abroad had been nothing but bad. The League of Nations was doing little and a number of countries had already shown themselves willing to recognise Italian Ethiopia. Haile Selassie accepted exile in Britain. He bought Fairfield House, a chunk of nineteenth-century Italianate brickwork in the regency spa town of Bath; smart enough – but still a long way from royal palaces and peasants kissing the ground.

The return of homegrown hero Robinson in May gave Harlem something to cheer about. He gave speeches to enthusiastic supporters, described his adventures, exaggerated a few dog fights, and pushed the idea of starting his own flight school. The African-American press loved him. A few days later he got an open limousine ride from Chicago Municipal Airport to the Southside, with an Ethiopian flag draped over his car and crowds lining the road.

The Black Eagle was less popular. On 18 June 1936 Hubert Julian's liner docked at Naples after a long journey from New York. He forced visa officials to wait an hour-and-a-half outside his cabin while he climbed into morning dress, adjusted his top hat to a jaunty angle, and found a red carnation for his buttonhole. Julian told the press that Mussolini had promised to sponsor a transatlantic flight. 'I thought of this flight the day the Ethiopian empire became Italian.'

Julian claimed to have become an Italian citizen under the name of Huberto Fauntleroyana Juliano. No one believed it. He hung around Rome hoping for an audience with Il Duce but the Fascist administration ignored him. Back in America, Julian told newsmen the visit had been a secret mission to assassinate Mussolini, which failed due to circumstances beyond his control. He named Malaku Bayen as co-conspirator, which annoyed the doctor so much the pair nearly had a fistfight when they ran into each other in Harlem.

'Another ... rascal ... in Ethiopia on wings for no other purpose than to gain information which he could sell to the Italian aggressors,' said Bayen.

By the next month Julian was leading a seven-piece orchestra, 'which he directs with continental finesse', according to *The Afro-American*. Then it was more interviews and talks full of digs at John Robinson and Ethiopian racism.

'Ethiopia is a conquered kingdom today because it refused to have confidence in anything black,' he said. 'Haile Selassie is a monarch without a throne because he placed a higher value on anything that came out of a white mouth above anything given him by his own flesh and blood.'

Other foreigners stayed loyal to the emperor but found the eyes of the world had moved on. Back home in Australia, Arnold Wienholt wrote up articles on the Italian occupation and sent them to newspaper contacts. The responses were polite but negative. The public had lost interest in Ethiopia. Now it was all about Spain.

*

Ethiopia was the dividing line between different generations of the European extreme right. The older cohort of monocled colonels worshipped hierarchy, throne and altar, despised organised labour and Bolshevism and saw prestige in non-white colonies. It was a reactionary world of exiled White Russians plotting in Paris cafés, former Freikorps officers shooting politicians in Berlin parks, cold-blooded invective in *Action française* newspapers, and red-faced British majors firing on political demonstrations in Indian marketplaces.

The newer generation had learned to distrust its elders back in the trenches of the First World War. It replaced the old Victorian certainties of king and country with a metanarrative born from modernity, cultural myth, and biological racism. Jackbooted junior officers taught themselves to see other hues of white as the eternal enemy and directed their colonial drives against fellow European nations. Swastika flags waved and Panzer tanks rolled; men shouted about *untermenschen* at Nürnberg rallies.

The invasion of Ethiopia had been Mussolini's attempt to stand with the older generation and earn their respect with an imperialist drive into Africa. Sanctions and international outrage soured that dream. By the time Addis Ababa fell he had switched loyalties to the New Order.

It all crystalised in Spain. On 18 July 1936 General Francisco Franco y Bahamonde and fellow army officers attempted to overthrow Spain's left-wing Popular Front government. The Nationalist insurgents believed the country was speeding towards anarchy, atheism and communism under the Popular Front's rule. The government and its supporters saw the rising as a Fascist assault on democracy.

On the side of the insurgents were conservatives, monarchists, devout Catholics, and the far right. The Popular Front could count on liberals, communists, socialists, and anarchists. The rising's effects were felt beyond Spain. The beleaguered Spanish government's cause became a rallying point for left-wingers across the world. As the Republican army staggered under the Nationalist onslaught, thirty-five thousand foreign volunteers from fifty countries joined the Popular Front's International Brigade units to fight against Franco.

Five times as many men from Italy, Nazi Germany, Morocco, and other nations joined the Nationalist forces. Hitler sent the Condor Legion, Mussolini formed a Blackshirt army, and Muslims in North Africa flocked to recruiting posts. Right-wing adventurers, ranging from fascists to monarchists to conservative Catholics, looked for a way in. Hilaire Du Berrier and De Wet tried to enlist as pilots but Nationalist representatives politely turned them down and muttered something about the Italians remembering them from Ethiopia.

Other foreigners with better pro-Fascist records had less trouble joining the Spanish rebels. Andrew Fountaine, conservative son of an English landowning family, had driven an ambulance with the British Red Cross unit in Ethiopia but fought for Franco in Spain. He would later become a leading member of the British far-right, open about his time helping a black emperor, '... though now I see I was on the wrong side,' he told reporters thirty years later.

Others would regret their involvement in Spain's civil war. Irishman General Eoin O'Duffy finally had the chance to send his followers into battle when Franco accepted them as the XV *bandera* of the Spanish Foreign Legion. The Irish unit had a disastrous time in the front line, nearly mutinied, and returned home with O'Duffy's reputation in tatters.

Konovalov offered his engineering skills to General Franco's army. The price extracted by the Italians was allowing the Russian's Ethiopian war memoir to be published out of Bologna in late 1936 as *Con le armate del Negus: Un bianco tra i neri* (With the Army of the Negus: A White Among the Blacks), with several chapters of pro-Fascist propaganda dumped in by a ghost writer. The book's dedication seemed to refer to Mussolini:

To the Italian soldier who showed to the world, at first sceptical and then amazed but always hostile, that glorifying in the new fascist climate, he has the ancient virtues of the Roman legionary.

Mussolini was impressed enough to recommend the book in his *Popolo d'Italia* newspaper. Konovalov convinced himself he was still being loyal to Haile Selassie. The book sold well. Another first-hand account of the Ethiopian war appeared in print the next year, this time in Spanish. Alejandro del Valle had written his memoirs.

The Cuban also managed to join Franco's Nationalists in the south of Spain early in the Civil War. After a few weeks the Italians found out about Ethiopia and Del Valle had to leave the battlefield in a hurry. Across the border in Portugal he linked up with some right-wing revolutionaries trying to overthrow the country's military dictatorship and taught them bomb-making techniques. German pilot Ludwig Weber was somewhere near Lisbon as well, training the Portuguese air force, having survived crashing his Junkers in Sudan.

Del Valle didn't spend long in Portugal. He booked a passage to Mexico with a boatload of South American refugees fleeing the Spanish fighting. The *Durango* made an unscheduled stop in Cuba on 29 October. The authorities were still looking for Del Valle after his activities in the ABC. He got ashore disguised as a sailor and his family managed to bribe Batista into forgetting any outstanding problems. Del Valle showed his loyalty to the government by taking a job in the customs service. 'As a special agent he was concerned with apprehending smugglers and took part in numerous risky raids,' wrote an impressed American journalist. 'It was Del Valle who arrested George Yukichi Ozawa, the Japanese who was masquerading as a naval attaché of the Nipponese legation in Havana and who recently was sentenced to a year and four months in the Isle of Pines federal prison.'

Del Valle soon got bored chasing smugglers. He wrote his Ethiopia war memoirs as a series of articles for the magazine *Carteles* ('larger and wider circulation throughout Latin America than any other magazine or weekly', boasted the advertising department) with the help of ghostwriter Arturo Alfonso Rosello. The magazine later compiled them into a paperback with a stapled-shut photograph section of mutilated Italian corpses. The publicity boys played up to Cuba's pro-Italian sentiment with the title *Un Hombre Blanco en el Infierno Negro* (A White Man in a Black Hell).

The editor of *Carteles* wrote an introduction fussing over the fact-checking done by the magazine. It should have done more. The book stayed within shouting distance of the truth but Del Valle liked to retell garbled stories he had heard second-hand (Mulugeta's death; Julian's air crash; Burgoyne's death; Haile

Selassie leaving Addis Ababa); and place himself at the centre of the action. His fantasies squirted clouds of ink around the realities of the war for a generation of Cuban readers.

'The narration of my eleven-month campaign in Ethiopia,' said Del Valle, 'and the extraordinary adventures that I lived in that black land, with death stalking me every second, may seem to the unbelieving reader, who has not left civilization for a single moment, exaggerations of a creative mind or a feverish fantasy.'

By the time the book was published in September 1937, Del Valle had organised a group of Cuban volunteers and was on his way back to Spain, planning to join the other side.

'Now he is returning to cast his lot with the loyalists,' said the American journalist, 'not, his friends explain, because of any particular political belief but because of his conviction that there he will find the hottest action.'

Another mercenary was equally keen not to let politics stand in the way of adventure and money. Hilaire du Berrier was a born mercenary and proud of it.

'It is the world's oldest profession,' he said, 'halfway point between a firing squad and a throne, nobler than diplomacy and fraught with danger.'

After the Nationalists turned him down in late 1936 Du Berrier joined the other side. He and De Wet signed up with the Spanish government as pilots for £180 a month plus £300 for each enemy plane downed. The pair took rooms at Madrid's Hotel Florida, heaving with foreign correspondents like George Steer, the British journalist shaky and depressed after the death of his wife in childbirth. De Wet nearly got shot calling for service in the hotel restaurant.

'Waiter!'

An angry man in white overalls and a pistol came over.

'Don't ever call me waiter,' he said. 'I am Comrade to you.'

Then he served them dinner.

The Spanish Civil War was an arena for gladiators of the left and right to hack away at each other. Nazi Germany and Fascist

Italy strengthened a shaky alliance eventually born in Ethiopia when both sent troops to help Franco. The Soviets funded the International Brigades and strengthened government ranks with experienced tank crews on fake passports. Some African-Americans joined the Brigades to get revenge for Haile Selassie.

'This ain't Ethiopia but it'll do,' said a newly arrived black volunteer, looking around Spain's sun-bleached landscape.

Most African-Americans who made it to Spain were communists able to put party loyalty ahead of doubts about the USSR's treatment of a black emperor. The rest of the community lacked their faith; bitterness over Soviet support for Mussolini capped the number of black volunteers at a hundred, a huge contrast to the tens of thousands who had offered to fight for Ethiopia.

By the time Franco's men declared victory on 1 April 1939 the Civil War had wrecked Spain and put both sides through the mincing machine. Du Berrier and De Wet were not around to see the end. They had been deported two years earlier. The Englishman had drunkenly bombed a town taken by the Republicans that morning; Du Berrier stayed sober but made his own mistakes, nearly shooting down an Air France passenger plane that resembled an Italian bomber. He was kicked out when someone outed him as a member of *Action française*. De Wet spent the rest of the thirties knocking around the cafés of Paris and Prague, scraping a living as a painter and journalist. His American friend went to China.

*

Around midnight on 7 July 1937 a Japanese army patrol got into a firefight with Chinese troops near the Marco Polo bridge outside Beijing. The shooting escalated and within weeks the two countries were at war. Japan saw a chance to expand its territory in Manchuria. Chiang Kai-Shek's Kuomintang government thought it could reunite the country. Kōdōha loyalists dropped their feud with the Tokyo establishment to join the invasion.

Du Berrier got a job with the Kuomintang as a pilot and airplane buyer. He brought in his old friend Vincent Schmidt, previously a flyer for the Spanish government. Schmidt found chaos when he arrived to join fellow foreigners in the 14th Volunteer Squadron. Orders were contradictory, ground crews incompetent, and the demoralised squadron spent its off-duty hours in Hankou's red light district. None of Schmidt's dawn patrols or bombing raids could hold back the Japanese.

Fellow Ethiopia veteran René Drouillet was in China as adviser to a General Wang, but saw little action. The Frenchman had previously flown around Spain, rescuing rich French families from Republican territory when the war got close.

Back in Dakota, Du Berrier's family hadn't heard from him for a while and was getting worried. China imposed sanctions on Mussolini during the invasion but everyone knew the Kuomintang air force had originally been trained by Italian pilots and Chiang Kai-Shek had modelled his politics on Fascism. The family wondered if someone had taken revenge for Ethiopia. Then Helen Berrier got a letter from Shanghai. Her brother gave a thumbnail sketch of his recent problems.

'Charged with being a Japanese spy, [I] was sacrificed in a typical Chinese political passe-passe [trick] in Hanow, November 1937, and was dismissed from Central Government Service. Barely escaped from the interior.'

The Chinese might have been right about the spying business. After losing his job Du Berrier headed straight for the gilded sleaze of Japanese-controlled Shanghai to work with Wang Jingwei, a former Kuomintang man now on Tokyo's side. Du Berrier brought weapons and did intelligence work for the Japanese. It got him a nice house with armed guards and the spare time to write travel pieces for *XXth Century*, an English-language magazine subsidised by Nazi Germany.

Du Berrier partied with conmen and blackmailers, abortionists and hitmen, and attempted to set up a male brothel on Avenue

Joffre for rich European women. He had a plan to blackmail his clients. Shanghai's corruption had seeped into his pores.

'It's hot, I'm tired,' he wrote to his sister. 'Shanghai is full of Jews, japs, and gunmen, and it's a toss-up which are worse. Law and order have gone with the winds and gambling joints and opium dives have taken their place.'

China still seemed a safe refuge when the Second World War began. In August 1939 Germany and the USSR agreed the Molotov–Ribbentrop pact. Ostensibly a non-aggression treaty, secret protocols divided Eastern Europe and the Baltic States between the two dictatorships. On 1 September the Third Reich invaded Poland. Britain and France declared war on Germany, and the resulting vortex sucked in most of the world.

The Soviet Union attacked Poland from the east in mid-September and the country was overrun by the end of the month. Stalin ate up Estonia, Latvia, and Lithuania before invading Finland in November. The Finnish battle hooked into the imagination of adventurers who leaned right and some set off for Helsinki to fight communism. Vincent Schmidt joined the Finnish air force but didn't see much fighting before returning to America and a place in General Eisenhower's headquarters as an intelligence officer. Carl von Rosen flew a bombing mission over Russian territory. Viking Tamm organised Swedish volunteers and commanded his men in a quiet section of the frontline. René Drouillet joined the Finns as a pilot but went to London after the fall of France to join Charles de Gaulle's forces under the nom de guerre 'Alain Montguelly'.

Finland also welcomed the Black Eagle. Hubert Julian joined the air force after convincing the Finnish military attaché in America he could stop the Soviets. He got the rank of captain and a boat ticket but the ceasefire had been signed by the time he arrived. Julian made one flight and returned home to walk around Harlem in his Finnish uniform. He challenged Herman Göring to an aerial duel; it was ignored. Julian put the uniform in his closet with the rest, became an American citizen, and sold used cars.

De Wet missed both China and Finland. He was in a German jail. The Englishman had been enjoying himself in Prague café society, painting and writing and newly married to a Russian exile. French spies asked him to smuggle out information about German troop movements in the Sudetenland. He was arrested when the Nazis occupied the rest of Czechoslovakia the following year. His wife killed herself in prison and De Wet spent the war behind bars, listening to prisoners being shot in the courtyard outside.

*

A few Ethiopia veterans managed to outrun the war as it rumbled towards them. Ludwig Weber quit Portugal in 1939 for the safety of Brazil where he became a businessman and continued to race. He retired to Switzerland in 1975 and died there sixteen years later. Vehip Pasha returned to Istanbul in 1938 after Atatürk died of cirrhosis. The general had two years to enjoy victory over his old political enemy before death carried him off. He was buried at Karacaahmet Cemetery in Istanbul among 700 years of turquoise-grey Ottoman tombstones.

Lieutenant-Colonel Léopold Reul did his best for peace with the *Ligue de l'Independence Nationale*, one of Nothomb's efforts that attempted to keep Belgium neutral as the French and Germans growled at each other over the border. More mainstream politicians shared Reul's concerns. Foreign Minister Paul Spaak used Ethiopia to justify his country's decision to stay out of the fighting.

'Remember Abyssinia,' he said, 'which was led to believe that by basing her defence upon a policy of collective security, she would be saved. Do you want that to happen to us?'

Hitler didn't care about neutrality. On 17 May 1940 the Nazis marched into Brussels. Reul's war and later life are obscure, as are those of his fellow mercenaries, although many members of the *Légion nationale* joined the resistance and De Fraipont seems to have been involved in hiding shot-down Allied airmen. Norman,

Viseur, and Frère had served as observers during the Spanish Civil War, and Norman would go on to fight in the Korean War. Major Auguste Dothée of the official mission escaped occupied Belgium to join the exile government in Britain and become military attaché in Tehran. He returned to Ethiopia as an ambassador years later.

Mussolini welcomed the war. He saw it as an opportunity to build a new Roman Empire around the Mediterranean. The Fascist leader wanted to grab some territory before the shooting stopped.

'I only need a few thousand dead,' he said, 'so that I can sit at the peace conference as a man who has fought.'

His army joined the Wehrmacht when it rolled into France and carved up the country. Military pride was short-lived. Italy suffered humiliating setbacks in Greece and Yugoslavia, forcing German troops to rescue them. An attempt to expand across East Africa from bases in Ethiopia backfired when British forces counter-attacked. Haile Selassie flew into Sudan to rally resistance among his people from across the border, accompanied by George Steer, now an intelligence officer in the British Army.

The jewel in Mussolini's empire fell quickly. A joint British and Ethiopian force under Colonel Orde Wingate took Addis Ababa in April 1941 and Haile Selassie returned to his capital the following month. Some collaborators were rewarded if they switched sides in time, like Ras Seyoum. Others ended up imprisoned, dead, or ostracised. 'I forgive you,' the emperor told Ras Getachew as he sentenced him to exile, 'but I do not know if God will.'

One of the men who helped to liberate Ethiopia was the Australian Arnold Wienholt. He had sailed to Aden when the war began, a tough sixty-two-year-old determined to find a role. His experience of Ethiopia got him a post in the British Army's Military Mission 101, a unit formed to foment guerrilla warfare in eastern Ethiopia. On 31 August 1940 Wienholt led a group over the border from Sudan to make contact with local loyalists. Ten days later Italian soldiers ambushed them. Wienholt was last seen crawling into the bush, badly wounded. His body was never found.

The war in Europe killed off another face from Ethiopia. Austrian Nazi photographer Franz Roth had covered the Spanish Civil War on the Francoist side and settled in Berlin working at the *Reichsministerium für Volksaufklärung und Propaganda*. When the war began he joined the *Leibstandarte SS Adolf Hitler* division as a war correspondent. He survived getting his skull split open by Greek bullets near Kastoria but his luck ran out when the war went global. In summer of 1941 Hitler tore up the Molotov–Ribbentrop Pact and invaded the Soviet Union; six months later a sneak attack on the Pearl Harbor naval base by Japan tipped America into the war. Roth followed the *Leibstandarte* into battle in the east and got a machine-gun bullet in the chest during the February 1943 Battle of Kharkov. The Waffen-SS awarded him a posthumous iron cross.

Mussolini's luck also ran out. That July, senior Italian Fascists voted him out of power and into prison in a desperate attempt to impress the British and American troops threatening to invade. Badoglio took over as prime minister.

Hilaire du Berrier initially remained untouched by the attack on Pearl Harbor. His contacts with Wang Jingwei, now leader of China's collaborationist government, left him free to wander Shanghai's nightclubs and opium dens. His writing was still being published in the *XXth Century* as late as February 1942, three months after America declared war on Japan. In November his usefulness ran out. Du Berrier spent the rest of the war in an internment camp and the effects of Japanese torture left his face partly paralysed.

The Japanese war effort had pockets of support in Du Berrier's homeland. The Ethiopian Pacific Movement, an African-American group formed during the Italian invasion, remembered Japan's support for the fallen emperor and preached neutrality in the war. Leader Robert O. Jordan went to prison for contacts with Japanese military figures. Even the UNIA went through a phase of using the slogan 'To Hell with Pearl Harbor' at its meetings.

Franz Roth's fellow Nazi Dr Valentin Schuppler had left Ethiopia at the end of May 1936 and returned to Austria after the Anschluss. He worked in a hospital during the war. Schuppler was back in Ethiopia by the 1950s and worked as a doctor in east Africa for the rest of his life. Muslim convert Harun al-Rashid Bey rejoined the German army when the war began. In 1944 he transferred as a *Standartenführer* (colonel) to the *Ostturkischer Waffen-Verband der SS*, a unit of Muslims recruited from occupied areas of the Soviet Union. He survived the war, tried and failed to emigrate to Ecuador, and died in 1963.

On the other side, Evelyn Waugh served in the Royal Marines and the Commandos. He was brave, calmly dodging Stuka dive bombers in the Battle for Crete, but unsuited to military life and unpopular with fellow officers. He had better luck than George Steer, who died in a jeep crash during the last Christmas of the war, but Waugh never found the heroic war he wanted. He was too much the cynical iconoclast.

'It was fun being pro-Italian when it was an unpopular and (I thought) losing cause,' he wrote to a friend after a visit to occupied Ethiopia in 1936. 'I have little sympathy with these exultant Fascists now.'

Waugh's most lasting achievement in wartime was to write the novel *Brideshead Revisited*, a creamy cocktail of nostalgia, faith, and social climbing. A character called Hooper represents the banality of modern man, the name possibly lifted from one of the Ethiopian Red Cross doctors. *Brideshead* made Waugh famous. He went on to international celebrity, cantankerous public appearances, and hard drinking. Waugh died at Easter 1966 after attending a Latin Mass and collapsing at his home.

*

On 28 April 1945 Mussolini was shot by a communist partisan at the gates of the Villa Belmonte in Mezzegra, northern Italy. Dramatic to the last, he pulled open his overcoat and told the executioner to shoot him in the chest. Il Duce had escaped imprisonment in 1943 with German help to lead a rump state of die-hards known as the Republic of Salò. Now that Fascist last stand was crumbling to dust along with the rest of Hitler's empire. Graziani was already organising Salò's surrender.

Soviet troops were closing in on Berlin. The Nazi invasion of the USSR had been swallowed up by the icy vastness of the east. On 30 April 1945 the Führer retired to his quarters in the Reich Chancellery bunker with long-time mistress Eva Braun, having married her earlier that day, and the couple committed suicide. Their bodies were cremated by members of the Waffen-SS outside the bunker as mortar shells rained down.

Three months later Japan's war finished in the flash of two atomic bombs dropped on Hiroshima and Nagasaki. Close to 200,000 people died. Japan surrendered, American troops moved in, and Kōdōha leader General Araki Sadao did ten years in prison for war crimes. He was released on health grounds and died in 1966.

Haile Selassie's pre-war enemies and allies were dead. He began to rebuild Ethiopia. His experiences had left him less keen on foreigners but in the post-war years the emperor invited back a select few to help with the reconstruction.

John Robinson rejoined the air force. The Brown Condor had spent the war as a civilian instructor at Tuskegee where he impressed fellow African-American pilots with his professionalism and a string of exaggerated stories about fighting the Italians. In Ethiopia he headed a team of instructors and mechanics in a programme to expand the country's air power. He had less control over his temper than in earlier years and in 1947 did three months in prison for a violent attack on Carl von Rosen. The Swede had returned to Ethiopia as chief instructor of the air force, a job Robinson wanted. Von Rosen stayed on until 1956 but intrigues among the royal court made life difficult and he returned to Sweden. By that time the Brown Condor had been dead for two years.

Despite the prison sentence, Robinson had retained support in high places. On release he was employed as private pilot for the Duke of Harar, grandson of Haile Selassie. Together they created Sultan Airways Ltd. On 13 March 1954, Robinson volunteered to fly a cross-country medical emergency but crashed en route. He died two weeks later in an Addis Ababa hospital and was buried with military honors.

Von Rosen went on to help end the Congo's Katanga secession as official pilot of UN chief Dag Hammarskjöld. He was on sick leave the day Hammarskjöld's plane crashed in Northern Rhodesia, killing everyone on board. Later the Swede switched sides and joined Biafran secessionists, dropping food to starving people and wiping out Nigerian planes on the ground with improvised bombs. He returned to Ethiopia and flew famine relief missions in Ogaden. Von Rosen was killed when rebels attacked the town of Gode on 13 September 1977.

Fellow Swede Viking Tamm had died two years earlier. He returned home from Finland a champion of guerrilla stay-behind tactics and eventually became a lieutenant-general. He managed to outlive fellow Ethiopia veteran René Drouillet by a year. The Frenchman had moved into air transport but couldn't stay still for long, living everywhere from Cannes to the Antibes. In 1974 Drouillet did his first skydive at seventy-six years old. That September he was speeding his car through the south of France when he swerved to avoid a donkey and flew off the road. He died in hospital.

The same decade saw the death of another mercenary. After Spain, Del Valle had returned to Cuba, married, and had two sons. In 1947 he was involved with an effort by Dominican exiles to invade their homeland and overthrow the regime of dictator and former jailbird President Rafael Trujillo. The plot fell apart and Del Valle moved to Mexico, putting his Texas A&M education to use as a rancher. His son Alejandro jr became involved with Cuban exile attempts to overthrow the new Castro regime and bled out on a Miami-bound fishing boat returning from the April 1961 Bay of Pigs fiasco. Del Valle died in Mexico in 1976.

White Russian exile Konovalov returned to Ethiopia and resumed his engineering job in the administration. His service in Spain and literary deals with Italy remained unknown or overlooked. Fellow Slav Adolf Parlesák never saw Ethiopia again. After returning to Brno he set off on more travels, travelling through Yemen (where he wrote about Shibam's mud skyscrapers), Japan, and China. His war years are obscure and he became a translator in communist Czechoslovakia. In 1948 he published *Habešská odyssea: čech ve službách habešského císaře* (Abyssinian Odyssey: A Czech in the Service of the Abyssinian Emperor), a well-written account of his time in Ethiopia. He died in Prague at the age of seventy-three in December 1981. Parlesák's friend Breyer disappeared from history, remembered only in the Czech's book and a few throwaway lines in Konovalov's writings.

John Robinson's old enemy made sure no one would ever forget him. Hubert Julian had failed to make the American air force during the war but discovered a talent for selling weapons when peace came. He became an arms dealer and supplied everyone from Dominica's Trujillo to Cuban dictator Fulgencio Batista. In 1961 he helped the secessionist state of Katanga, dodging bullets when the United Nations tried to shut down the country by force. The UN arrested him at Elisabethville airport smuggling in a gas mask and a sten gun. Congolese authorities wanted an execution but Julian dodged the noose to be deported back to America. He kept himself in the headlines, even posing with Mohammed Ali, until his death in 1983.

Hilaire du Berrier never returned to Ethiopia. His version of events became more exaggerated as the years went by, with claims to have flown combat missions and been awarded a medal by Haile Selassie. After Du Berrier's release from the Japanese prison camp he went on to inform on former Shanghai friends for the OSS, an early version of the CIA, using the name Abdullah de

Berrière, which he claimed to have picked up converting to Islam before the war.

He lived a long and adventurous life: there were rumours of a plot to overthrow Charles de Gaulle just after the war; involvement in Indochina affairs before returning to America in the late 1950s and allying with the fanatically anti-communist John Birch Society; friendship with General Edwin Walker, a retired army officer and Society member best remembered today for having been shot at by Lee Harvey Oswald in the weeks before the assassination of President John F. Kennedy; advising segregationist George Wallace; and narrowly escaping death in 1983 by missing his check-in with Korean Airlines flight KAL-007, shot down by Soviet fighters when it strayed off its flight path. He retired to Monaco to publish the *H du B Report* newsletter, full of right-wing commentary about the New World Order and the European Union, until his death in October 2002.

His friend Hugh De Wet returned to London after the war, remarried and made a career as a writer and sculptor. His bust of Dylan Thomas is on display at London's Royal Festival Hall. De Wet had a still in his studio that produced pure alcohol. He drank himself to death on 16 January 1975.

*

Haile Selassie's post-war attempts to modernise Ethiopia while keeping its traditions intact were as unsuccessful as his earlier efforts. The *rases* associated modernity with Italian bombs and poison gas, and did their best to cripple his plans. A progressive tax scheme was abandoned, a land tax was paid mostly by the poor and the aristocracy kept its privileges. A revised constitution passed in 1955 gave a measure of democracy without abandoning any of the emperor's power. Both democrats and traditionalists disliked it.

An Ethiopian contingent went to fight in the Korean War and many died at Pork Chop Hill; a UN peacekeeping unit in

Katanga got a reputation for looting and rape. Haile Selassie tried expansionist imperialism by declaring Eritrea a rogue province and sending in troops. It set off a long war. International criticism was muted out of respect for his diplomatic ability to balance pro-western policies with support for decolonialisation.

By the 1970s Haile Selassie was the longest serving head of state still in power. The same decade saw a famine that killed at least 80,000 and accusations of war crimes in Eritrea. Opposition figures were imprisoned, censorship was near absolute. There were rumours the emperor was struggling with dementia. His most loyal lieutenants had died years before: Ras Kassa in 1954; Ras Seyoum in 1960, having been forgiven his collaboration.

The emperor was still sharp enough to order the death of the king cut from *Macbeth* when the play was performed in case it gave anyone ideas. That didn't stop a group of Marxist army officers, known as the Derg, overthrowing him in February 1974. They put him under house arrest in the royal palace. They tried to make Haile Selassie's son Crown Prince Asfa Wossen emperor, but he refused to accept the crown. Ras Imru had friends among the Derg but also stayed loyal to the monarchy. When Asfa Wossen protested over the murder of sixty former officials of the Imperial Government in November, the Marxists turned Ethiopia into a republic.

On 28 August the next year, the Derg announced that Haile Selassie had died after a prostate operation. It was widely believed he had been murdered, with rumours about a brutal strangulation circulating in Addis Ababa. No one knew with any certainty what had happened to the emperor until his bones were discovered in 1992 under a concrete slab in the palace.

He was finally reburied on 5 August 2000 in a lavish ceremony by the Ethiopian Orthodox Church. The government refused to call the ceremony a state funeral. Ethiopia remains a republic.

SELECT BIBLIOGRAPHY

Balázs, Szélinger, *Magyarország és Etiópia: Formális és informális kapcsolatok a 19. század második felétől a II. Világháborúig* (Doktori Értekezés, Szegedi Tudományegyetem Bölcsészettudományi Kar, 2008)

Bertonha, João Fábio, *O Fascismo e os Imigrantes Italianos no Brasil* (Edipucrs, 2001)

Brendon, Piers, *The Dark Valley: A Panorama of the 1930s* (Johnathan Cape, 2000)

Bridgeman, Brian, *The Flyers* (Self Publishing Association, 1989)

Clarke III, J Calvitt, *Alliance of the Colored Peoples: Ethiopia & Japan Before World War II* (Boydell & Brewer Ltd, 2011)

Clarke III, J Calvitt, *Feodor Konovalov and the Italo-Ethiopian War (Part I)* (World War II Quarterly, vol.5 no.1, 2008)

Clarke III, J Calvitt, *Feodor Konovalov and the Italo-Ethiopian War (Part II)* (World War II Quarterly, vol. 5 no.2, 2008)

Consuegra Sanfiel, Alberto, *De Latinoamérica al Medio Oriente: Alineamientos y compromisos frente al segundo conflicto ítalo-abisinio (1935-1936)* (Humania del Sur. Año 8, No. 15, Julio-Diciembre, 2013)

Del Valle, Alejandro & Alfonso Roselló, Arturo, *Un Hombre Blanco en el Infierno Negro* (Maza, Caso y cía, 1937)

Erlich, Haggai, *Haile Selassie and the Arabs: 1935-1936* (Northeast African Studies, New Series, Vol. 1, No. 1, 1994)

Gebrekidan, Fikru, *In Defense of Ethiopia: A Comparative Assessment of Caribbean and African American Anti-Fascist Protests, 1935-1941* (Northeast African Studies New Series, Vol. 2, No. 1, 1995)

McMahon, Cian, *Eoin O'Duffy's Blueshirts and the Abyssinian Crisis* (History Ireland, Volume 10, Issue 2, 2002)

Mockler, Anthony, *Haile Selassie's War: The Italian-Ethiopian Campaign, 1935-1941* Mockler (Random House, 1984)

Nizamoğlu, Yüksel, İtalya-Habeşistan Savaşı: Vehip Paşa ve Türkiye (Sosyal Bilimler Araştırmaları Dergisi, II, 2011)

Nugent, John Peer, *The Black Eagle* (Bantam, 1971)

Othen, Christopher, *Franco's International Brigades: Adventurers, Fascists, and Christian Crusaders in the Spanish Civil War* (Hurst, 2013)

Parlesák, Adolf, *Habešská Odyssea: čech ve službách habešského císaře* (Toužimský a Moravec, 1948)

Prijac, Lukian (ed.), *Les Relations Entre L'Ethiopie et les Nations étrangères: Histoire Humaine et Diplomatique (des Origines à Nos Jours)* (LIT Verlag Münster, 2015)

Scheere, David, *Léopold Reul in Ethiopië: van officiële naar officieuze militaire samenwerking – Konden huurlingen de formele coöperatie voortzetten?* (Vrije Universiteit Brussel Thesis, 2014)

Stannard, Martin, *Evelyn Waugh: Volume 1 – The Early Years 1903-1939* (Flamingo, 1993)

Steer, George, *Caesar in Abyssinia* (Hodder & Stoughton, 1936)

Sundiata, Ibrahim K, *Brothers and Strangers: Black Zion, Black Slavery, 1914–1940* (Duke University Press, 2004)

Tucker, Philip Thomas, *Father of the Tuskegee Airmen: John C Robinson* (Potomac Books, 2012)

Ventresco, Fiorello B, *Italian-Americans and the Ethiopian Crisis* (Italian Americana, Vol. 6, No. 1, Fall/Winter 1980)

Wasserstein, Bernard, *Secret War in Shanghai: Treachery, Subversion and Collaboration in the Second World War* (Profile Books, 1998)

Waugh, Evelyn, *Waugh in Abyssinia* (Penguin Modern Classics, 2000)

NOTES

Introduction

'This is the best ...' Death at Dessye (Time, 16 December 1935)

'Dozens of helpless women ...' Bomb Comes Within Six Feet of Killing Ethiopian Emperor (The Pittsburgh Press, 7 December 1935)

'We cannot permit our ...' Ethiopia Unbound: Studies in Race Emancipation, Hayford (Cass, 1969) pxxv

'The Abyssinian maintains that ...' Brothers and Strangers: Black Zion, Black Slavery, 1914–1940, Sundiata (Duke University Press, 2004) p294

'Things in Africa had ...' O fascismo e os imigrantes italianos no Brasil, Bertonha (EDIPUCRS, 2001) p256

'Thousands of mercenaries and ...' A 'Foreign Legion' for Mussolini? A Transnational Experience of Fascist Volunteers during the Ethiopian War, Bertonha (http://research.uni-leipzig.de/eniugh/congress/fileadmin/eniugh2011/dokumente/Fascism_Transnational_and_Bertonha_2011_03_25.pdf)

'You take too much ...' Haile Selassie's War: The Italian-Ethiopian Campaign, 1935-1941, Mockler (Random House, 1984) p59

'He was notorious for ...' Evelyn Waugh: Volume 1 – The Early Years 1903-1939, Stannard (Flamingo, 1993) p406]

'Now he was back ...' Eyewitness, Monks (Frederick Muller, 1955) p37

1. The Emperor's Pal

'I am Melaku Bayen ...' The Black Eagle, Nugent (Bantam, 1971) p41

'He crossed into America ...' The Black Eagle, p9

'Julian and Garvey were ...' Beyond Blackface: African Americans and the Creation of American Popular Culture, 1890-1930, Brundage (University of North Carolina Press, 2011) p313 n34

'Those French pilots are ...' The Black Eagle, p70

'Brother, once I got ...' Race and U.S. Foreign Policy from 1900 Through World War II, Krenn (Taylor & Francis, 1998) p157

'The emperor-elect is ...' The Black Eagle, p59

'Around 100 African-Americans ...' Brothers and Strangers: Black Zion, Black Slavery, 1914–1940, p289
'Even UNIA members – whose ...' Anthem: Social Movements and the Sound of Solidarity in the African Diaspora, Redmond (NYU Press, 2013) p21
'No great man is ...' The Black Eagle, p61
'I wanted to give ...' The Black Eagle, p63
'They have more planes ...' Hubert Fauntleroy Julian (1897-1983), Barrière (http://www.crezan.net/pag_aby/abyssinia_pil_julian.html)
'I can state categorically ...' The Black Eagle, p69-70
'I will never return ...' The Black Eagle, p70

2. No Darker Than a Spaniard
'I did not know ... ' Evelyn Waugh: 1924-1966, Wilson (Fairleigh Dickinson Univ Press, 1996) p48
'The Abyssinians had nothing ... ' Waugh in Abyssinia, Waugh (Penguin Modern Classics, 2000) p24
'Half man, half snake ...' Haile Selassie's War: The Italian-Ethiopian Campaign, 1935-1941, p7
'They are beginning the ...' Remote People, Waugh (Penguin, 1985) p44
'Like many of the ...' Ethiopia as an Image: The Czechoslovak and European Press of the 1920s and Early 1930s, Zahorik (Asian and African Studies, 17 (1), 2008)
'If you were ever ...' Story of Lynchings in the US Enflames Listening Abyssinians (The Afro-American, 10 January 1931)
'Waugh took a long ...' Evelyn Waugh: Volume 1 – The Early Years 1903-1939, p254

3. Hot Macaroni
'By the end of ...' Haile Selassie's War: The Italian-Ethiopian Campaign, 1935-1941, p39
'When you want to ...' Haile Selassie's War: The Italian-Ethiopian Campaign, 1935-1941, p40
'The advisers made such ...' *Biographie belge d'Outre-Mer* Vol. VIII (Academie Royale Des Sciences D'outre-Mer, 1998) p101
'The sending of a ...' Léopold Reul in *Ethiopië: van officiële naar officieuze militaire samenwerking – Konden huurlingen de formele coöperatie voortzetten?* Scheere (Vrije Universiteit Brussel Thesis, 2014)
'Soon the Swede had ...' *Svenska officerare i kejsarens tjänst*, Carlomagno (http://www.popularhistoria.se/artiklar/svenska-officerare-i-kejsarens-tjanst/)
'You may not stay ...' *Svenska officerare i kejsarens tjänst*
'They had huge retinues ...' Caesar in Abyssinia, Steer (Hodder & Stoughton, 1936) p34
'Most of my chiefs ...' Haile Selassie's War: The Italian-Ethiopian Campaign, 1935-1941, p58
'It is better to live ...' Duce! A biography of Benito Mussolini, Collier (Viking Press, 1971) p447

4. Return of the Black Eagle

'I can write better ...' http://www.quotes.net/quote/8760

'Hey, these ain't no ...' The Black Eagle, p74

'Do as you like ...' Ibid, p81

'Italy, of course, is ...' Ibid, p83

'He was planning to ...' Ibid, p83

'After all, India is ...' Ibid, p83

'Not many journalists would ...' Reporting It All: A. J. Liebling at one hundred, Remnick (New Yorker, 29 March 2004) http://www.newyorker.com/magazine/2004/03/29/reporting-it-all

'Remember,' said Julian, 'no ...' The Black Eagle, 84

'I would have been ...' Marcus Garvey: Life and Lessons, Hill (University of California Press, 1987) plvii

'A very considerable degree ...' British West Indian Reaction to the Italian-Ethiopian War: An Episode in Pan-Africanism, Weisbord (Caribbean Studies, Vol. 10, No. 1, April 1970)

'More peaceful campaigners raised ...' In Defense of Ethiopia: A Comparative Assessment of Caribbean and African American Anti-Fascist Protests, 1935-1941, Gebrekidan (Northeast African Studies New Series, Vol. 2, No. 1, 1995)

'The Ethiopians' lack of ...' In Defense of Ethiopia: A Comparative Assessment of Caribbean and African American Anti-Fascist Protests, 1935-1941, Gebrekidan (Northeast African Studies New Series, Vol. 2, No. 1, 1995)

'The former French colony ...' *De Latinoamérica al Medio Oriente: Alineamientos y compromisos frente al segundo conflicto ítalo-abisinio* (1935-1936), *Consuegra Sanfiel* (Humania del Sur. Año 8, No. 15, Julio-Diciembre, 2013)

'Twenty years ago Negroes ... In Defense of Ethiopia: A Comparative Assessment of Caribbean and African American Anti-Fascist Protests, 1935-1941, Gebrekidan (Northeast African Studies, New Series, Vol. 2, No. 1, 1995)

'A letter to Jamaica's ...' In Defense of Ethiopia: A Comparative Assessment of Caribbean and African American Anti-Fascist Protests, 1935-1941, Gebrekidan (Northeast African Studies New Series, Vol. 2, No. 1, 1995)

'In the name of ...' *Habešská Odyssea: čech ve službách habešského císaře*, Parlesák (Toužimský a Moravec, 1948) p25

'IL DUCE NOTE,' ran ...' The Black Eagle, p84

'I would like to ...' The Black Eagle, p84

'The Ethiopians frown on ...' Ethiopian Emperor Reported Cool to Colonel Julian (The Afro-American, 20 April 1935)

'Every morning he led ...' The Black Eagle, p86

5. The Great White Hopeless

'Why don't you fight ...' Why Go To Ethiopia? (Chicago Defender, 27 July 1935)

'Professional Negrophile busybodies and ...' Views and Reviews (Pittsburgh Courier, 7 December 1935)

'By the time Louis ...' US National Archives, State Department Decimal Files 1930-1939, 884.142/25, Memorandum of Paul H. Ailing, Division of Near Eastern Affairs, September 5, 1935

'A group calling itself ...' Harlem Renaissance Lives, ed. Gates jr. & Higginbotham (OUP, 2009) p236

'War is to man …' The Sociology of War and Violence, Malešević (Cambridge University Press, 2010) p292
'Everything is hotsy-totsy …' Left Hooks (The Pittsburgh Courier, 29 June 1935)]

6. Murdering Our Own Mother
'Perhaps tomorrow, maybe the …' *Habešská Odyssea*, p7
'I learnt to abhor …' The Flyers, Bridgeman (Self Publishing Association, 1989) p53
'These station police are …' Abyssinia on the Eve, Farago (Putnam 1935) p16
'If I had a …' *Habešská Odyssea*, p22
'His two divisions and …' Haile Selassie's War: The Italian-Ethiopian Campaign, 1935-1941, p54
'That was another Italy …' *Magyarország és Etiópia: Formális és informális kapcsolatok a 19. század második felétől a II. Világháborúig*, Balázs (Doktori Értekezés, Szegedi Tudományegyetem Bölcsészettudományi Kar, 2008)
'The journalists are lousy …' Evelyn Waugh: Volume 1 – The Early Years 1903-1939, p403
'Addis Ababa stuck to …' London Throngs Watch War Acts (The Nassau Daily Review, 5 October 1935)
'Letters simply poured into …' Ethiopia Stretches Forth Across the Atlantic: African American Anticolonialism during the Interwar Period, Munro (Left History, vol.13 no.2, 2008)
'It is the duty …' Ethiopia and World Politics, Padmore (The Crisis, May 1935)
'Murdering our own mother …' A British Fascist in the Second World War: The Italian War Diary of James Strachey Barnes, 1943-45, ed. Baldoli & Fleming (Bloomsbury Publishing, 2014) p8
'Tomorrow?' asked De Wet …' The Flyers, p57

7. The Bargain Basement Aristocrat
'Make your friends on …' Secret War in Shanghai: Treachery, Subversion and Collaboration in the Second World War, Wasserstein (Profile Books, 1998) p31
'There was a sporting …' Remembrance of Things Paris: Sixty Years of Writing from Gourmet, ed. Reichl (Random House, 2009) p259
'In brief,' said Du …' Remembrance of Things Paris: Sixty Years of Writing from Gourmet, p261
'By the autumn of …' Waugh in Abyssinia, p85
'Europeans paid off spies …' Waugh in Abyssinia, p83
'He bought water paints …' http://freepages.genealogy.rootsweb.ancestry.com/~lgcool/berrier/harold1906.html
'He came to Iowa from …' http://freepages.genealogy.rootsweb.ancestry.com/~lgcool/berrier/harold1906.html
'When I was nine …' http://www.isegoria.net/2010/07/north-dakotan-monarchist/
'He combined the promiscuous …' Secret War in Shanghai: Treachery, Subversion and Collaboration in the Second World War, p30
'The Riviera was agog …' Chicagoan Challenges Italian to Rapier Duel (Pittsburgh Post-Gazette, 26 July 1935)

'Dirt ... three sheep ... four ...' Describes Life on Boat Trip to Scene of War (Chicago Tribune, 9 October 1935)

8. *Two Bohemian Adventurers*
'Ras Kassa sends you ...' *Habešská Odyssea*, p61
'About 200 pupils of ...' Ibid, p34
'The Italians cannot win ...' Ibid, p39
'I feel sorry for ...' http://www.jahmusic.net/2011/03/cesi-a-habesska-valka/
'Our young intellectuals, who ...' http://www.jahmusic.net/2011/03/cesi-a-habesska-valka/
'The diplomacy led to ...' *Historia stosunków polsko-etiopskich* http://www.addisabeba.msz.gov.pl/pl/wspolpraca_dwustronna/historia_stosunkow_polsko_etiopskich/tytul_strony
'As soon as the ...' The European Consequences of the Italian Aggression against Ethiopia, Réti (Rivista di Studi Politici Internazionali, Nuova Serie, Vol. 74, No. 3 (295), Luglio-Settembre 2007)
'I am a moral ...' *Magyarország és Etiópia: Formális és informális kapcsolatok a 19. század második felétől a II. Világháborúig*, Balázs (Doktori Értekezés, Szegedi Tudományegyetem Bölcsészettudományi Kar, 2008)
'Will the Italians use ...' *Habešská Odyssea*, p52
'I have with this ...' Ibid, p55
'Abyssinia! ... We waited for ...' Ibid, p62
'When are you coming ...' Ibid, p64

9. *The Man from Chicago*
'Mr Waugh,' he said ...' Waugh in Abyssinia, p110
'We have been patient ...' Haile Selassie's War: The Italian-Ethiopian Campaign, 1935-1941, p61
'Nine-tenths confidence plus ...' How to Fly (The Flyer's Manual): A Practical Course of Training in Aviation, Gordon, Re Vley, & Lewis (P. Elder, 1917) p83
'He asked me if ...' Father of the Tuskegee Airmen: John C Robinson, Tucker (Potomac Books, 2012) p97
'He is a quiet, capable ...' Fiasco in Ethiopia, Hubbard (Harper & Brothers, 1936) p311
'I applaud your theory ...' The Battle of Adwa: African Victory in the Age of Empire, Jonas (Harvard University Press, 2011) p283
'I can readily see ...' Father of the Tuskegee Airmen: John C Robinson, p111
'Ethiopian aviation is headed ...' The Black Eagle, p84
'It is a prodigious lie ...' The Black Eagle, p88
'I dident mind being ...' Father of the Tuskegee Airmen: John C Robinson, p131
'Nurse unupblown,' he telegraphed ...' Evelyn Waugh: Volume 1 – The Early Years 1903-1939, p409

10. *Haile Selassie's Fascist Friends*
'In the last two ...' *Les Relations Entre L'Ethiopie et les Nations étrangères: Histoire Humaine et Diplomatique (des Origines à Nos Jours)*, ed. Prijac (LIT Verlag Münster, 2015) p186, n63

'Europeans in general,' said ...' Ethiopia Has not Begun to Fight (Milwaukee Journal, 19 November 1935)

'Reul was too much ...' Ibid

'On the Italian side ...' Ibid

'It was the Emperor's ...' The Black Eagle, p90

'To fight on the ...' The Black Eagle, pp90-91

'This character from an ...' http://www.crezan.net/pag_aby/abyssinia_1935 html

'That could never happen ...' Paris Wilder than Ethiopia – Julian (The Afro-American, 7 December 1935)

'I'm sorry for the ...' The Black Eagle, p94

'Believe me, it moves ...' Ethiopia Has not Begun to Fight (Milwaukee Journal, 19 November 1935)

'A democratic regime must ...' The European Right: A Historical Profile, ed. Roger and Weber (University of California Press, 1965) p148

'It had king worship ...' Belgium and the Holocaust: Jews, Belgians, Germans, Mikhman (Berghahn Books, 1998) p173 n23

'Will the Belgian government ...' *Les Relations Entre L'Ethiopie et les Nations étrangères: Histoire Humaine et Diplomatique (des Origines à Nos Jours)*, p186

'Emperor very unhappy over ...' Léopold Reul in *Ethiopië: van officiële naar officieuze militaire samenwerking – Konden huurlingen de formele coöperatie voortzetten?* Scheere (Thesis, Vrije Universiteit Brussel, 2014)

'Such behavior has never ...' Haile Selassie's War: The Italian-Ethiopian Campaign, 1935-1941, p59 n1

'It encountered two extremely ...' Ethiopia Has not Begun to Fight (Milwaukee Journal, 19 November 1935)

'Before such a situation ...' Ethiopia Has not Begun to Fight (Milwaukee Journal, 19 November 1935)

11. Doctors and Prostitutes

'He eats too little ...' Dollfuss Was Tiny But Bold (Milwaukee Journal, 26 July 1934)

'In my opinion, sacrificing ...' 'The European Consequences of the Italian Aggression against Ethiopia', Réti *(Rivista di Studi Politici Internazionali, Nuova Serie*, Vol. 74, No. 3 (295), Luglio-Settembre 2007)

'You don't see anyone ...' Nazis Muff Their Biggest Chance, Dollfuss' Death Unites All Austria (Milwaukee Journal, 26 July 1934)

'Nature has made Dessye ...' Confusion in the Palace (The Sydney Morning Herald, 5 December 1935)

'What next? Is it ...' London Throngs Watch War Acts (The Nassau Daily Review, 5 October 1935)

'Have much appreciated your ...' Evelyn Waugh: Volume 1 – The Early Years 1903-1939, p414

'Adventurers of obscure origins ...' *Un Hombre Blanco en el Infierno Negro*, Del Valle & Alfonso Roselló (Maza, Caso y cía, 1937) p33

'Schuppler found himself working ...' Parallel Lives In Ethiopia – Two Hungarian Doctors in The 1920s And 1930s, Balázs (https://www.academia.edu/4045312/

Parallel_Lives_-_Two_Hungarian_Doctors_in_Ethiopia_in_the_1920s_
and_1930s)
'Small ambulance brigades were ...' Swedes in Haile Selassie's Ethiopia, Norberg
(Scandinavian Institute of African Studies,1977) p160
'Captain Rudolf Brunner had ...' Addis Ababa (St Louis Post-Dispatch,
5 November 1935)
'Outside, Adventist Dr Ragnar ...' Confusion in the Palace (The Sydney Morning
Herald, 5 December 1935)
'A bomb fell within ...' Bomb Comes Within Six Feet of Killing Ethiopian
Emperor (7 December 1935, The Pittsburgh Press)
'The war correspondents' camp ...' 'Camp in Flames' (7 December 1935, Reading
Eagle)
'The less foreigners visit ...' Ras Desta: An Able Ethiopian Chief (The Times,
26 February 1937)

12. Bohemians on the Frontline
'The Italians are coming ...' *Habešská Odyssea*, p120
'What a miracle,' he ...' Ibid, p121
'The Abyssinians hate work ...' Ibid, p122
'Everyone will now be ...' The Black Eagle, p89
'White dogs invaded our ...' *Habešská Odyssea*, p108
'In another month we'll ...' Ibid, p84
'Your brain has turned ...' Ibid, p92
'You cannot go to ...' Ibid, p104
' ... urgently and earnestly asks ...' Ibid, p110
'The sea of fiery campfires ...' Ibid, p138

13. Peace to Men of Good Will
'In 1929 a Dr ...' Reds and Whites in Ethiopia before the Italo-Ethiopian War of
1935 and 1936, Calvitt Clarke III (http://fch.fiu.edu/FCH-2009/Calvitt_reds_
and_whites_in_ethiopia.htm)
'We have shed blood ...' Feodor Konovalov and the Italo-Ethiopian War (Part I),
Calvitt Clarke III (World War II Quarterly, vol.5 no.1, 2008)
'These are the positions ...' Feodor Konovalov and the Italo-Ethiopian War
(Part I), Calvitt Clarke III (World War II Quarterly, vol.5 no.1, 2008)
'In all of the ...' *Habešská Odyssea*, p166
'The more we try ...' Doctor Tells of War Horror (The Afro-American, 2 May 1936)
'Brophil had been ...' Ibid
'I'm still alive ...' Ibid
'The whole thing was ...' Ibid
'Not the best accompaniment ...' Death from the Ethiopian Sky (The Spectator,
23 April 1936)
'Ras Kassa was a ...' Feodor Konovalov and the Italo-Ethiopian War (Part I),
Calvitt Clarke III (World War II Quarterly, vol.5 no.1, 2008)
'About half an hour ...' *Habešská Odyssea*, p178

14. Our Cuban Friend

'I would rather die ...' Off to Spain (Harrisburg Sunday Courier, 8 August 1937)

'Cuban youth, reportedly heir ...' Admits Own 'Kidnapping' (The Daily Times Rochester and Beaver, 26 April 1935)

'I have in my ...' *Un Hombre Blanco en el Infierno Negro*, p3

'The Diario de La ...' *Cuba: El Diario De La Marina, Los «Misioneros De Mussolini» y La Intelectualidad Cubana Proitaliana Durante El Segundo Conflicto Ítalo-Abisinio (1935-1936)*, Consuegra Sanfiel (*Memoria y Sociedad* 18, n. 36, 2014)

'It was leprous!' said ...' *Un Hombre Blanco en el Infierno Negro*, p13

'After the age of ...' Ibid, p51

'I saw many of ...' Ibid, p53

'Why do you want ...' Ibid, p63

'The emperor has told ...' Ibid, p69

'They worry less about ...' Ibid, p79

'The seven men were mutilated ...' Ibid, p105

15. Ravaging Bayonets

'*Den Irske Mussolini* ...' Collection List No.166: Eoin O'Duffy papers (http://www.nli.ie/pdfs/mss%20lists/166_Eoin%20O'Duffy%20Papers%20Collection%20List.pdf)

'Irish fascists would not ...' Franco's International Brigades: Adventurers, Fascists, and Christian Crusaders in the Spanish Civil War, Othen (Hurst, 2013) p121

'A huge farce – there ...' Eoin O'Duffy's Blueshirts and the Abyssinian Crisis, McMahon (History Ireland, Volume 10, Issue 2, 2002)

'After fifteen years in ...' Ibid

'The dockers of Dublin ...' Ibid

'I do not think ...' Ibid

'The most picturesque medley ...' *Magyarország és Etiópia: Formális és informális kapcsolatok a 19. század második felétől a II. Világháborúig*, Balázs (Doktori Értekezés, Szegedi Tudományegyetem Bölcsészettudományi Kar, 2008)

'Mussolini copied fascism from ...' The Veiled Garvey: The Life and Times of Amy Jacques Garvey, Taylor (University of North Carolina Press, 2003) p99

'The newspapers in Rome ...' Alliance of the Colored Peoples: Ethiopia & Japan Before World War II, Calvitt Clarke III (Boydell & Brewer Ltd, 2011) p114

'The Ministry suggested the ...' A 'Foreign Legion' for Mussolini? A Transnational Experience of Fascist Volunteers during the Ethiopian War, Dr. João Fábio Bertonha (http://research.uni-leipzig.de/eniugh/congress/fileadmin/eniugh2011/dokumente/Fascism_Transnational_and_Bertonha_2011_03_25.pdf)

'Adwa was an Italian ...' Ibid

'The Ministry broke down ...' Ibid

'In addition, fascist political ...' *De Latinoamérica al Medio Oriente: Alineamientos y compromisos frente al segundo conflicto ítalo-abisinio (1935-1936)*, Consuegra Sanfiel (*Humania del Sur*, Año 8, No. 15, Julio-Diciembre, 2013)

'In June 1935, 400 ...' Ibid

'The Negus sent cannibals ...' 'The Green Shirts and Others', Nagy-Talavera (The Center for Romanian Studies, 2001) p150 n.65

'The low-flying planes ...' 'The Green Shirts and Others', p150 n.65

'Eighty of the newspapers ...' Italian-Americans and the Ethiopian Crisis, Ventresco (Italian Americana, Vol. 6, No. 1, Fall/Winter 1980)

'A 700-strong crowd ...' Ibid

'Over 800 Americans would ...' Ibid

'Fascist propaganda films were ...' *O Fascismo e os Imigrantes Italianos no Brasil,* p277 n.15

'This insatiable octopus, sucking ...' *O Fascismo e os Imigrantes Italianos no Brasil,* p191

16. Bohemian Attack

'Our aircraft are fast ...' *Habešská Odyssea,* p218

'How are you going ...' Ibid, p181

'You know, we went ...' Ibid, p183

'We are fighting for ...' Ibid, p184

'Every Abyssinian is a ...' Ibid, p192

'Their camps are not ...' Feodor Konovalov and the Italo-Ethiopian War (Part II), Calvitt Clarke III, (World War II Quarterly, vol.5 no.2, 2008)

'Their strength is in ...' Ibid

'At four o'clock in ...' *Habešská Odyssea,* p190

'Against the organised fire ...' The Dark Valley: A Panorama of the 1930s, Brendon (Johnathan Cape, 2000) p278

'Well, well,' said Breyer ...' *Habešská Odyssea,* p205

'Our patients may have ...' Death from the Ethiopian Sky (The Spectator, 23 April 1936)

'The Red Cross emblem ...' Doctor Tells of War Horror (The Afro-America, 2 May 1936)

'The survival in Ethiopia ...' Brothers and Strangers: Black Zion, Black Slavery, 1914–1940, p296

'They had no chance ...' Review of the Week (Chicago Tribune, 16 February 1936)

17. Black Dragons at the Barricades

'Excuse me for the ...' The Dark Valley: A Panorama of the 1930s, p385

'Rising sun flags went ...' Revolt in Japan: The Young Officers and the February 26, 1936 Incident, Shillony (Princeton University Press, 1973) p59

'The Young Officers of ...' The Dark Valley: A Panorama of the 1930s, p191

'Every single bullet must ...' The Dark Valley: A Panorama of the 1930s, p375

'It has been my ...' Alliance of the Colored Peoples: Ethiopia and Japan Before World War II, Calvitt Clarke (Boydell & Brewer Ltd, 2011) p83

'Japaniser poet Blatta Gabra-Egziabher ...' Honour in African History, Iliffe (Cambridge University Press, 2005) p258

'He who accepts it ...' Alliance of the Colored Peoples: Ethiopia and Japan Before World War II, p9

'We shall never have ...' Ibid, p81

'I understand that the ...' Ibid, p86

'Fairyland Ethiopia Will Receive ...' Ibid, p88

'The press ignored most ...' The Dark Valley: A Panorama of the 1930s, p386

'The Japanese rising sun ...' Kita Ikki and the Making of Modern Japan: A Vision of Empire, Tankha (University of Hawaii Press/University of Delhi Press, 2006) p293

'Plans have been made ...' Alliance of the Colored Peoples: Ethiopia and Japan Before World War II, p90

'Italy picked up on ...' Alliance of the Colored Peoples: Ethiopia and Japan Before World War II, p89

'Hitherto, Caucasian peoples have ...' Proceedings of the XVth International Conference of Ethiopian Studies, Hamburg, July 20-25 2003, ed. Uhlig (Otto Harrassowitz Verlag, 2006) p225

'Abyssinia [...] is now menaced ...' Proceedings of the XVth International Conference of Ethiopian Studies, Hamburg July 20-25 2003, p227

'Prominent black newspaper the ...' Ethiopian, Italian Armies Face Each Other in Africa' (Chicago Defender, 13 July 1935)

'Your fathers, mothers, brothers ...' The Dark Valley: A Panorama of the 1930s, p388

'I'd rather not ...' The Dark Valley: A Panorama of the 1930s, p388

18. Our Cuban Friend Under Fire

'The shells are defective ...' Un Hombre Blanco en el Infierno Negro, p123

'This is what Mulugeta ...' Ibid, p137

'For me the League ...' Ibid, p137

'We found 80,000 liras ...' Ibid, p129

'Here's the formula,' Del ...' Ibid, p146

'Every day was a ...' Ibid, p134

'Your tent's gone,' said ...' Haile Selassie's War: The Italian-Ethiopian Campaign, 1935-1941, p87

'Wake up Geneva. It ...' Bombing Wrecks Briton's Hospital (New York Post, 16 January 1936)

'The Montreal Gazette reported ...' Plot to Kill Negus Bared (Montreal Gazette, 20 February 1936)

'How could it have ...' Feodor Konovalov and the Italo-Ethiopian War (Part I), Calvitt Clarke III (World War II Quarterly, vol.5 no.1, 2008)

19. Bohemians on the Run

'That's awful,' he said ...' Habešská Odyssea, p204

'He signed a statement ...' News Denied by Ethiopian (The Milwaukee Journal, 18 February 1936)

'Why not mark the ...' Habešská Odyssea, p243

'Countless European officers, who ...' Habešská Odyssea, p243

'The officials have begun ...' Father of the Tuskegee Airmen: John C Robinson, p159

'Never, during the conversations ...' League of Nations Official Journal, Volume 17 (League of Nations, 1936) p779

'Situation desperate,' Frère cabled ...' Haile Selassie's War: The Italian-Ethiopian Campaign, 1935-1941, p93

'We have to retreat ...' Habešská Odyssea, p251

'There are the old ...' Feodor Konovalov and the Italo-Ethiopian War (Part II), Calvitt Clarke III, (World War II Quarterly, vol.5 no.2, 2008)
'His words exude confident ...' *Habešská Odyssea*, p272
'But Your Majesty,' said ...' *Habešská Odyssea*, p273

20. Nazi Ethiopia

'I can tell you ...' Is Tomorrow Hitler's? 200 Questions on the Battle of Mankind, Knickerbocker (Reynal & Hitchcock, 1941) p26
'Their Ethiopian blood gave ...' Caesar in Abyssinia, p180
'On 24 December 1934 ...' What Hitler Knew: The Battle for Information in Nazi Foreign Policy, Shore (Oxford University Press, 2005) p69
'Weber was closemouthed enough ...' Mussolini's War: Fascist Italy's Military Struggles from Africa and Western Europe to the Mediterranean and Soviet Union 1935-45, Joseph (Helion and Company, 2010) p21
'When the *Reichsluftfahrtministerium* officially ...' Girding for Battle: The Arms Trade in a Global Perspective, 1815-1940, ed. Stoker jr & Grant (Praeger, 2003), p164
'Steffen tried to pitch ...' Girding for Battle: The Arms Trade in a Global Perspective, 1815-1940, p162
'Despite being a member ...' Ethiopia Stretches Forth across the Atlantic: African American Anticolonialism during the Interwar Period, Munro (Left History, Fall/Winter 2008)
'Does your anti-imperialism ...' The Black Pacific Narrative: Geographic Imaginings of Race and Empire between the World Wars, Taketani (Dartmouth College Press, 2014) p70
'Russia is showing increasingly ...' Ethiopia in Broader Perspective: Papers of the XIIIth International Conference of Ethiopian Studies Kyoto 12-17 December 1997, ed. Fukui, Kurimoto, & Shigeta (Shokado Book Sellers, 1997) p703
'Keep away from Africa ...' *Paranoie fasciste? Il volontariato in favore dell'Etiopia durante la guerra del 1935-1936*, Berthona (*Diacronie: Studi di Storia Contemporanea*, No. 14, 2, 2013)
'A last shipment of ...' Caesar in Abyssinia, p360
'Mussolini is a leader ...' *De Latinoamérica al Medio Oriente: Alineamientos y compromisos frente al segundo conflicto ítalo-abisinio* (1935-1936), Consuegra Sanfiel (*Humania del Sur, Año 8*, No. 15, Julio-Diciembre, 2013)

21. Tradition, Honour, Patriarchy

'The entrenchments of their ...' Feodor Konovalov and the Italo-Ethiopian War (Part II), Calvitt Clarke III, (World War II Quarterly, vol.5 no.2, 2008)
'It was obvious the ...' Ibid
'Ils sont trés braves ...' Ibid
'War brings out the ... ' *Magyarország és Etiópia: Formális és informális kapcsolatok a 19. század második felétől a II. Világháborúig*, Balázs (Doktori Értekezés, Szegedi Tudományegyetem Bölcsészettudományi Kar, 2008)
'To be brutally frank ...' Italian-Americans and the Ethiopian Crisis, Ventresco (Italian Americana, Vol. 6, No. 1, Fall/Winter 1980)
'I am happy we ...' Feodor Konovalov and the Italo-Ethiopian War (Part II), Calvitt Clarke III, (World War II Quarterly, vol.5 no.2, 2008)

'En route, I thought ...' Ibid
'Your Majesty, all this ...' Ibid
'Clearly, this was the ...' Ibid

22. *The Turkish Defence*

'The government in Ankara ...' Italo-Turkish Relations between Two Wars: The Impact of the Ethiopian Crisis, Di Casola (Il Politico, Vol. 62, No. 2, Aprile-Giugno 1997)

'May God help you ...' Haile Selassie and the Arabs: 1935-1936, Erlich (Northeast African Studies, New Series, Vol. 1, No. 1, 1994)

'The builder of modern ...' Haile Selassie and the Arabs: 1935-1936, Erlich (Northeast African Studies, New Series, Vol. 1, No. 1, 1994)

'Nabil Ismail Daud, a ...' *Paranoie fasciste? Il volontariato in favore dell'Etiopia durante la guerra del 1935-1936*, Berthona (*Diacronie: Studi di Storia Contemporanea*, No. 14, 2, 2013)

'Vehip Pasha is a ...' *İtalya-Habeşistan Savaşı: Vehip Paşa ve Türkiye*, Nizamoğlu (*Sosyal Bilimler Araştırmaları Dergisi*, II, 2011)

'For some reason, they ...' Ibid

'[The empire] was taken ...' Evelyn Waugh: Volume 1 – The Early Years 1903-1939, p395

'The usurper, the tyrant ...' Haile Selassie and the Arabs: 1935-1936, Erlich (Northeast African Studies, New Series, Vol. 1, No. 1, 1994)

'Ethiopia is an ancient ...' *De Latinoamérica al Medio Oriente: Alineamientos y compromisos frente al segundo conflicto ítalo-abisinio* (1935-1936), *Consuegra Sanfiel* (*Humania del Sur, Año 8*, No. 15, Julio-Diciembre, 2013)

'I am ready now in ...' Haile Selassie and the Arabs: 1935-1936, Erlich (Northeast African Studies, New Series, Vol. 1, No. 1, 1994)

'Leave the Abyssinians alone ...' Haile Selassie and the Arabs: 1935-1936, Erlich (Northeast African Studies, New Series, Vol. 1, No. 1, 1994)

'Monsignor Cole, Bishop of ...' The Catholic Missions, British West African Nationalists, and the Italian Invasion of Ethiopia, 1935-36, Asante (African Affairs, Vol. 73, No. 291, April 1974)

'Going and taking something ...' Ibid

'Italian spies first noticed ...' *Palestina*, V. V., U. F. and L. V. V. (*Oriente Moderno*, Anno 15, Nr. 12, Dicembre 1935)

'Tārik Bey liked to ...' Caesar in Abyssinia, p190

'Tārik Bey was born ...' *Palestina*, V. V., U. F. and L. V. V. (Oriente Moderno, Anno 15, Nr. 12, Dicembre 1935)

'Hands Off Abyssinia! ...' *De Latinoamérica al Medio Oriente: Alineamientos y compromisos frente al segundo conflicto ítalo-abisinio* (1935-1936), Consuegra Sanfiel (*Humania del Sur, Año 8*, No. 15, Julio-Diciembre, 2013)

'Kumalo said he could ...' 'Picked Zulu Braves May Fight Italy' (The Singapore Free Press and Mercantile Advertiser, 23 August 1935)

'There were lawyers, there ...' Haile Selassie's War: The Italian-Ethiopian Campaign, 1935-1941, p89

'The defences thought up ...' Léopold Reul in *Ethiopië: van officiële naar officieuze militaire samenwerking – Konden huurlingen de formele coöperatie voortzetten?* Scheere (Vrije Universiteit Brussel Thesis, 2014)

'An African Verdun ...' *İtalya-Habeşistan Savaşı: Vehip Paşa ve Türkiye*, Nizamoğlu (*Sosyal Bilimler Araştırmaları Dergisi*, II, 2011)
'Out there will be ...' The War: Water Will Win, Stallings (*Time*, 14 October 1935)

23. *A Little Scrap*
'This is an order ...' Arnold Wienholt: Man and Myth, Siemon (University of Queensland PhD thesis, 1993) p227
'Journalist and radio broadcaster ...' The Campion Society & Catholic Social Militancy in Australia, 1929-1939, Jory (Harpham, 1986) p71
'Australia was as black ...' Australian Catholics and the Abyssinian War, Kneipp (Journal of Religious History, Volume 10, Issue 4, December 1979)
'There were thousands upon ...' Arnold Wienholt: Man and Myth, Siemon (Univeristy of Queensland PhD thesis, 1993) p231
'Take me away this ...' Telegram from Guernica: The Extraordinary Life of George Steer, War Correspondent, Rankin (Faber & Faber, 2012) pXX
'Let's go. They're more ...' *Habešská Odyssea*, p284
'The little scrap seemed ...' Arnold Wienholt: Man and Myth, Siemon (Univeristy of Queensland PhD thesis, 1993) p232
'A poetic genius of ...' Caesar in Abyssinia, p181
'The general was calling ...' The War: Water Will Win, Stallings (Time, 14 October 1935)
'Glad to see you ...' Ibid
'The general seemed happier ...' Ibid
'Why do you ask ...' Ibid

24. *Saboteurs and Spies*
'But alcohol changed the ...' The Flyers, p59
'Who are you?' drawled ...' http://hankduval.com/index.php/mnu_dewetfamily/biographies/251-21-hugh-william-arthur-oloff-de-wet-born-apr-2,-1912
'Only a skilled hand ...' Plot to Kill Negus Bared (The Montreal Gazette, 20 February 1936)
'Count Maurice de Roquefeuil ...' Spying For Italy (The West Australian, 18 September 1935)
'A wild rider, sniper ...' My Lives in Russia, Fischer (Harper, 1944)
'He had a third ...' Дело о педофилах союзного значения, Жирнов (http://www.kommersant.ru/doc/2040573)
'Adolf Parlesák heard about ...' *Habešská Odyssea*, p65
'Military experts gasped at ... ' Leading Mountain Attack (The Chicago Defender, 28 April 1936)

25. *Swedish Die-Hards*
'Only twelve Italians prisoners ... ' Between Bombs and Good Intentions: The Red Cross and the Italo-Ethiopian War 1935-1936, Rainer Baudendistel (Berghahn Books, 2006) p229
'Badoglio was seventy-five ...' Haile Selassie's War: The Italian-Ethiopian Campaign, 1935-1941, p127
'I have done my ...' Haile Selassie's War: The Italian-Ethiopian Campaign, 1935-1941, p130

'More government money paid ...' Caesar in Abyssinia, p60

'He was happy to ...' Ethiopia Mobilizes (Hope Star, 26 September 1935)

'It was with a ...' Haile Selassie's War: The Italian-Ethiopian Campaign, 1935-1941, p125

'They are prepared to ...' Haile Selassie's War: The Italian-Ethiopian Campaign, 1935-1941, p134

'This is the end ...' Haile Selassie's War: The Italian-Ethiopian Campaign, 1935-1941, p135

'My country,' said a ...' Haile Selassie's War: The Italian-Ethiopian Campaign, 1935-1941, p136

'The government is gone ...' *Habešská Odyssea*, p293

'We wait until the ...' *Habešská Odyssea*, p296

26. March of the Iron Will

'The chief of police ...' Ethiopia at Bay, Spencer (Algonac, MI: Reference Publications, 1984) p65

'The Virgin in the ...' Caesar in Abyssinia, p385

'He had been bombed ...' Caesar in Abyssinia, p323

'Where are your soldiers ...' Caesar in Abyssinia, p336

'Open the doors ...' http://www.crezan.net/pag_aby/abyssinia_avi_w33.html

'Both Legations had their ...' The Memoirs of Cordell Hull, Vol. I, Hull (New York: MacMillan, 1948), pp. 468-69

'De Halpert, a sixtysomething ...' The Red Cross in Abyssinia (The Times, 26 June 1936)

'They don't know what ...' Prevail: The Inspiring Story of Ethiopia's Victory over Mussolini's Invasion, 1935-1941, Pearce (Skyhorse Publishing, 2014) p496

'I had just thirty ...' Forgot Grandmother's Spoons (The New York Sun, 8 May 1936)

'The column advanced slowly ...' Feodor Konovalov and the Italo-Ethiopian War (Part II), Calvitt Clarke III, (World War II Quarterly, vol.5 no.2, 2008)

'There was nothing spectacular ...' The Education of a Correspondent, Matthews (New York: Harcourt Brace, 1946), pp. 62-63

'Around forty foreigners directly ...' *Paranoie fasciste? Il volontariato in favore dell'Etiopia durante la guerra del 1935-1936 (Diacronie: Studi di Storia Contemporanea*, No. 14/2, 2013) – João Fábio Bertonha has found an Italian report that claims 200 foreigners helped the Ethiopians during the war, 85 of them in a military capacity; it's a possible figure although the breakdown of nationalities indicates a more likely mix of double counting, mislabelled Red Cross members, and inclusion of departed military missions.

'If deserters are accepted ...' Nomads in the Shadows of Empires: Contests, Conflicts and Legacies on the Southern Ethiopian-Northern Kenyan Frontier, Oba (BRILL, 2013) p177

'From the moment they ...' Caesar in Abyssinia, p315

'During the war at ...' South Africa and the Italo-Ethiopian War 1935-6, Dedering (The International History Review, Volume 35, 2013); a more in-depth look at casualty figures can be found at http://necrometrics.com/20c300k.htm#Eth35

Aftermath

'To some degree, all ...' Ethiopia Deals With Legacy of Kings and Colonels (The
New York Times, 31 December 1995)

'Ethiopia cannot be controlled ...' *İtalya-Habeşistan Savaşı, Vehip Paşa ve
Türkiye*, Nizamoğlu (*Sosyal Bilimler Araştırmaları Dergisi, II*, 2011)

'À la porte les ...' The Rape of Ethiopia 1936, Barker (Ballantine Books, 1971) p133

'Von Rosen had flown ...' Between Bombs and Good Intentions: The Red Cross
and the Italo-Ethiopian War 1935-1936, p63

'A day later we ...' *Un Hombre Blanco en el Infierno Negro*, p278

'I thought of this ...' Italy Adopted by Black Eagle (New York Sun, 18 June 1936)

'Another ... rascal ... in Ethiopia ...' The Colonial Caribbean in Transition:
Essays on Postemancipation Social and Cultural History, Brereton & Yelvington
(University Press of Florida, 1999) p217

'By the next month ...' Julian Leads Band in Ofay Hot Spot (The Afro-American,
20 February 1937)

'Ethiopia is a conquered ...' 'I Am No Traitor' Says Julian, 'And I Told the Truth
but Others Lied' (The Afro-American, 22 August 1936)

'... though now I see ...' Winning Fights in the Streets (The Times, 26 May 1961)

'To the Italian soldier ...' *Con le armate del Negus: Un bianco tra i neri*,
Konovalov & Miccichè (Nicola Zanichelli, 1938) p26

'As a special agent ...' Off to Spain (Harrisburg Sunday Courier, 8 August 1937)

'He wrote his Ethiopia ...' http://havanajournal.com/culture/entry/
carteles_cuban_magazine_from_1938/

'The narration of my ...' *Un Hombre Blanco en el Infierno Negro*, p1

'Now he is returning ...' Off to Spain (Harrisburg Sunday Courier, 8 August
1937)

'It is the world's ...' The Redpath Bureau Presents Hilaire du Berrier, (leaflet, n.d)

'Du Wet nearly got ...' The Flyers, p68

'This ain't Ethiopia but ...' The Marcus Garvey and Universal Negro Improvement
Association Papers, Vol. X: Africa for the Africans, 1923–1945, Garvey
(University of California Press, 2006) pC

'Charged with being a ...' Secret War in Shanghai, p32

'It's hot, I'm tired ...' Secret War in Shanghai, p33

'Remember Abyssinia,' he said ...' Belgium Remembers Abyssinia; Reasons for
Neutrality (The Daily News, 19 October 1936)

'I only need a ...' *L'Italia nella seconda guerra mondiale*, Badoglio (Mondadori,
1946) p37

'I forgive you,' the ...' https://en.wikipedia.org/wiki/Getachew_Abate

'Even the UNIA went ...' 'Yellow' and 'Black': Japanese-Inspired Sedition among
African Americans Before and During World War II, Lewin (http://fch.fiu.edu/
FCH-1998/Lewin-Yellow%20and%20Black1-1998.htm)

'It was fun being ...' Modernism and World War II, MacKay (Cambridge
University Press, 2007) p133

INDEX